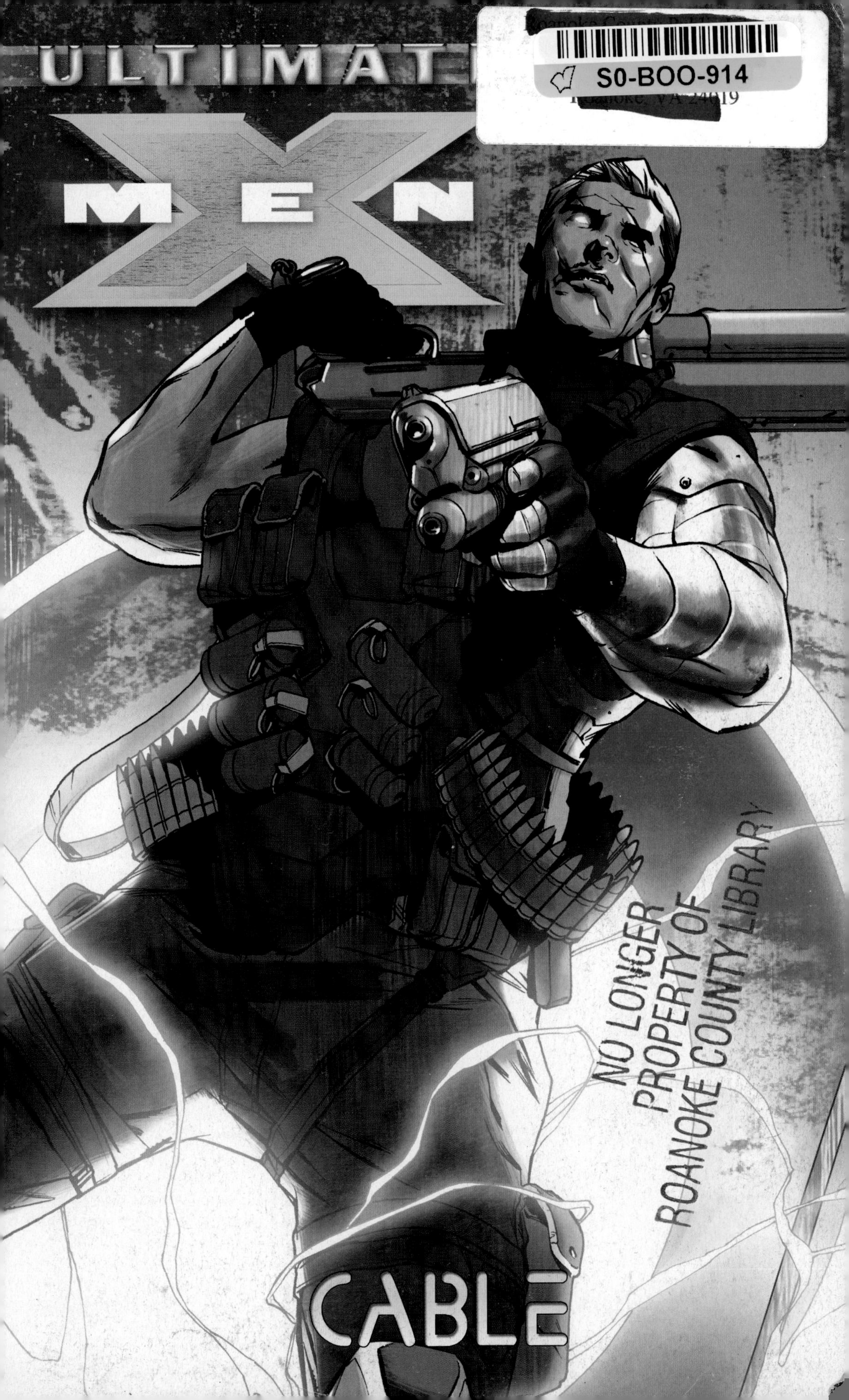
ULTIMAT
X
MEN
CABLE

ULTIMATE X-MEN

CABLE

WRITER
Robert Kirkman

ART (ISSUES #75-76 & 78)
Ben Oliver

PENCILS (ISSUES #77, 79 & 80)
Yanick Paquette

INKS (ISSUES #77, 79 & 80)
Serge LaPointe

COLORS
**Jason Keith &
Stephane Peru (Issues #77, 79 & 80)**

COVERS
**Michael Turner and Aspen, Ben Oliver
(with Richard Isanove on #78) &
Yanick Paquette (with Serge LaPointe
& Stephane Peru)**

"EXTRACURRICULAR"
WRITER
Sean McKeever
PENCILER
Mark Brooks
INKS
Jaime Mendoza
COLORS
John Rauch

LETTERS
Virtual Calligraphy's Joe Caramagna
ASSOCIATE EDITOR
John Barber
EDITOR
Ralph Macchio

COLLECTION EDITOR
Jennifer Grünwald
ASSISTANT EDITORS
Michael Short & Cory Levine
ASSOCIATE EDITOR
Mark D. Beazley
SENIOR EDITOR, SPECIAL PROJECTS
Jeff Youngquist
SENIOR VICE PRESIDENT OF SALES
David Gabriel

PRODUCTION
Jerron Quality Color
VICE PRESIDENT OF CREATIVE
Tom Marvelli

EDITOR IN CHIEF
Joe Quesada
PUBLISHER
Dan Buckley

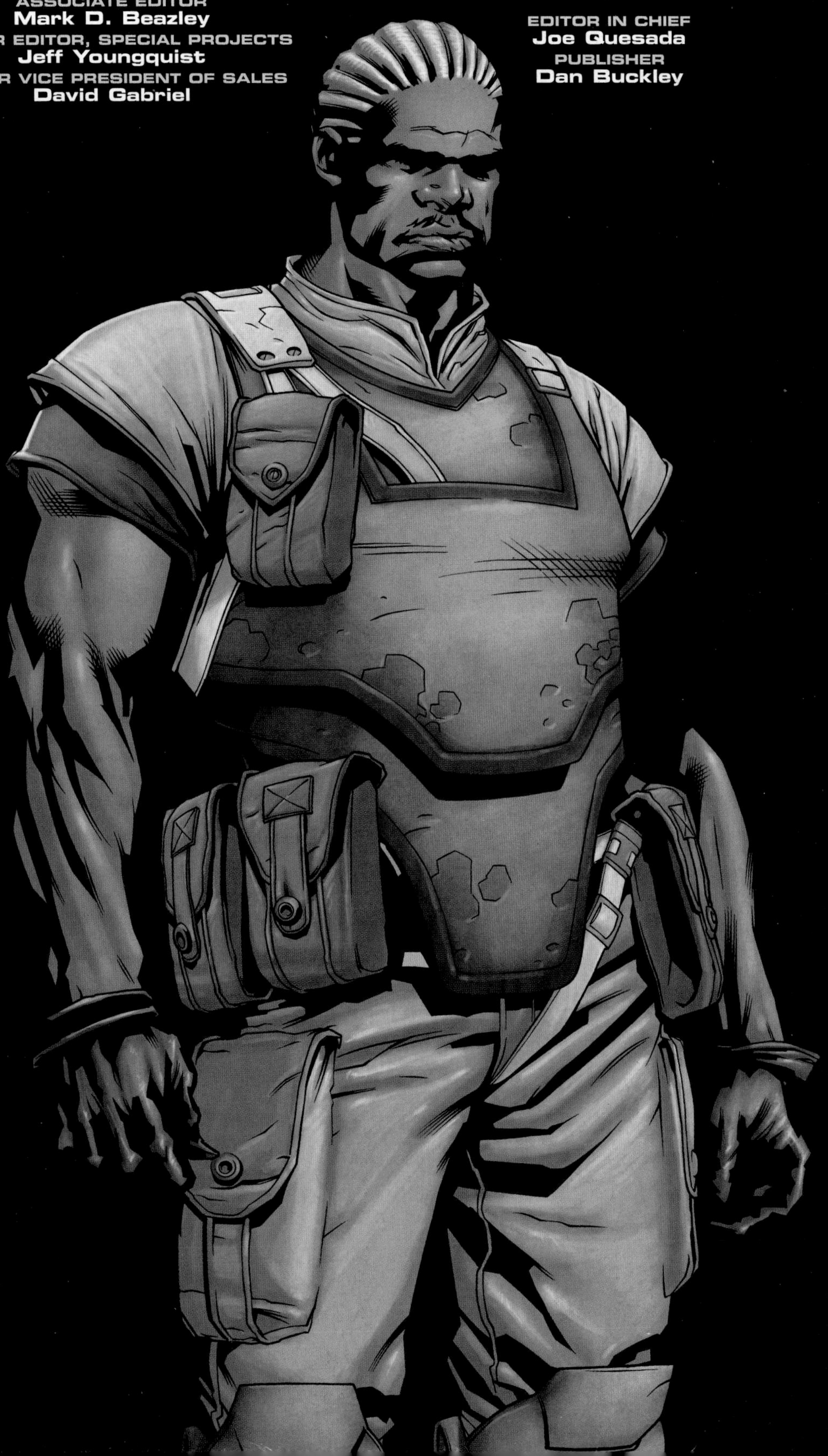

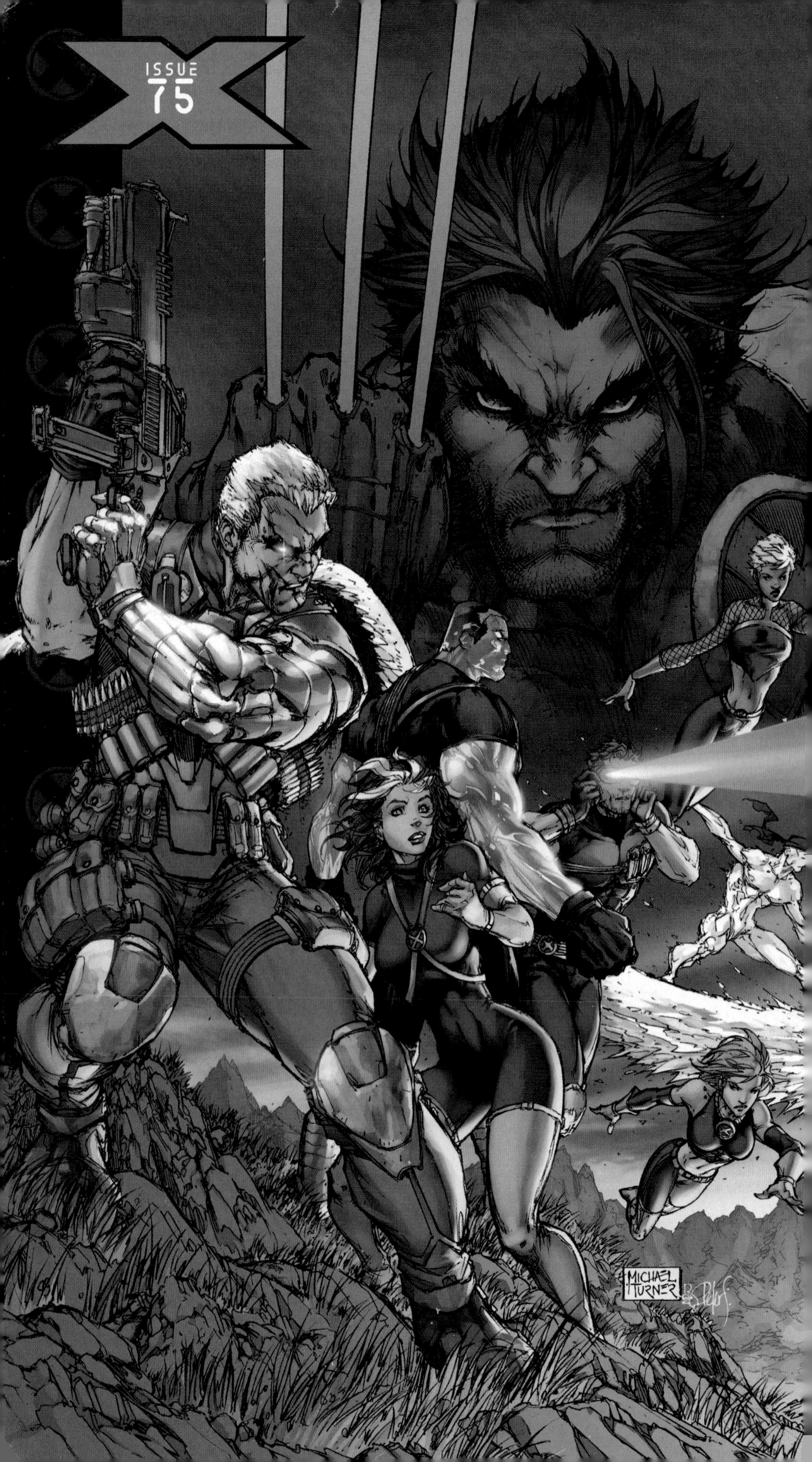
ISSUE
75
MICHAEL TURNER

PREVIOUSLY IN ULTIMATE X-MEN:

Born with strange and amazing abilities, the X-Men are young mutant heroes,
sworn to protect a world that fears and hates them.

Their ranks have recently taken a hit. Nightcrawler has snapped--forcing Xavier to keep him in a trance, inactive.
As a result, Dazzler has quit the team.

A new addition to the X-Men, Magician, revealed himself to be evil--trying to kill the X-Men before he was stopped.

Rogue's powers have returned after Gambit's abilities, which she absorbed (and retained) upon his death, faded
away unexpectedly. Once again, she cannot make physical contact with anyone.

Now is not a happy time for the students of Xavier's School for Gifted Children.

CABLE

PART 1 (OF 4)

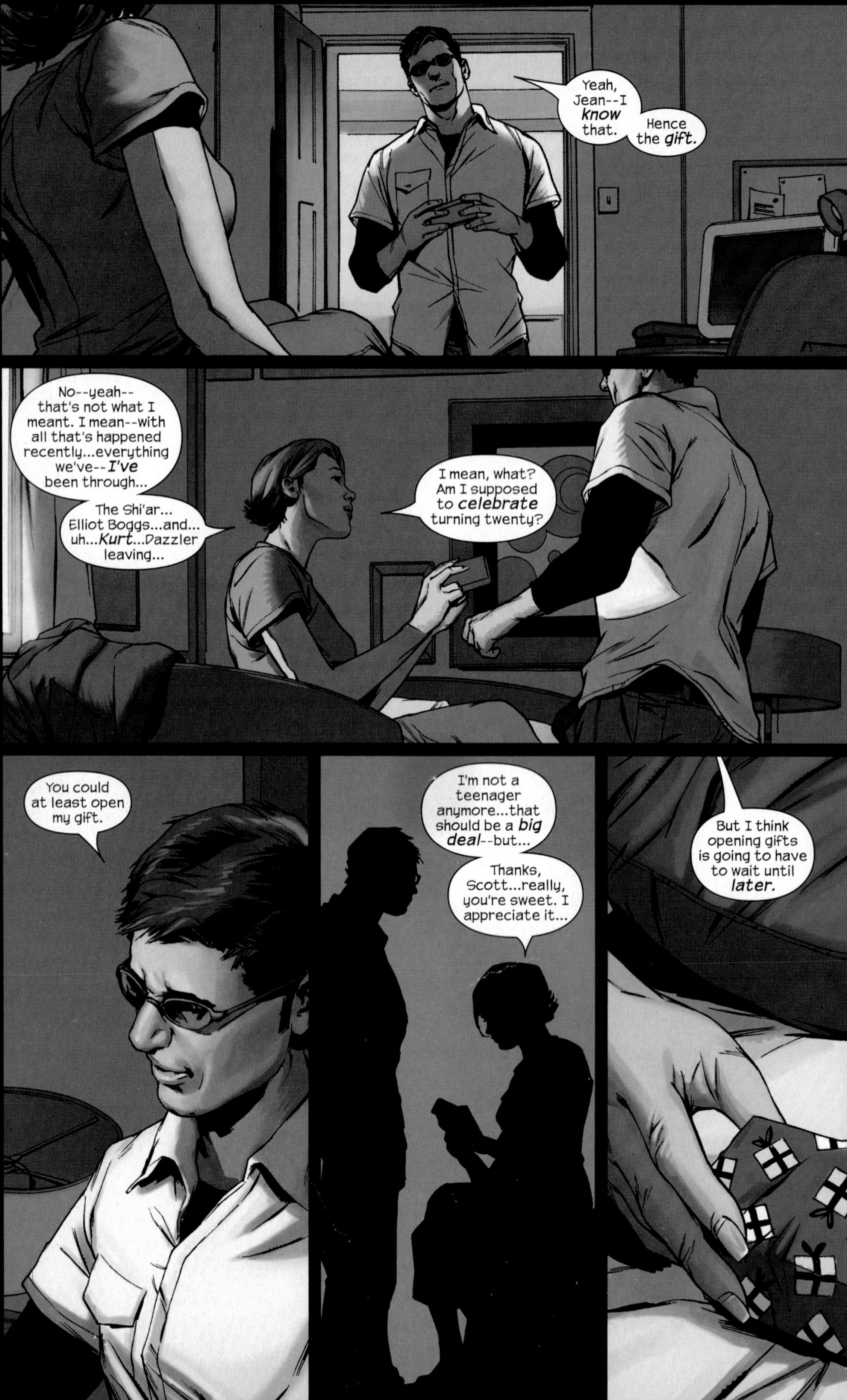
Yeah, Jean--I *know* that.
Hence the *gift.*
No--yeah--that's not what I meant. I mean--with all that's happened recently...everything we've--*I've* been through...
The Shi'ar... Elliot Boggs...and... uh...*Kurt*...Dazzler leaving...
I mean, what? Am I supposed to *celebrate* turning twenty?
You could at least open my gift.
I'm not a teenager anymore...that should be a *big deal*--but...
Thanks, Scott...really, you're sweet. I appreciate it...
But I think opening gifts is going to have to wait until *later.*

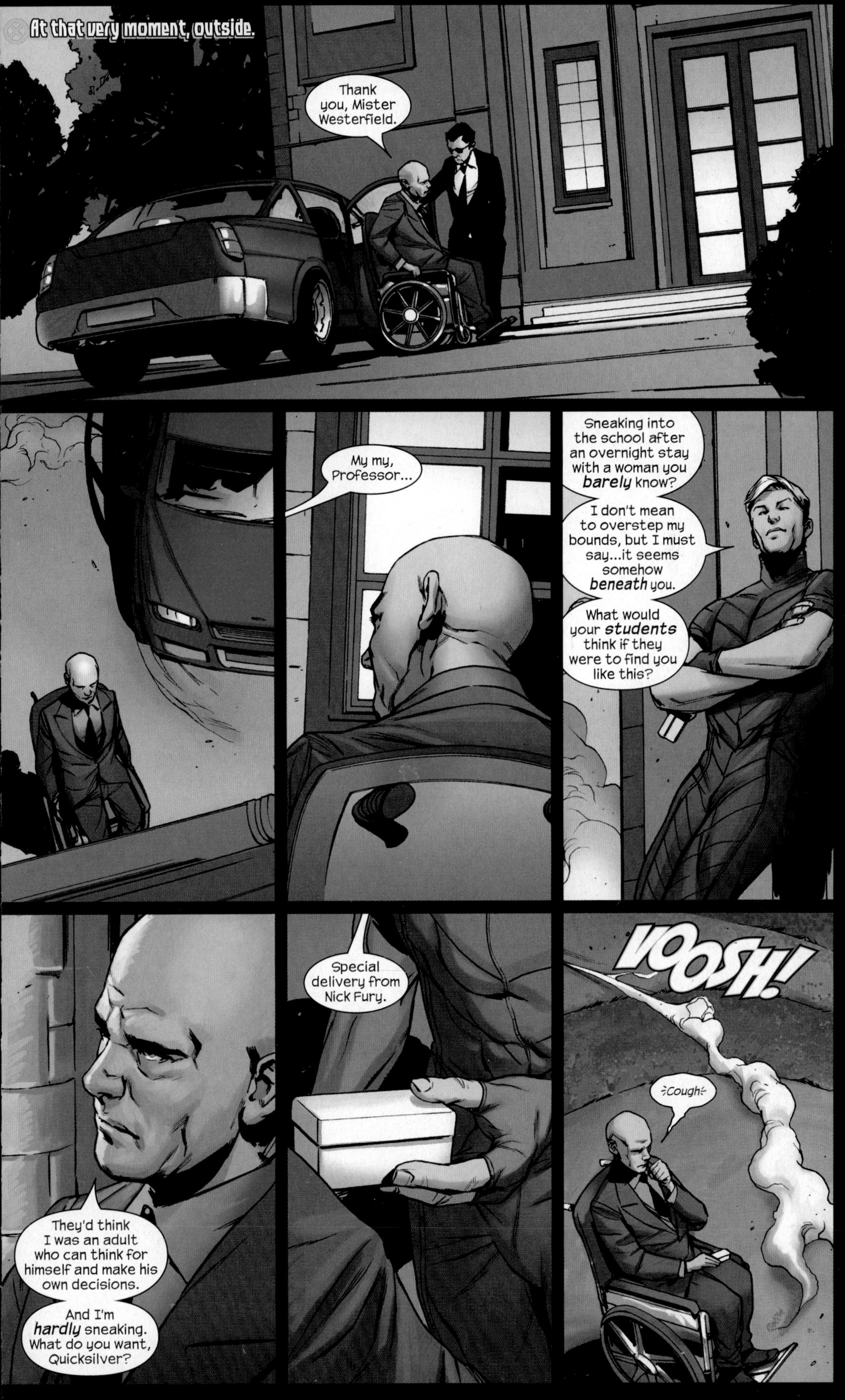
At that very moment, outside.
Thank you, Mister Westerfield.
My my, Professor...
Sneaking into the school after an overnight stay with a woman you *barely* know?
I don't mean to overstep my bounds, but I must say...it seems somehow *beneath* you.
What would your *students* think if they were to find you like this?
They'd think I was an adult who can think for himself and make his own decisions.
And I'm *hardly* sneaking. What do you want, Quicksilver?
Special delivery from Nick Fury.
VOOSH!
Cough

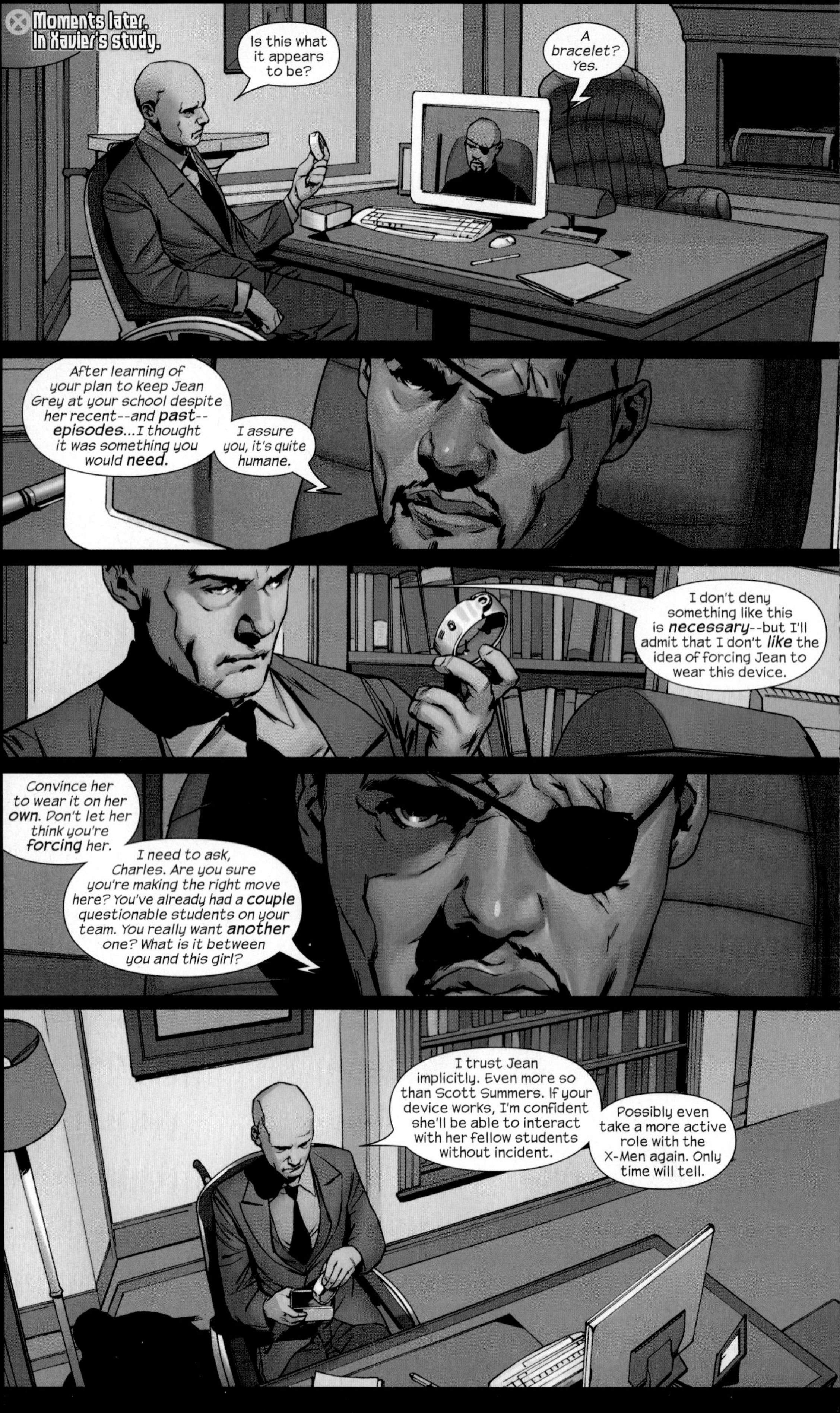
Moments later. In Xavier's study.
Is this what it appears to be?
A bracelet? Yes.
After learning of your plan to keep Jean Grey at your school despite her recent--and past--episodes...I thought it was something you would need.
I assure you, it's quite humane.
I don't deny something like this is necessary--but I'll admit that I don't like the idea of forcing Jean to wear this device.
Convince her to wear it on her own. Don't let her think you're forcing her.
I need to ask, Charles. Are you sure you're making the right move here? You've already had a couple questionable students on your team. You really want another one? What is it between you and this girl?
I trust Jean implicitly. Even more so than Scott Summers. If your device works, I'm confident she'll be able to interact with her fellow students without incident.
Possibly even take a more active role with the X-Men again. Only time will tell.

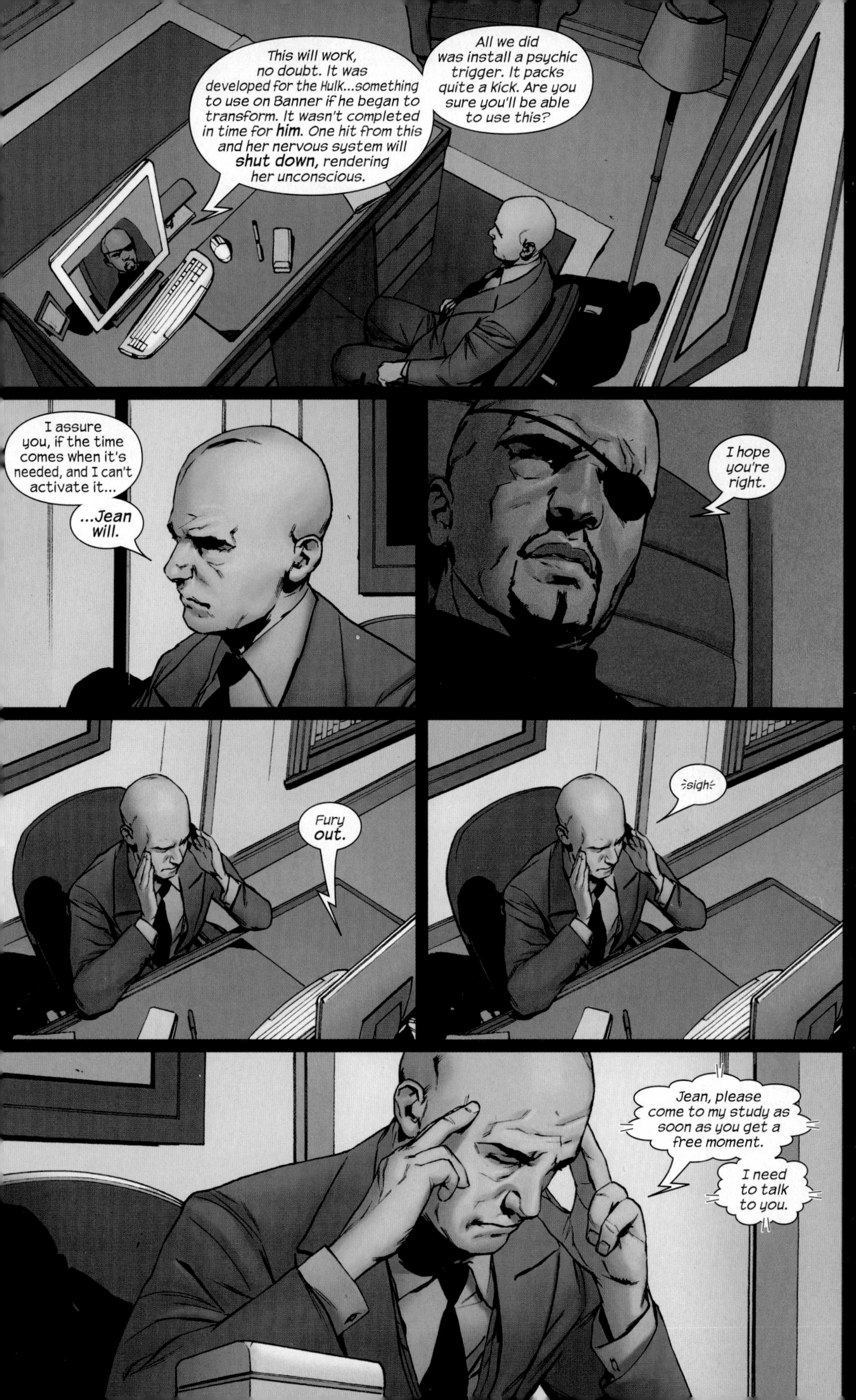
This will work, no doubt. It was developed for the Hulk...something to use on Banner if he began to transform. It wasn't completed in time for him. One hit from this and her nervous system will shut down, rendering her unconscious.
All we did was install a psychic trigger. It packs quite a kick. Are you sure you'll be able to use this?
I assure you, if the time comes when it's needed, and I can't activate it...
...Jean will.
I hope you're right.
Fury out.
sigh
Jean, please come to my study as soon as you get a free moment.
I need to talk to you.

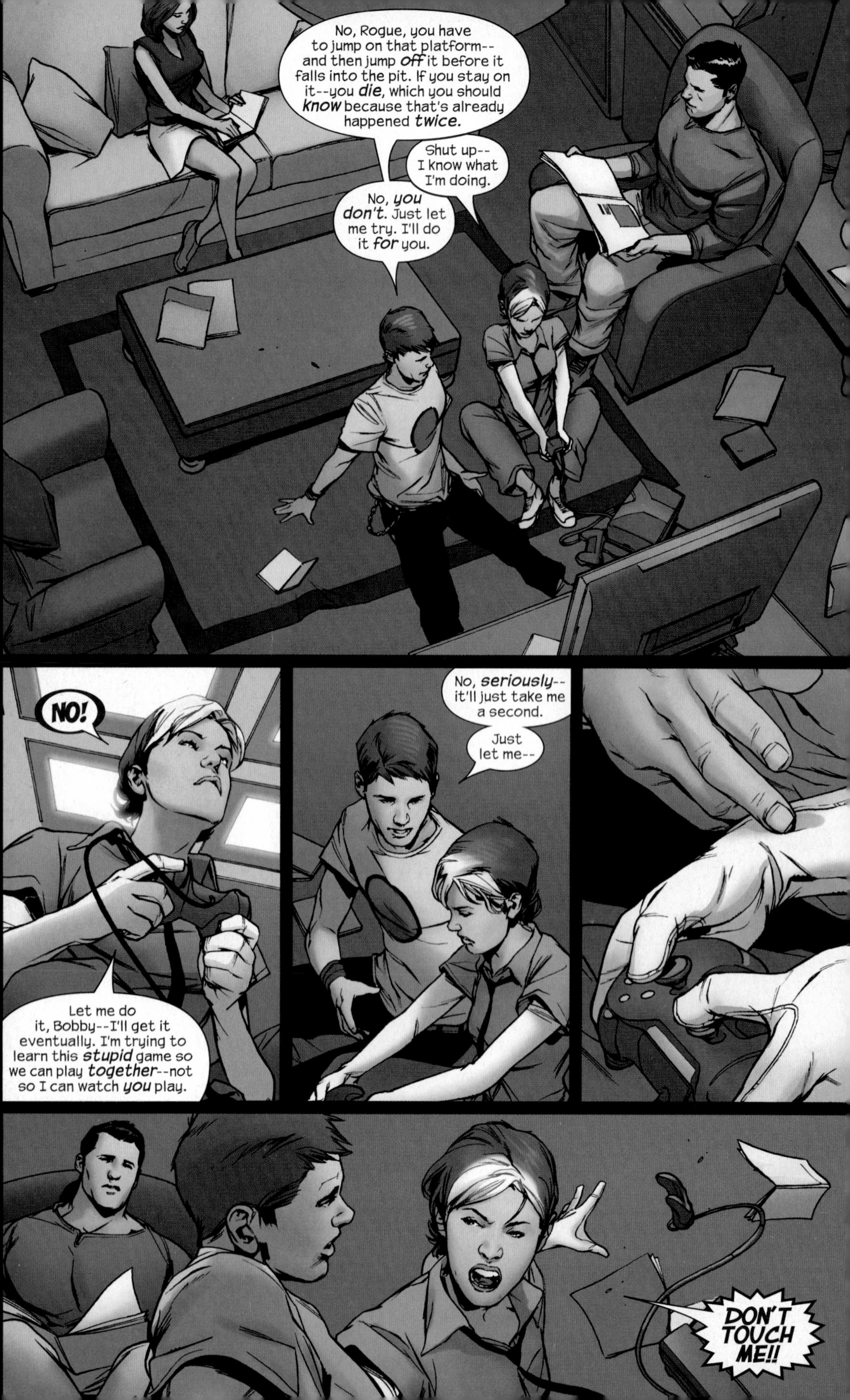
No, Rogue, you have to jump on that platform-- and then jump off it before it falls into the pit. If you stay on it--you die, which you should know because that's already happened twice.
Shut up-- I know what I'm doing.
No, you don't. Just let me try. I'll do it for you.
NO!
Let me do it, Bobby--I'll get it eventually. I'm trying to learn this stupid game so we can play together--not so I can watch you play.
No, seriously-- it'll just take me a second.
Just let me--
DON'T TOUCH ME!!

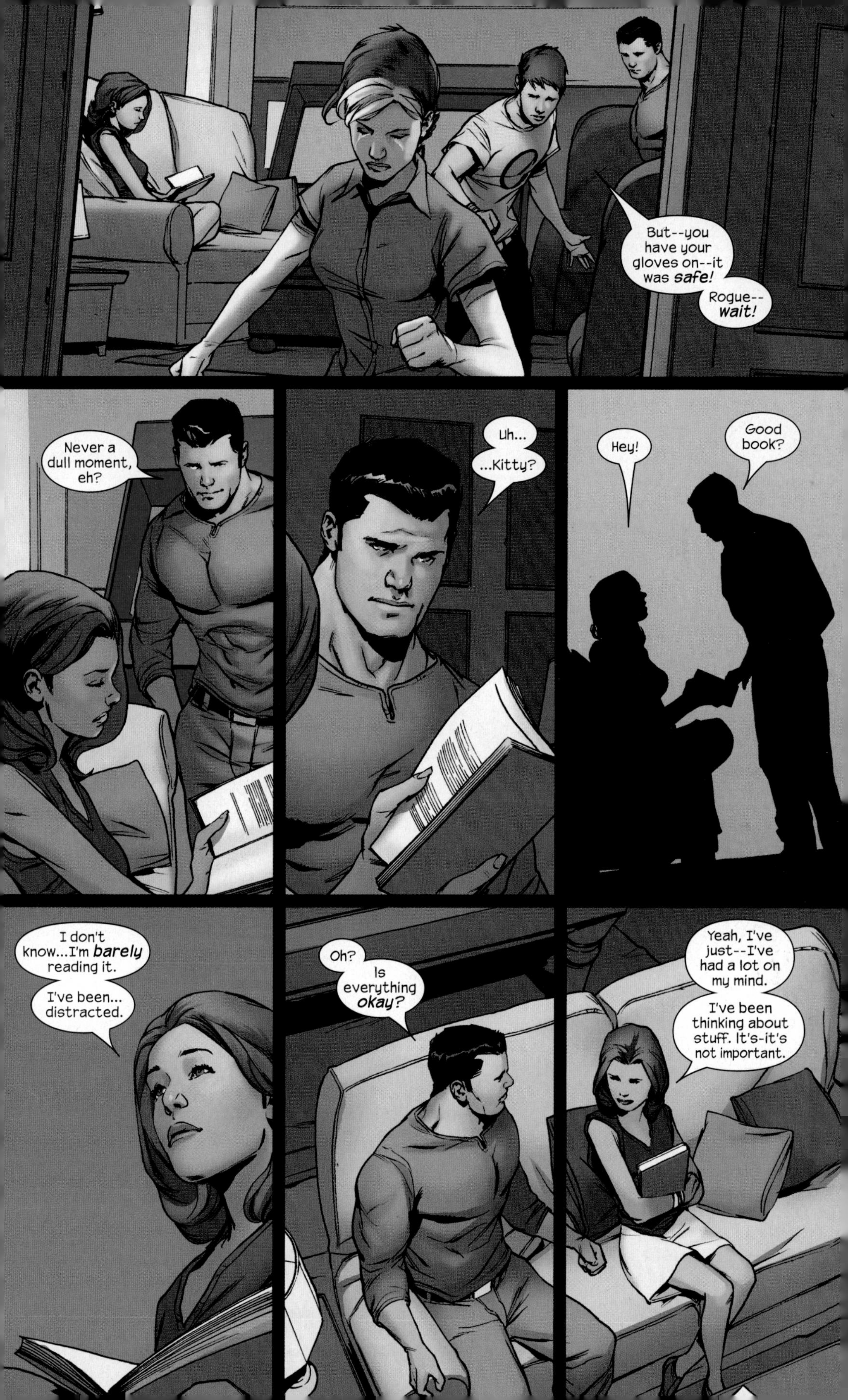

But--you have your gloves on--it was *safe!*
Rogue-- *wait!*
Never a dull moment, eh?
Uh...
...Kitty?
Hey!
Good book?
I don't know...I'm *barely* reading it.
I've been... distracted.
Oh?
Is everything *okay?*
Yeah, I've just--I've had a lot on my mind.
I've been thinking about stuff. It's-it's not important.

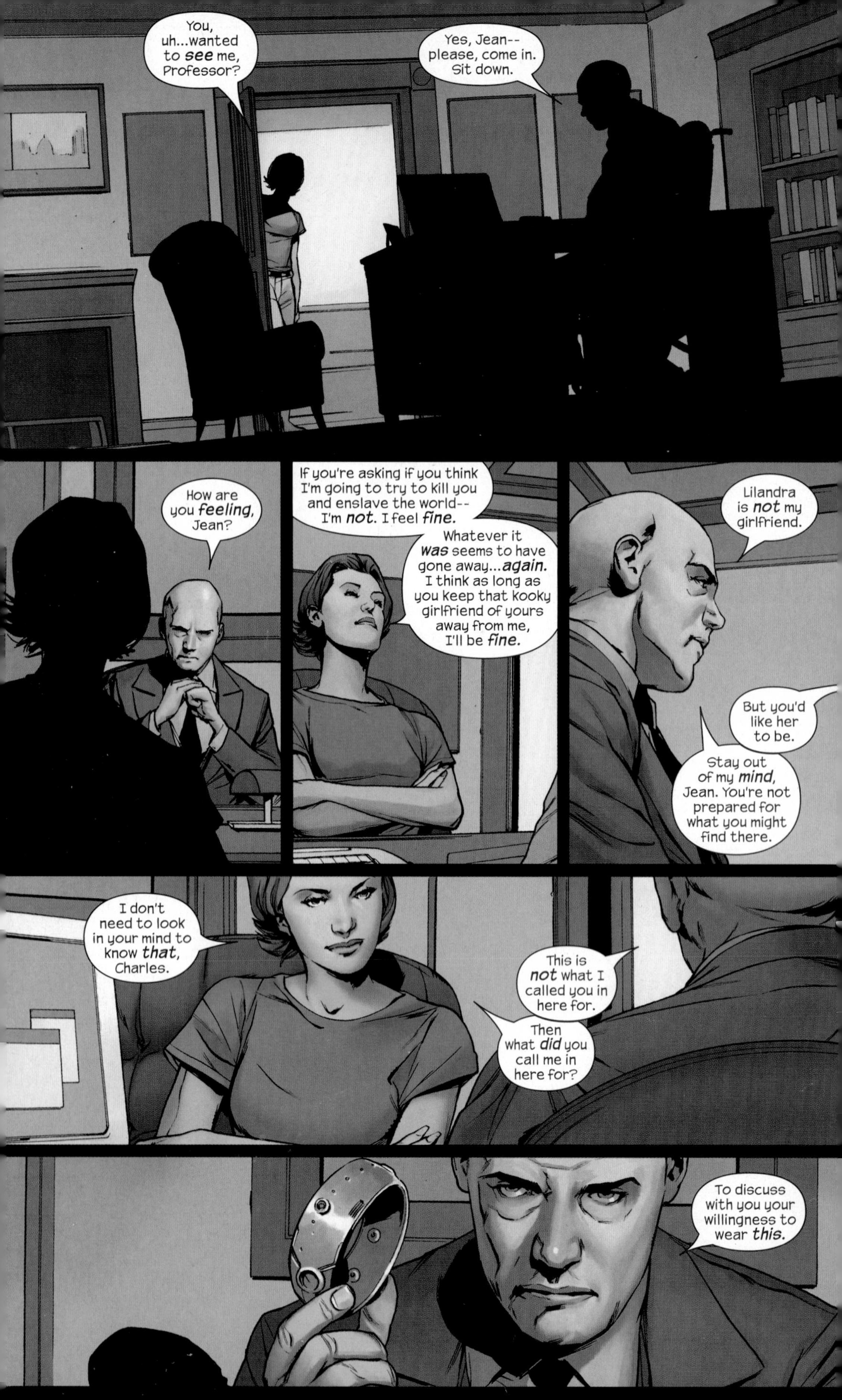
You, uh...wanted to see me, Professor?
Yes, Jean-- please, come in. Sit down.
How are you feeling, Jean?
If you're asking if you think I'm going to try to kill you and enslave the world-- I'm not. I feel fine.
Whatever it was seems to have gone away...again. I think as long as you keep that kooky girlfriend of yours away from me, I'll be fine.
Lilandra is not my girlfriend.
But you'd like her to be.
Stay out of my mind, Jean. You're not prepared for what you might find there.
I don't need to look in your mind to know that, Charles.
This is not what I called you in here for.
Then what did you call me in here for?
To discuss with you your willingness to wear this.

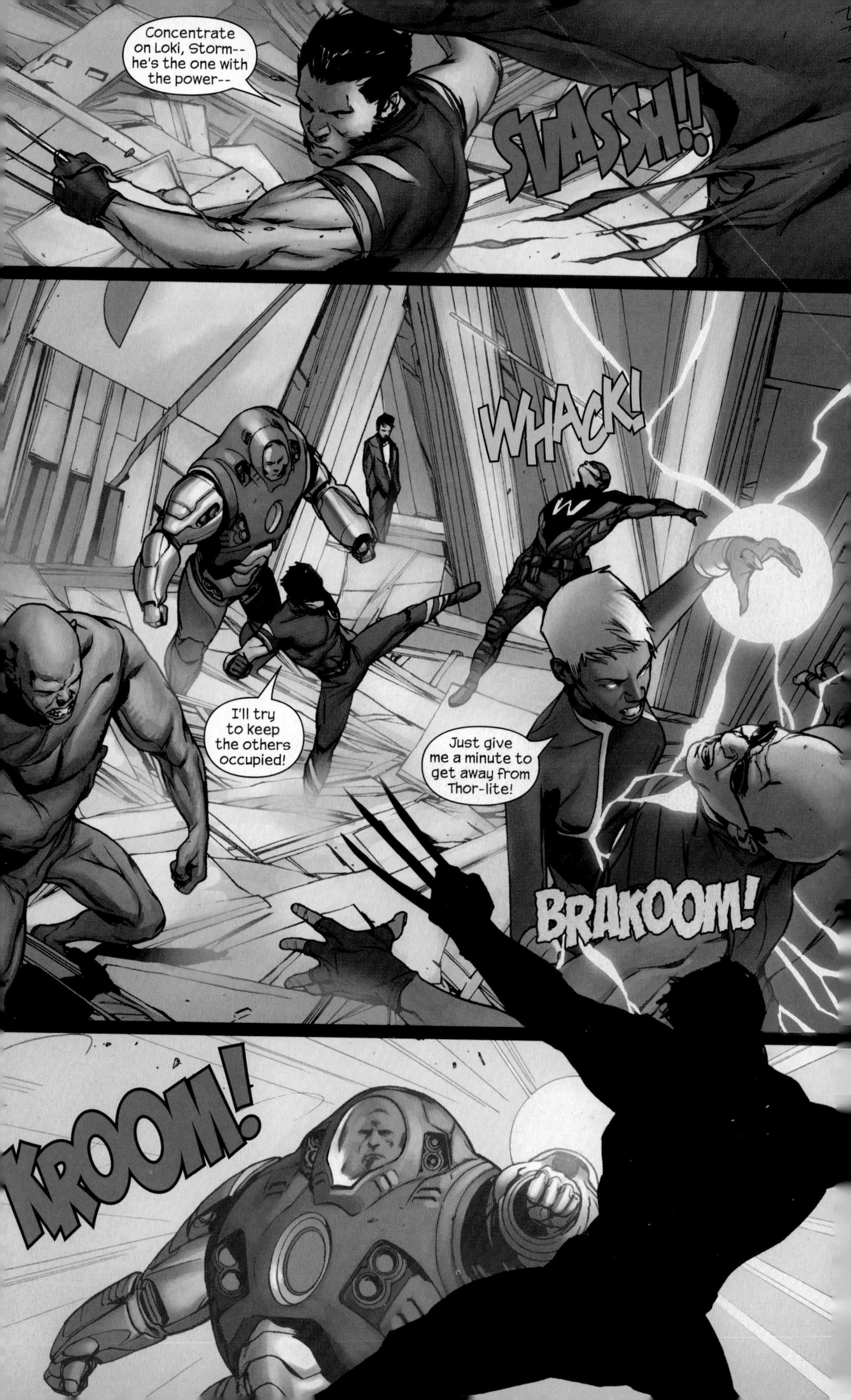

Concentrate on Loki, Storm--he's the one with the power--
SNASSH!!
WHACK!
I'll try to keep the others occupied!
Just give me a minute to get away from Thor-lite!
BRAKOOM!
KROOM!

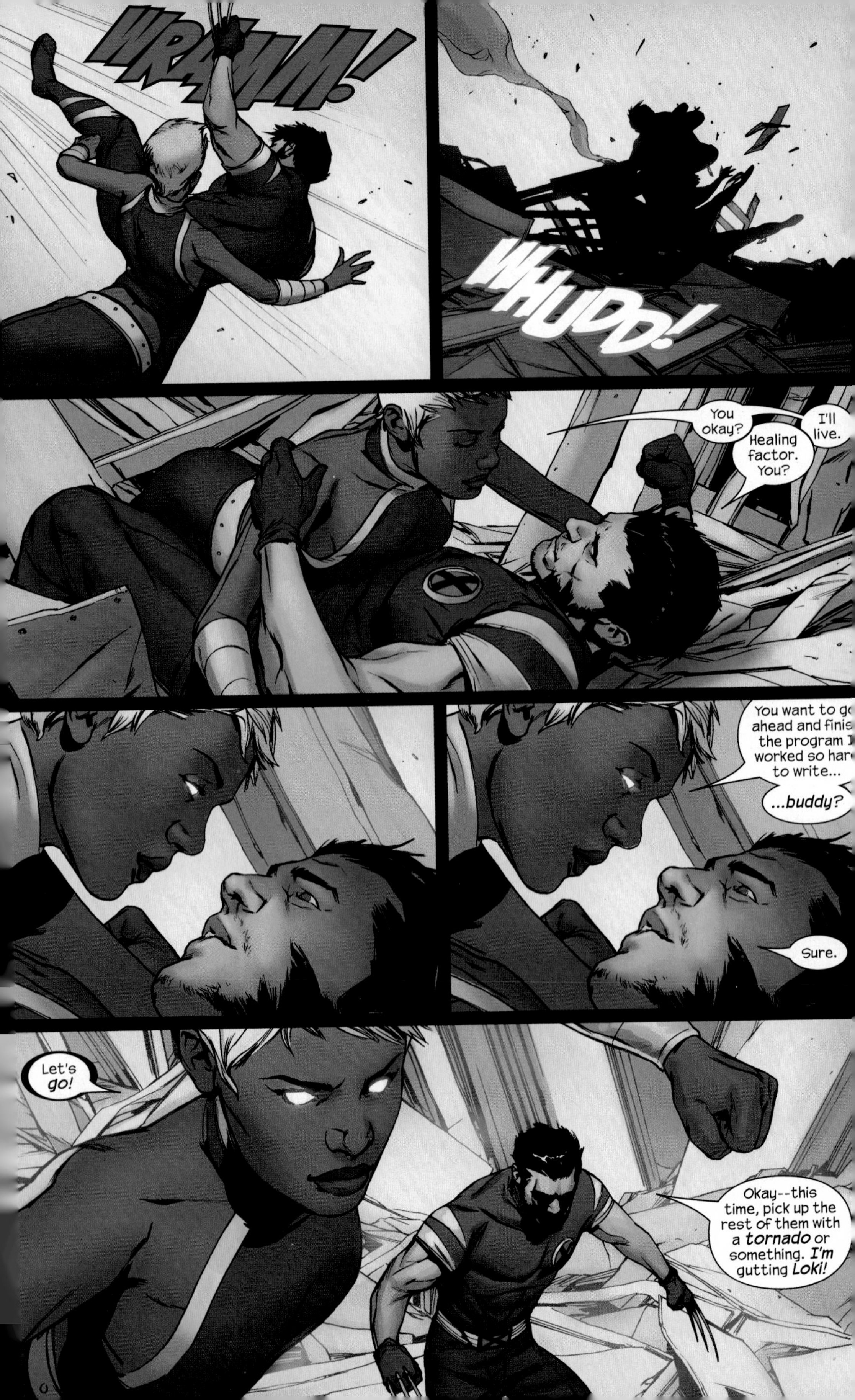
WRAAMM!
WHUDD!
You okay?
I'll live.
Healing factor. You?
You want to go ahead and finish the program I worked so hard to write...
...buddy?
Sure.
Let's go!
Okay--this time, pick up the rest of them with a tornado or something. I'm gutting Loki!

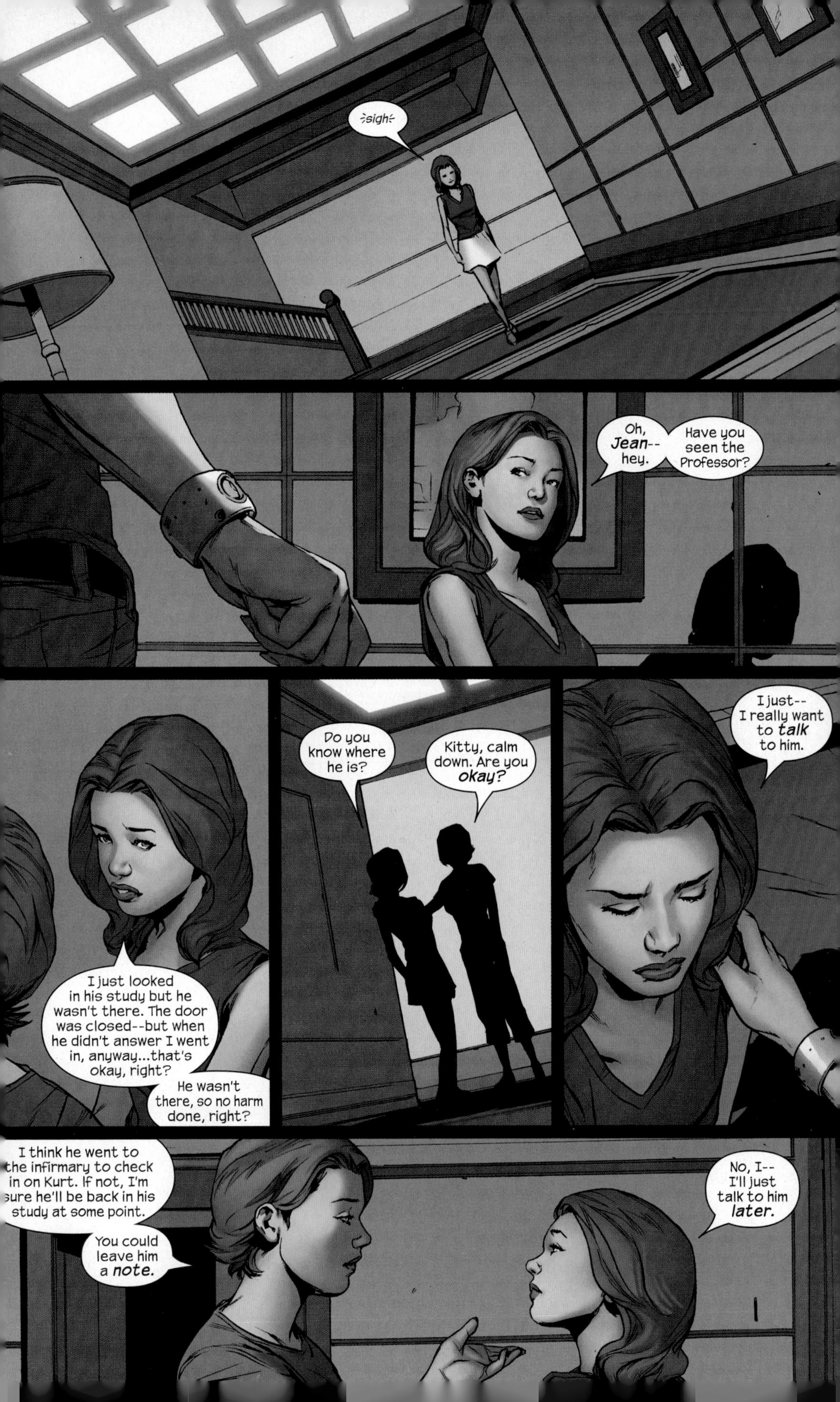

-sigh-
Oh, Jean-- hey.
Have you seen the Professor?
I just looked in his study but he wasn't there. The door was closed--but when he didn't answer I went in, anyway...that's okay, right?
He wasn't there, so no harm done, right?
Do you know where he is?
Kitty, calm down. Are you okay?
I just-- I really want to talk to him.
I think he went to the infirmary to check in on Kurt. If not, I'm sure he'll be back in his study at some point.
You could leave him a note.
No, I-- I'll just talk to him later.

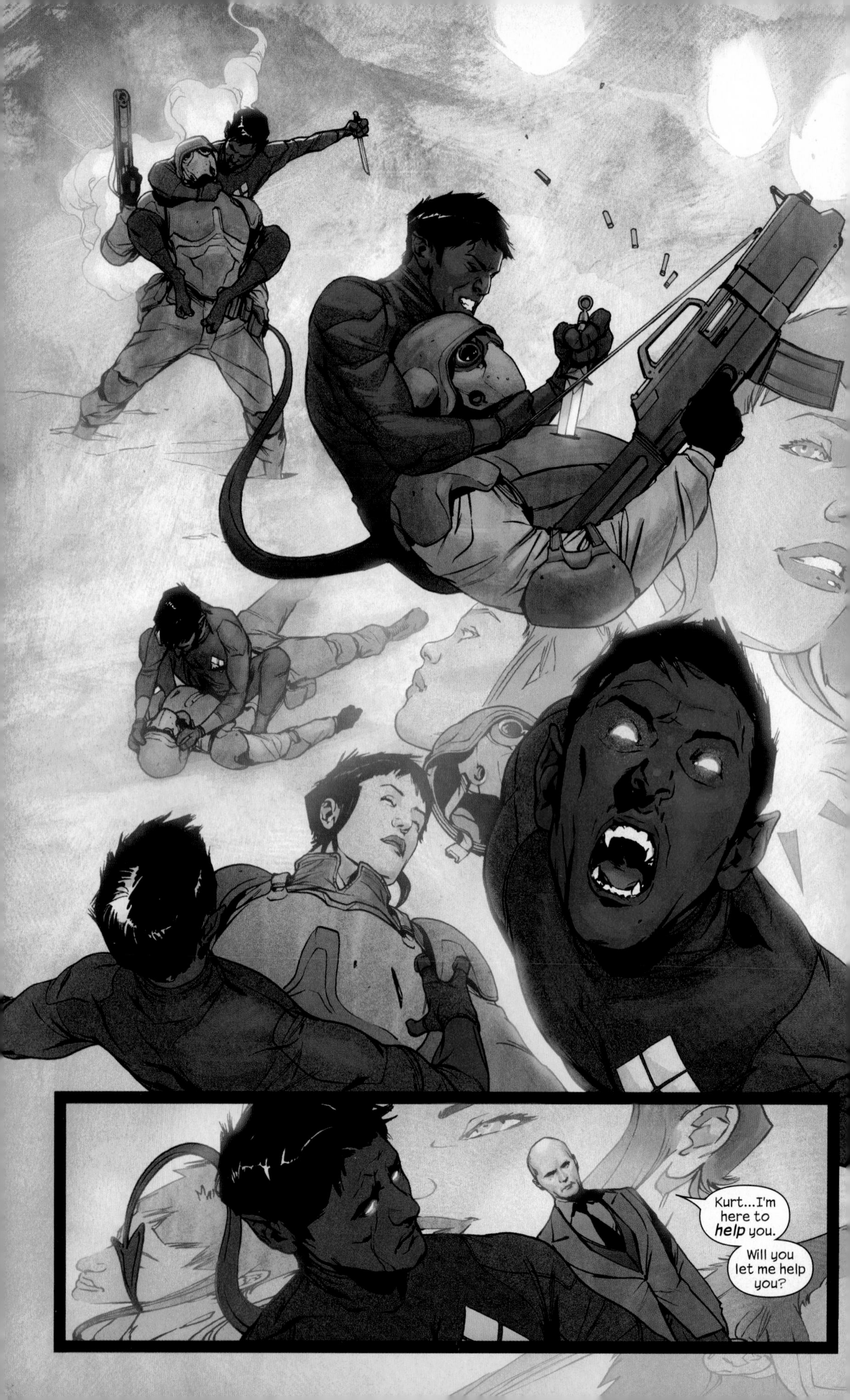
Kurt...I'm here to **help** you.
Will you let me help you?

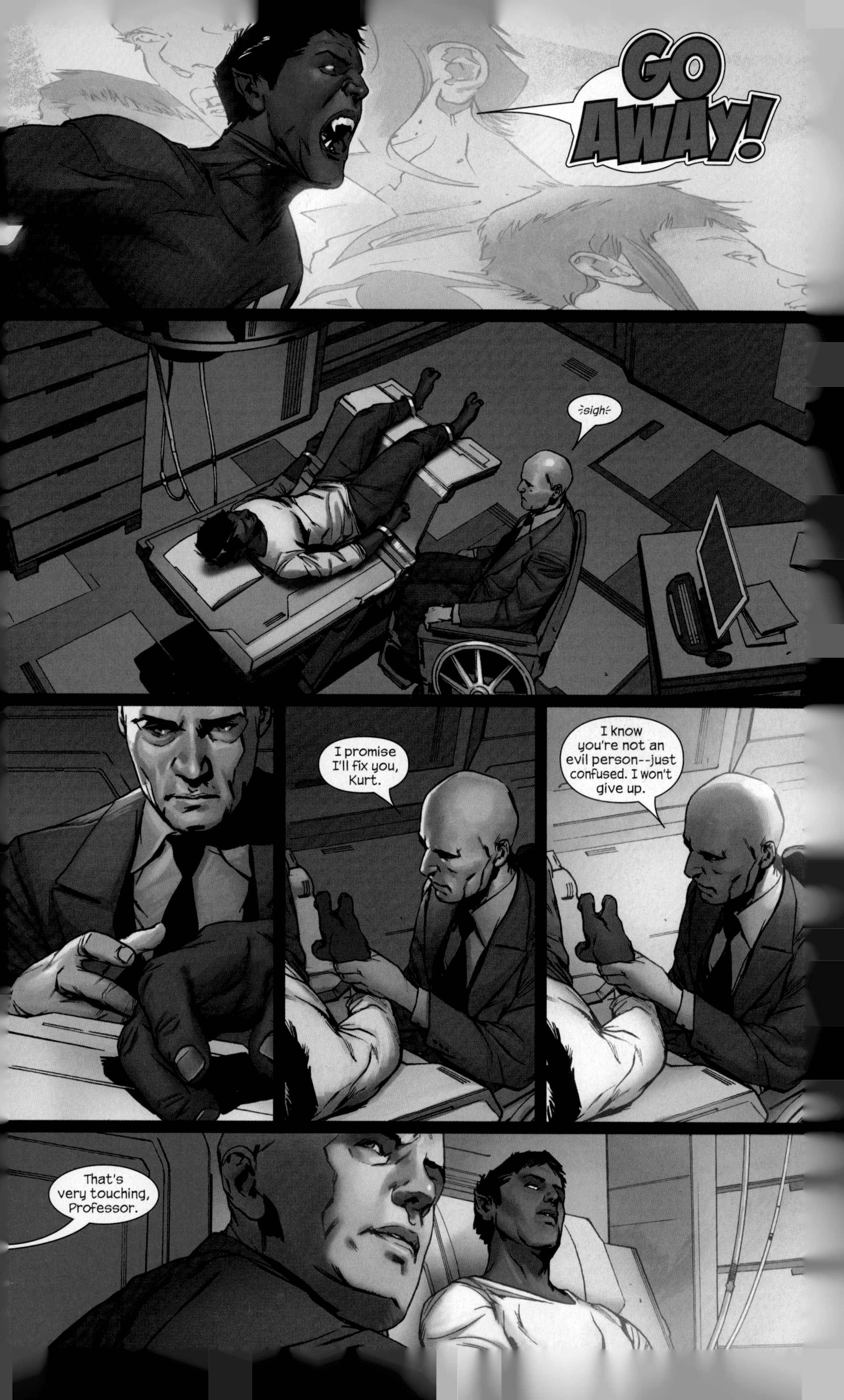
GO AWAY!
sigh
I promise I'll fix you, Kurt.
I know you're not an evil person--just confused. I won't give up.
That's very touching, Professor.

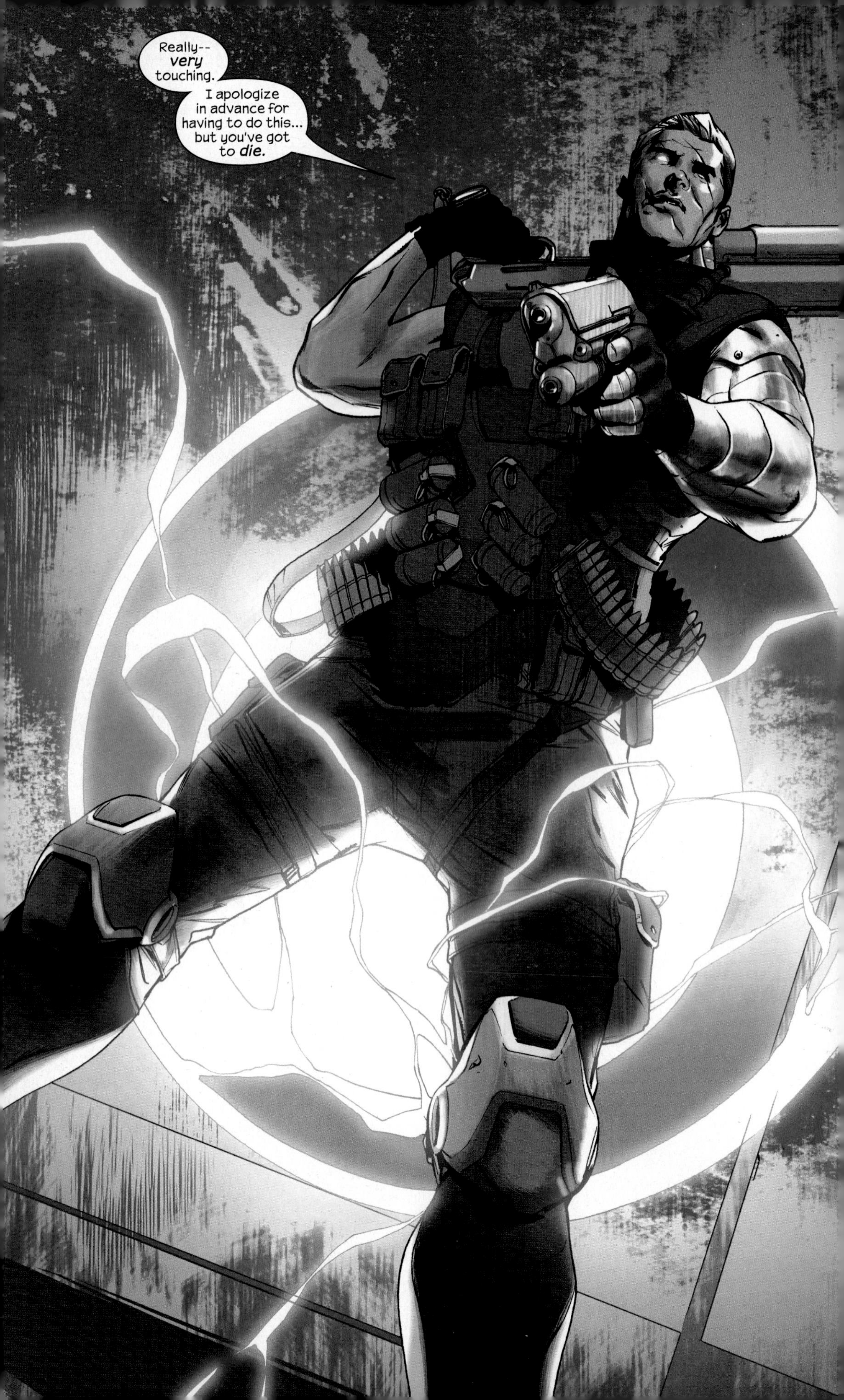
Really-- very touching.
I apologize in advance for having to do this... but you've got to die.

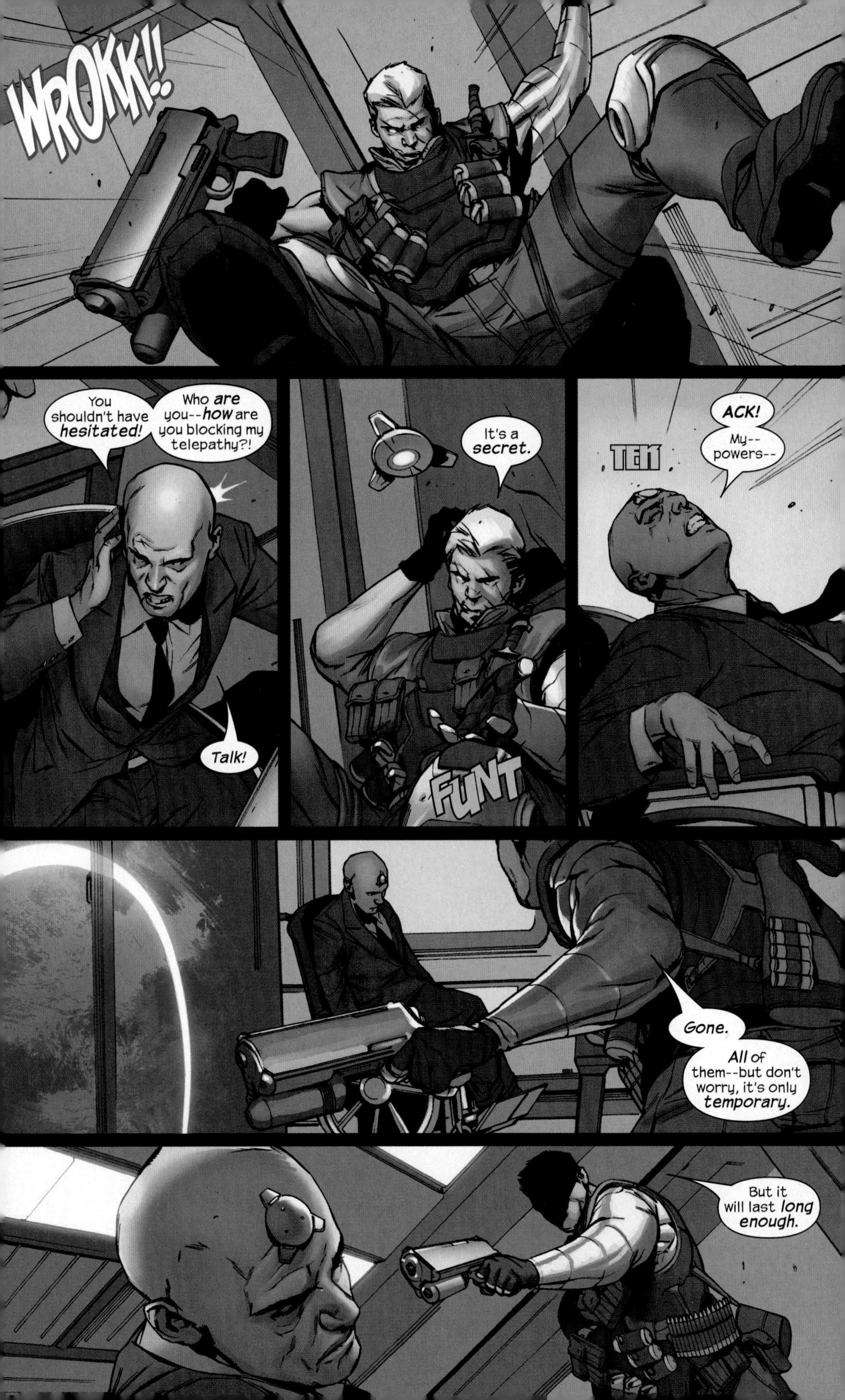
WROKK!!
You shouldn't have hesitated!
Who are you--how are you blocking my telepathy?!
Talk!
It's a secret.
FUNT
TEK
ACK! My--powers--
Gone.
All of them--but don't worry, it's only temporary.
But it will last long enough.

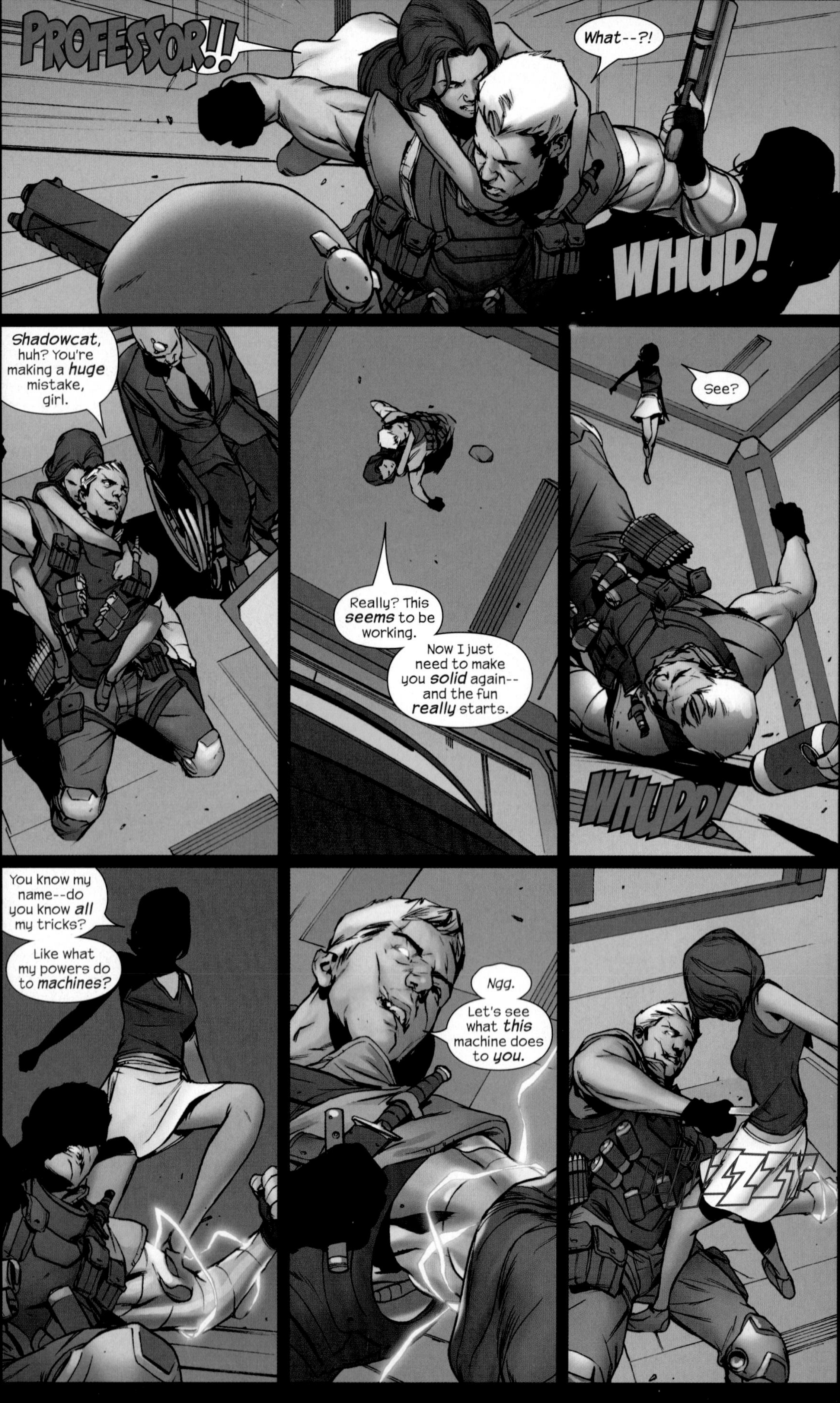
PROFESSOR!!
What--?!
WHUD!
Shadowcat, huh? You're making a huge mistake, girl.
Really? This seems to be working.
Now I just need to make you solid again--and the fun really starts.
See?
WHUDD!
You know my name--do you know all my tricks?
Like what my powers do to machines?
Ngg.
Let's see what this machine does to you.

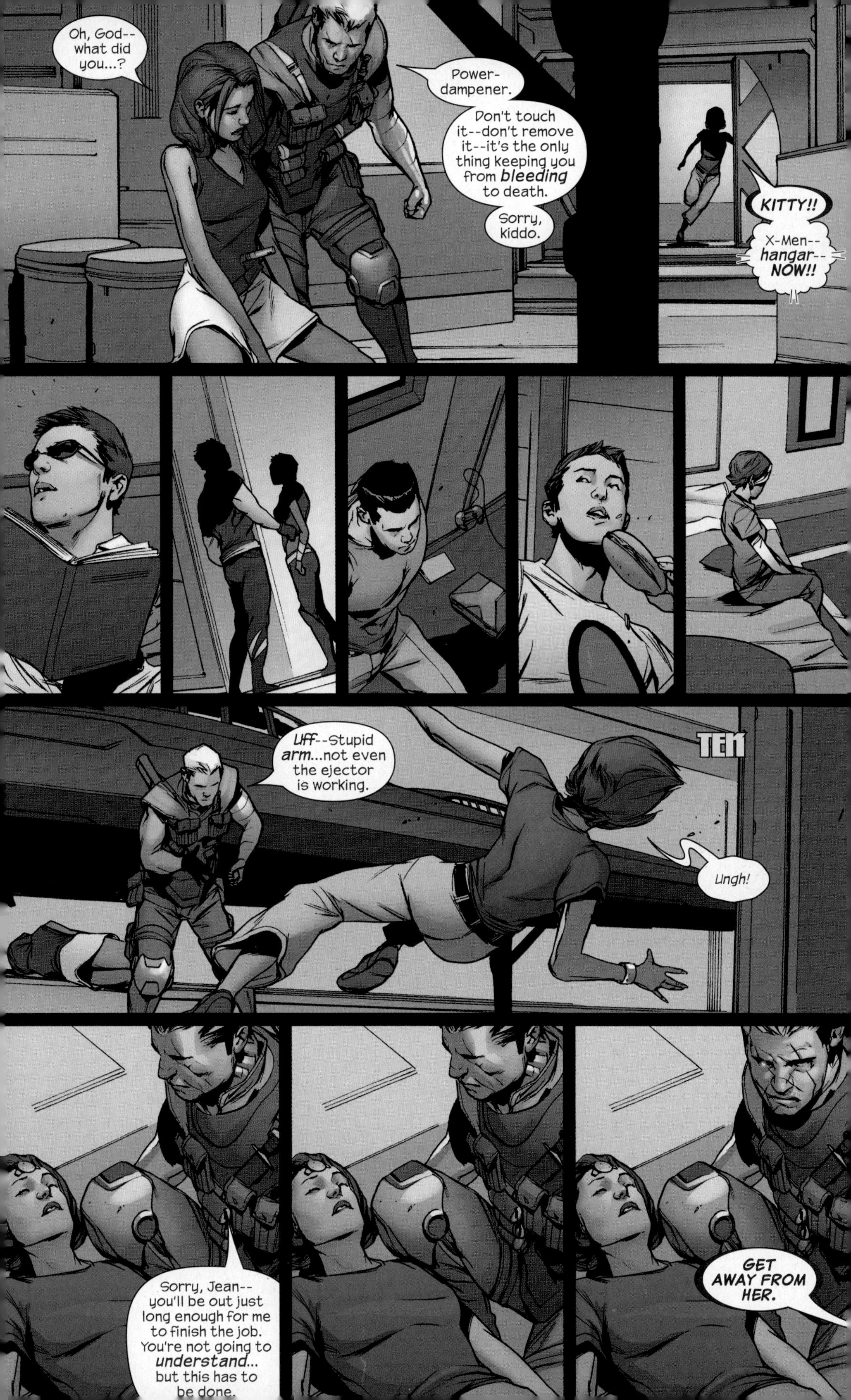
Oh, God--
what did
you...?
Power-
dampener.
Don't touch
it--don't remove
it--it's the only
thing keeping you
from *bleeding*
to death.
Sorry,
kiddo.
KITTY!!
X-Men--
hangar--
NOW!!
Uff--Stupid
arm...not even
the ejector
is working.
TEN
Ungh!
Sorry, Jean--
you'll be out just
long enough for me
to finish the job.
You're not going to
understand...
but this has to
be done.
GET
AWAY FROM
HER.

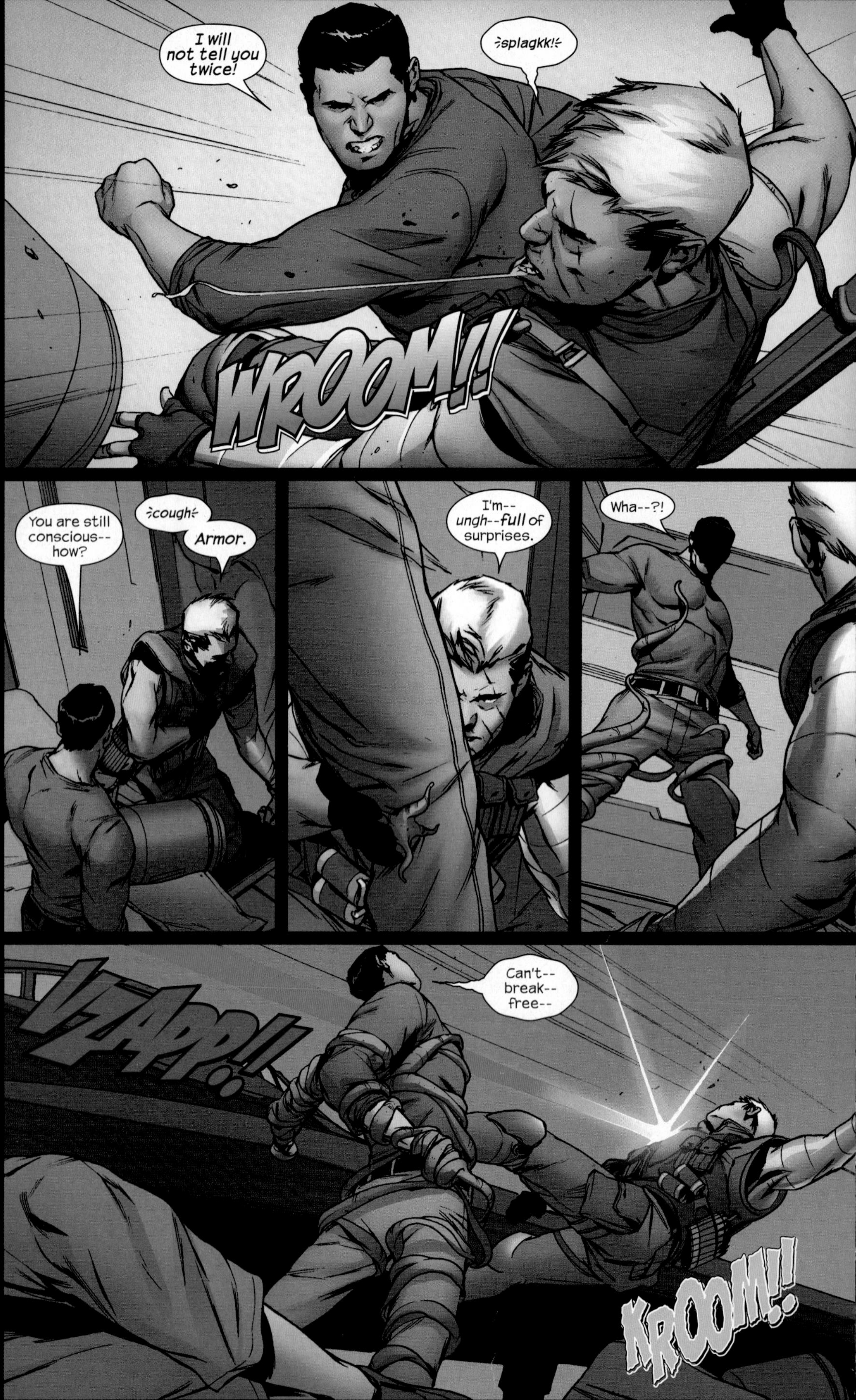
I will not tell you twice!
-splagkk!-
WROOM!!
You are still conscious--how?
-cough-
Armor.
I'm--ungh--full of surprises.
Wha--?!
VZAPP!!
Can't--break--free--
KROOM!!

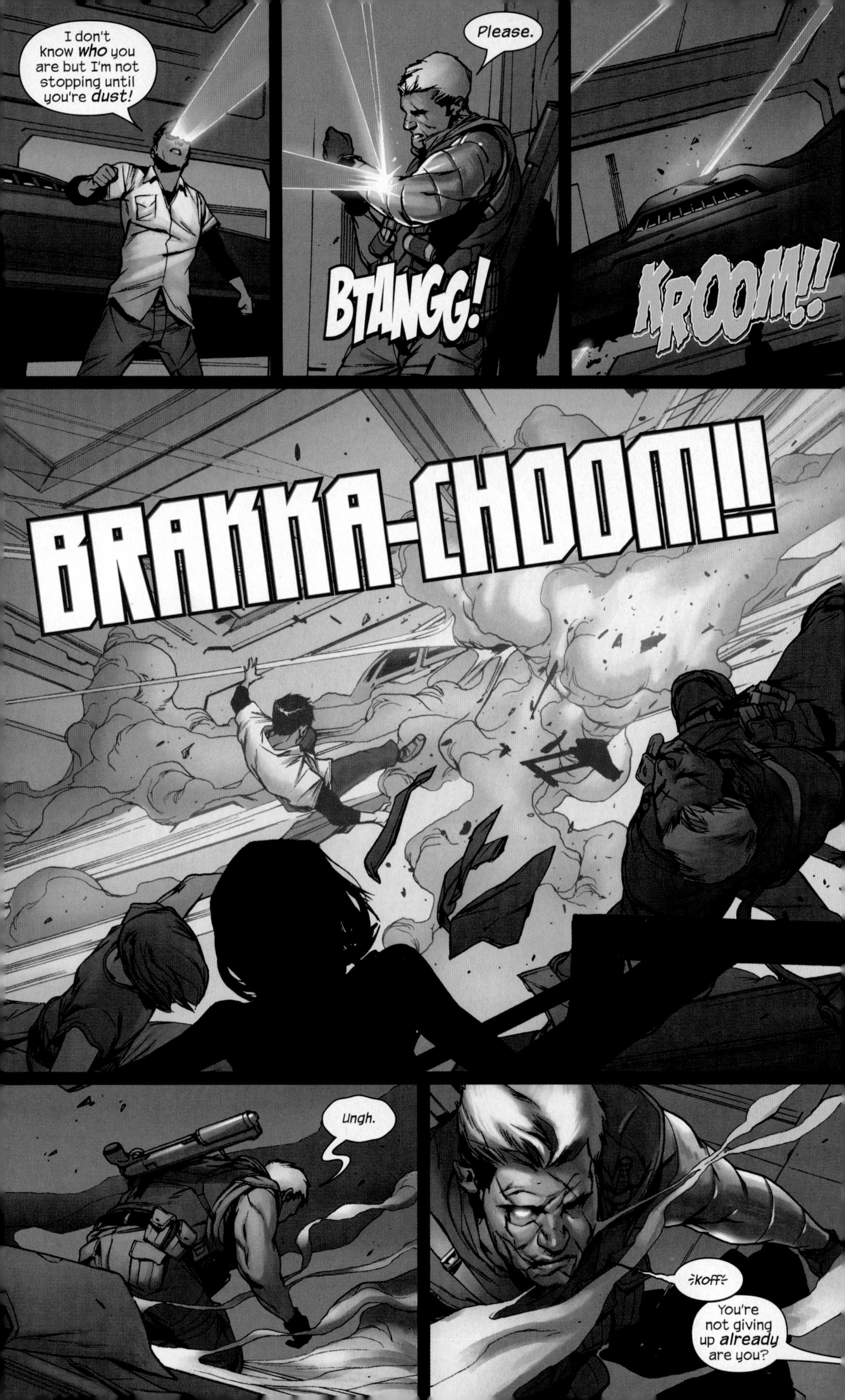
I don't know who you are but I'm not stopping until you're dust!
Please.
BTANGG!
KROOM!!
BRAKKA-CHOOM!!
Ungh.
koff
You're not giving up already are you?

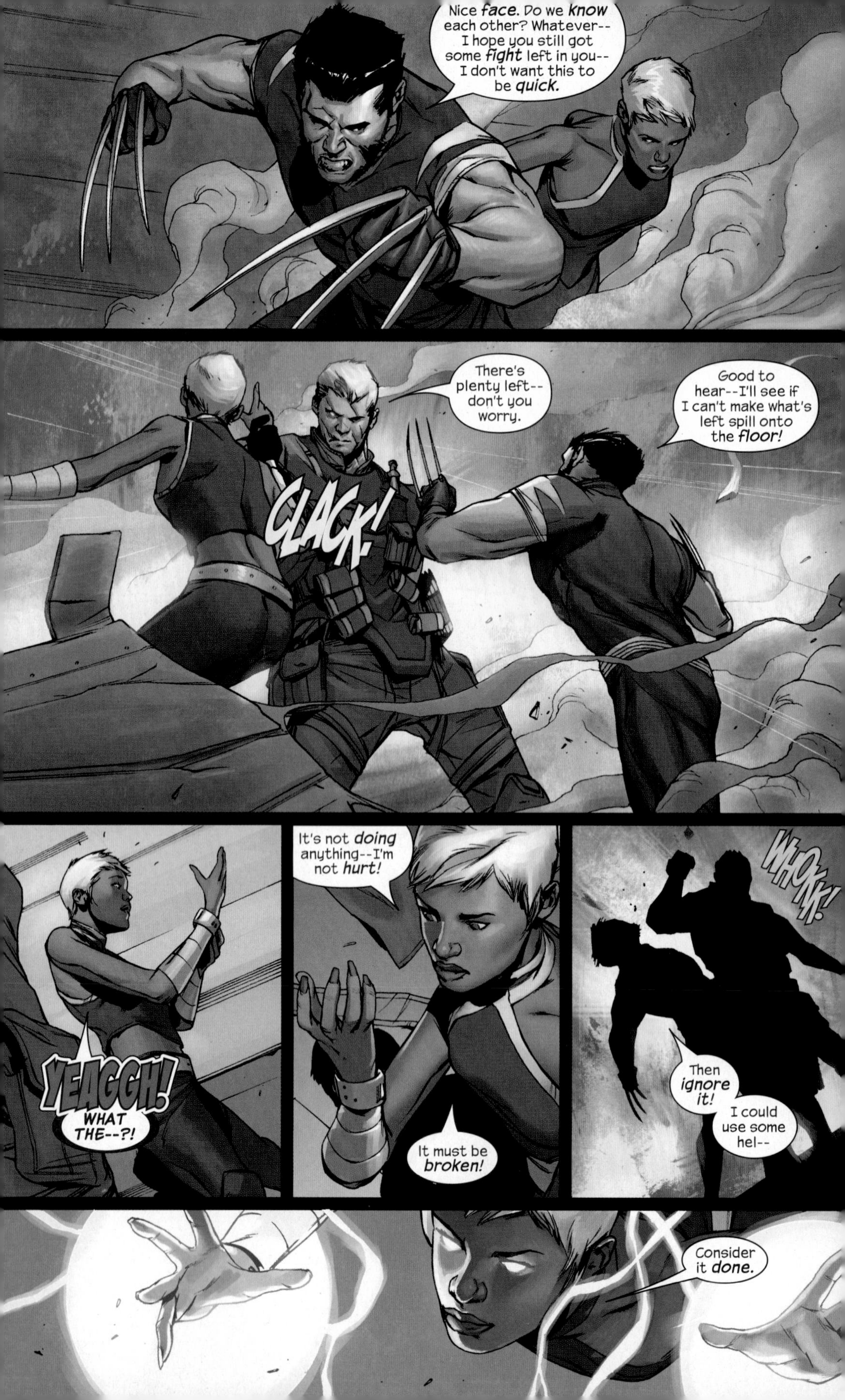
Nice face. Do we know each other? Whatever-- I hope you still got some fight left in you-- I don't want this to be quick.
There's plenty left-- don't you worry.
Good to hear--I'll see if I can't make what's left spill onto the floor!
CLACK!
YEAGGH! WHAT THE--?!
It's not doing anything--I'm not hurt!
It must be broken!
WHOKK!
Then ignore it!
I could use some hel--
Consider it done.

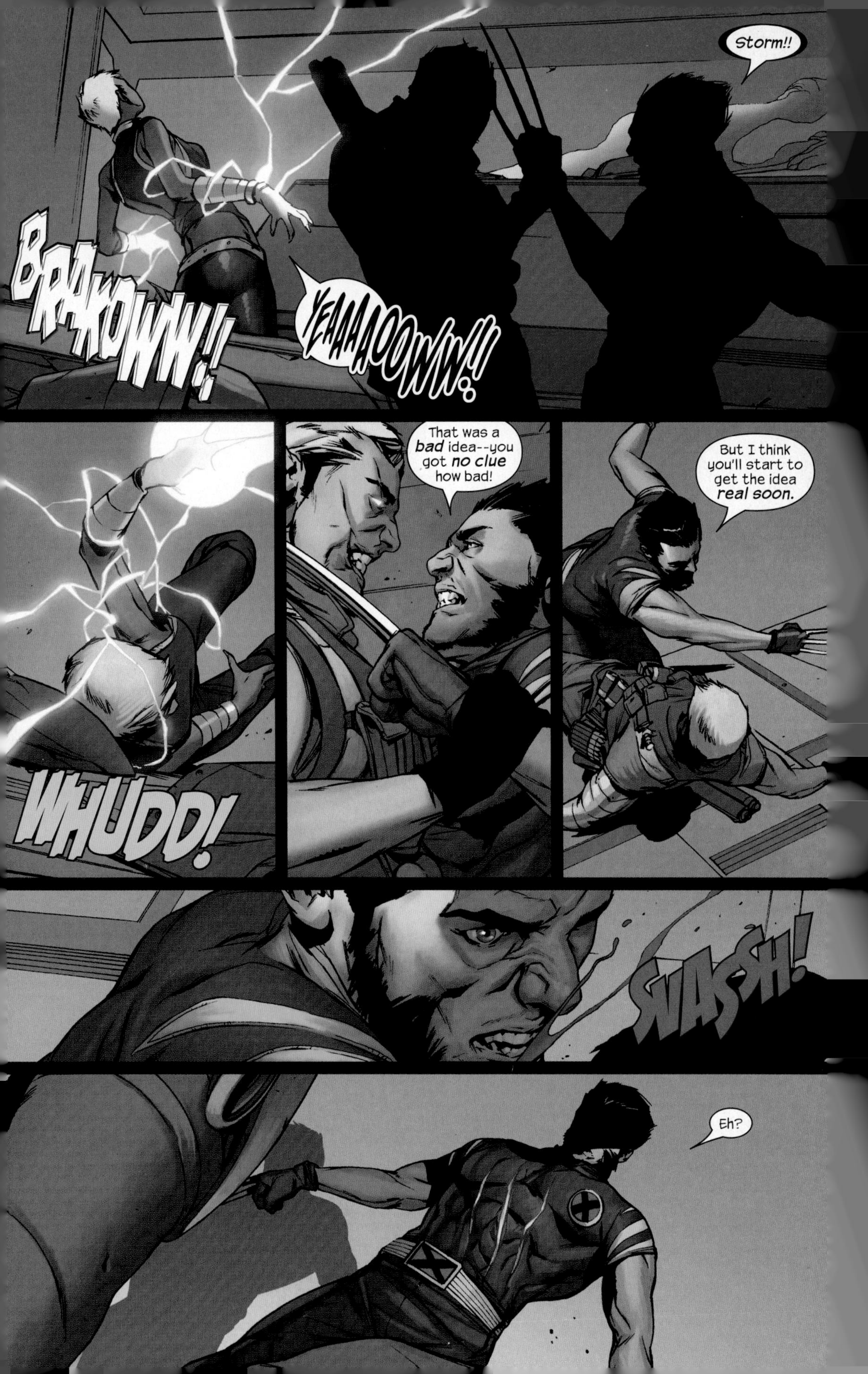
Storm!!
BRAKOWW!!
YEAAAAOOWW!!
WHUDD!
That was a bad idea--you got no clue how bad!
But I think you'll start to get the idea real soon.
SWASH!
Eh?

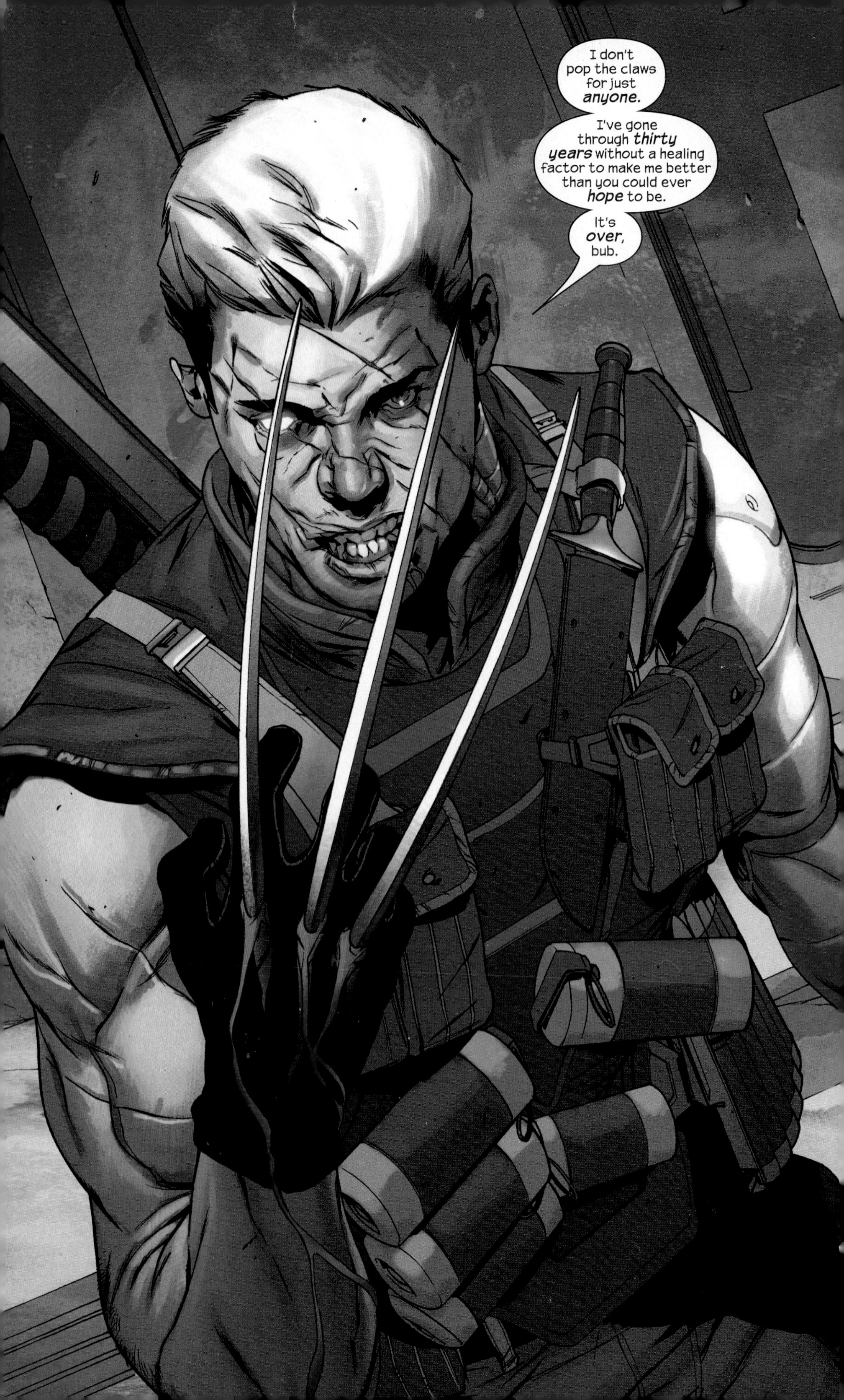
I don't pop the claws for just *anyone.*
I've gone through *thirty years* without a healing factor to make me better than you could ever *hope* to be.
It's *over,* bub.

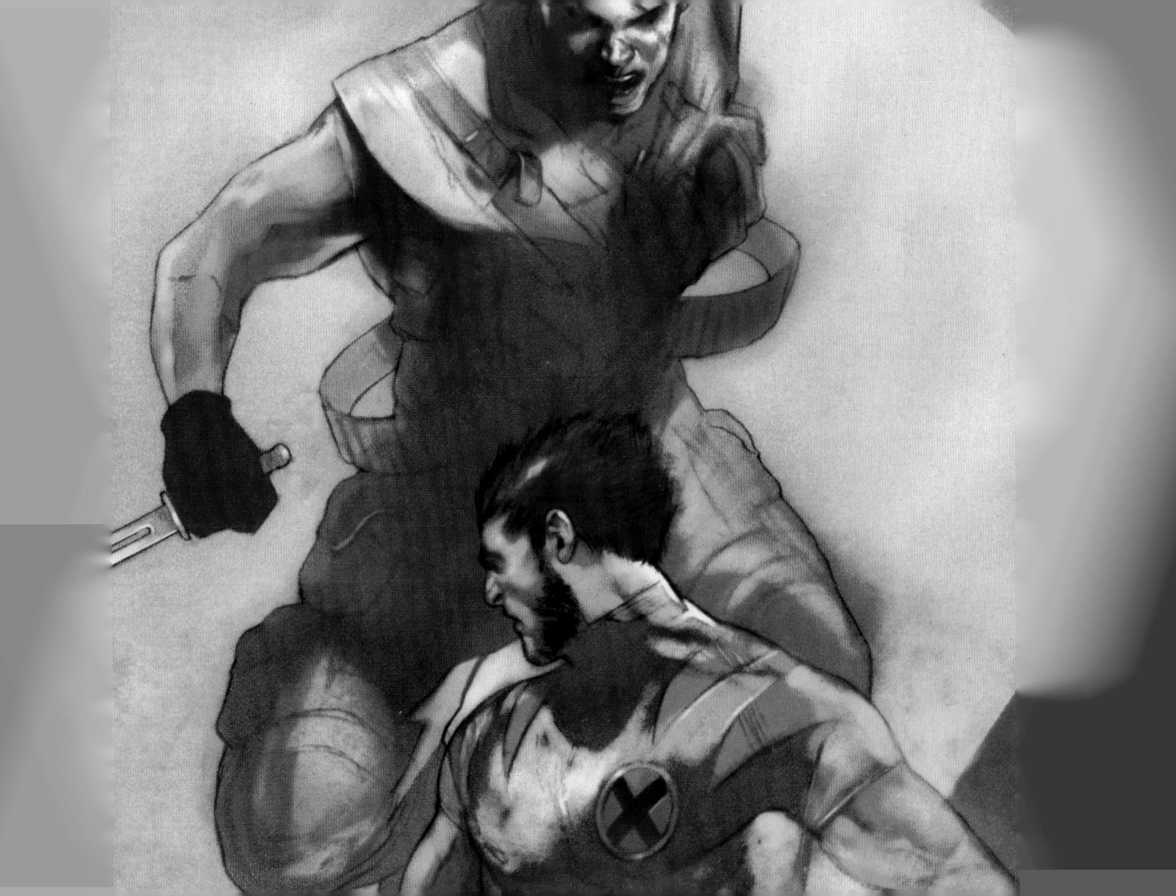

CABLE PART 2 (OF 4)

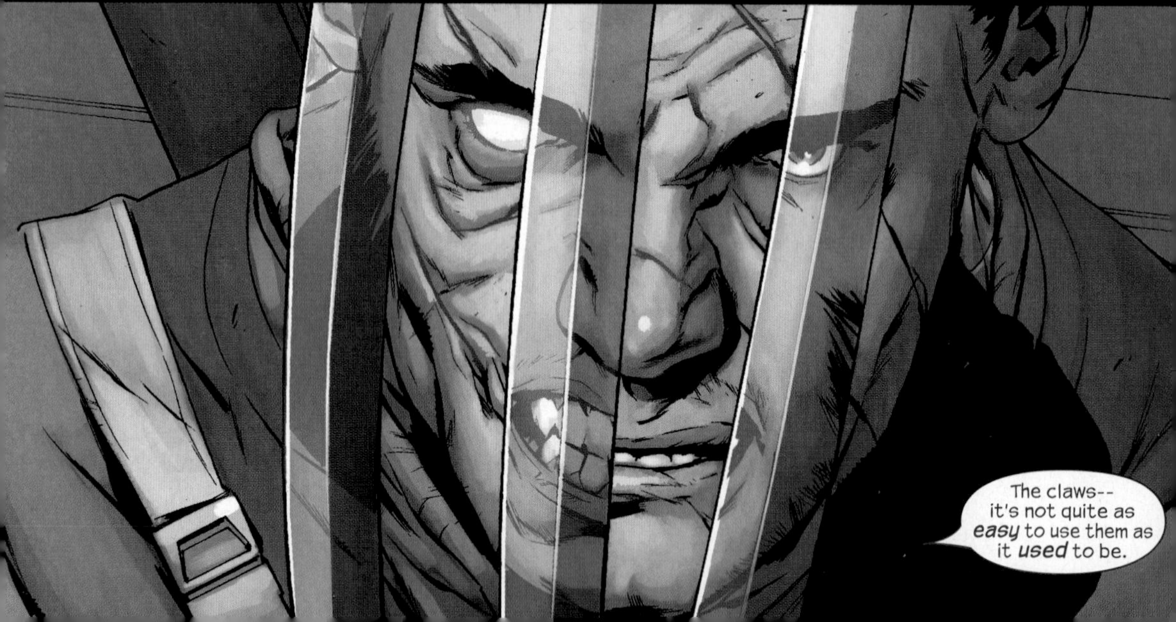
The claws-- it's not quite as *easy* to use them as it *used* to be.

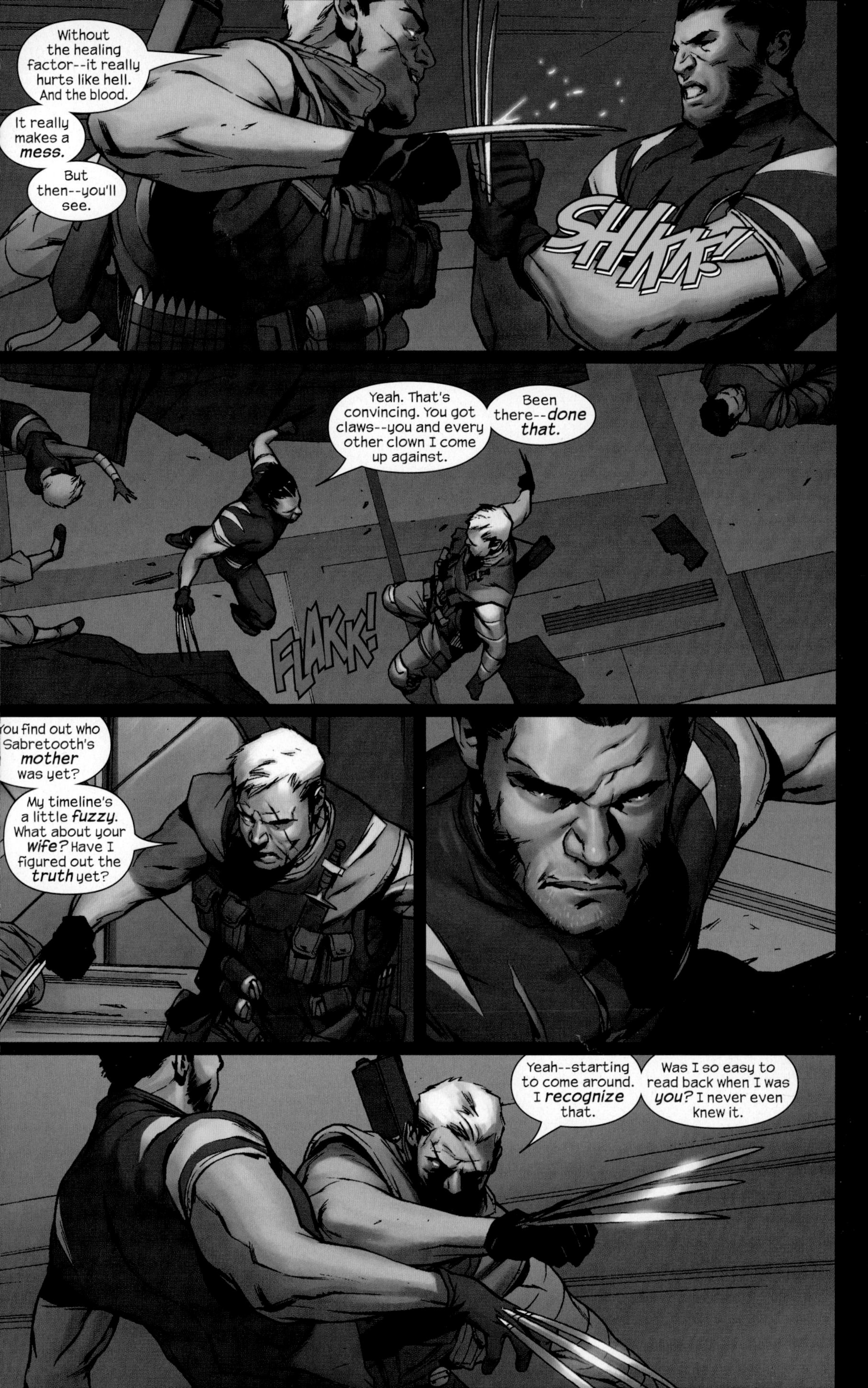
Without the healing factor--it really hurts like hell. And the blood.
It really makes a *mess.*
But then--you'll see.
SHIKK!
Yeah. That's convincing. You got claws--you and every other clown I come up against.
Been there--*done that.*
FLAKK!
You find out who Sabretooth's *mother* was yet?
My timeline's a little *fuzzy.* What about your *wife?* Have I figured out the *truth* yet?
Yeah--starting to come around. I *recognize* that.
Was I so easy to read back when I was *you?* I never even knew it.

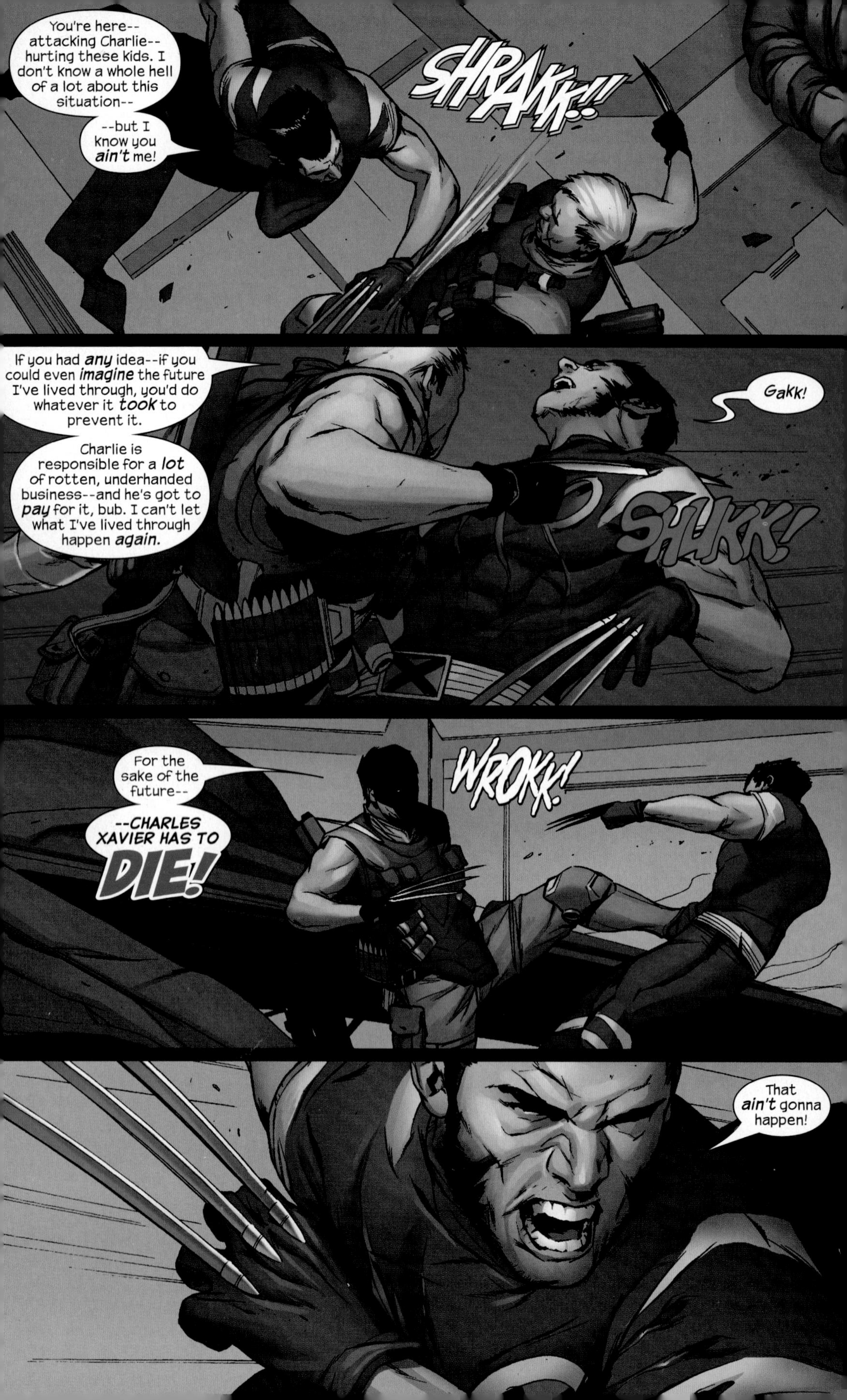
You're here--attacking Charlie--hurting these kids. I don't know a whole hell of a lot about this situation--
--but I know you ain't me!
SHRAKK!!
If you had any idea--if you could even imagine the future I've lived through, you'd do whatever it took to prevent it.
Charlie is responsible for a lot of rotten, underhanded business--and he's got to pay for it, bub. I can't let what I've lived through happen again.
Gakk!
SHUKK!
For the sake of the future--
--CHARLES XAVIER HAS TO DIE!
WROKK!
That ain't gonna happen!

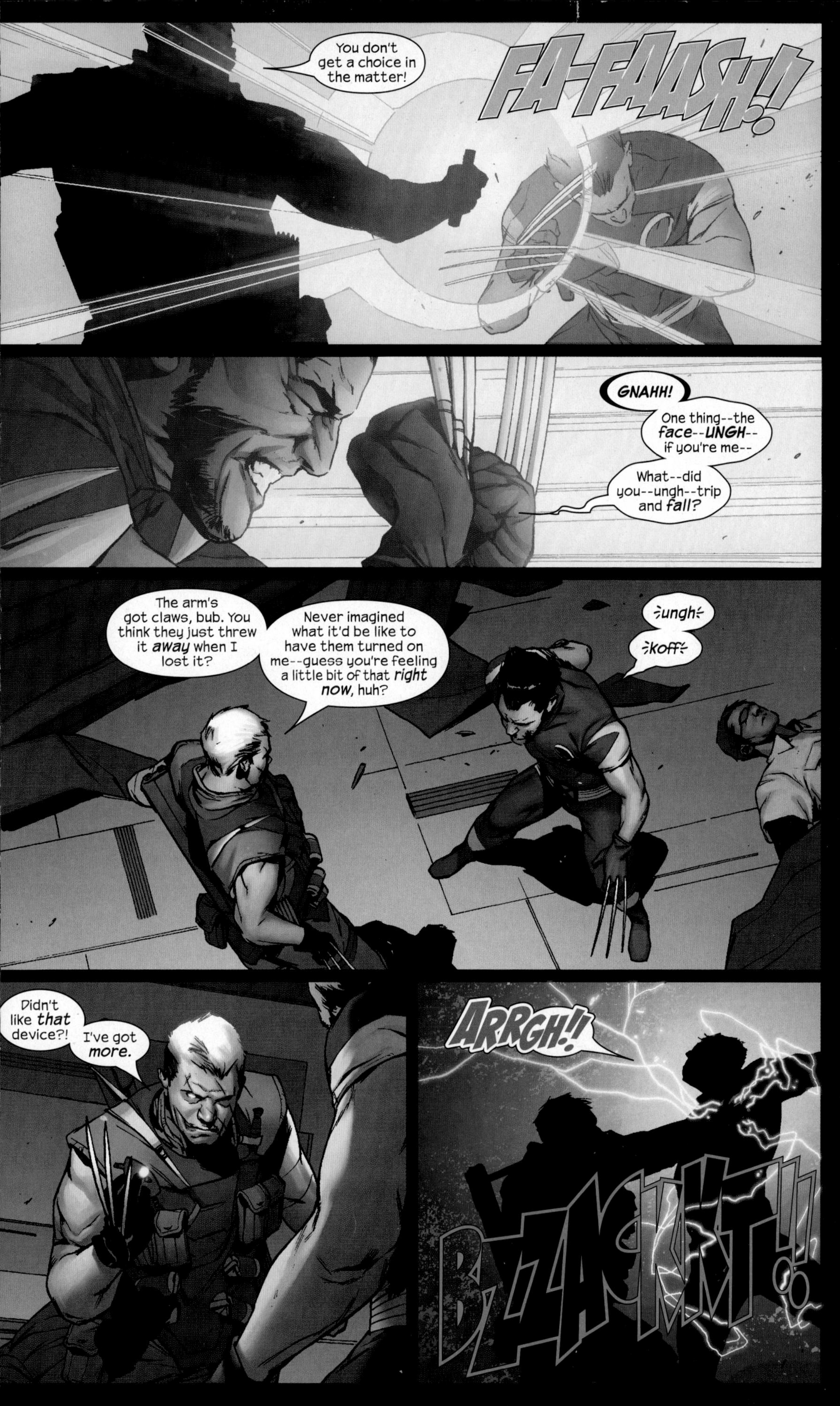
You don't get a choice in the matter!
FA-FAASH!!
GNAHH!
One thing--the face--UNGH--if you're me--
What--did you--ungh--trip and fall?
The arm's got claws, bub. You think they just threw it away when I lost it?
Never imagined what it'd be like to have them turned on me--guess you're feeling a little bit of that right now, huh?
ungh
koff
Didn't like that device?!
I've got more.
ARRGH!!
BZACKKT!!

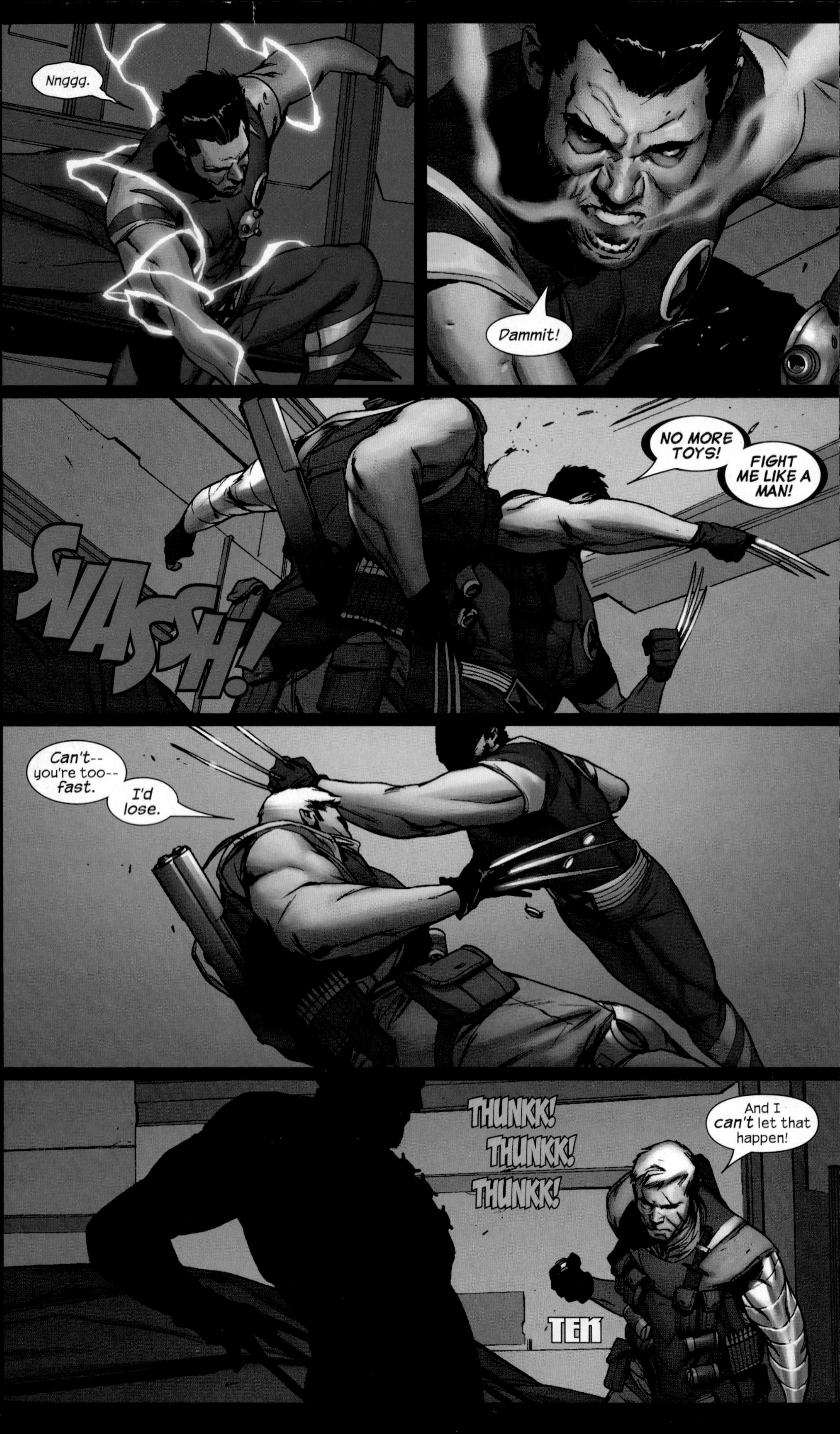
Nnggg.
Dammit!
NO MORE TOYS!
FIGHT ME LIKE A MAN!
SNASH!
Can't-- you're too-- fast.
I'd lose.
THUNKK!
THUNKK!
THUNKK!
And I can't let that happen!
TEN

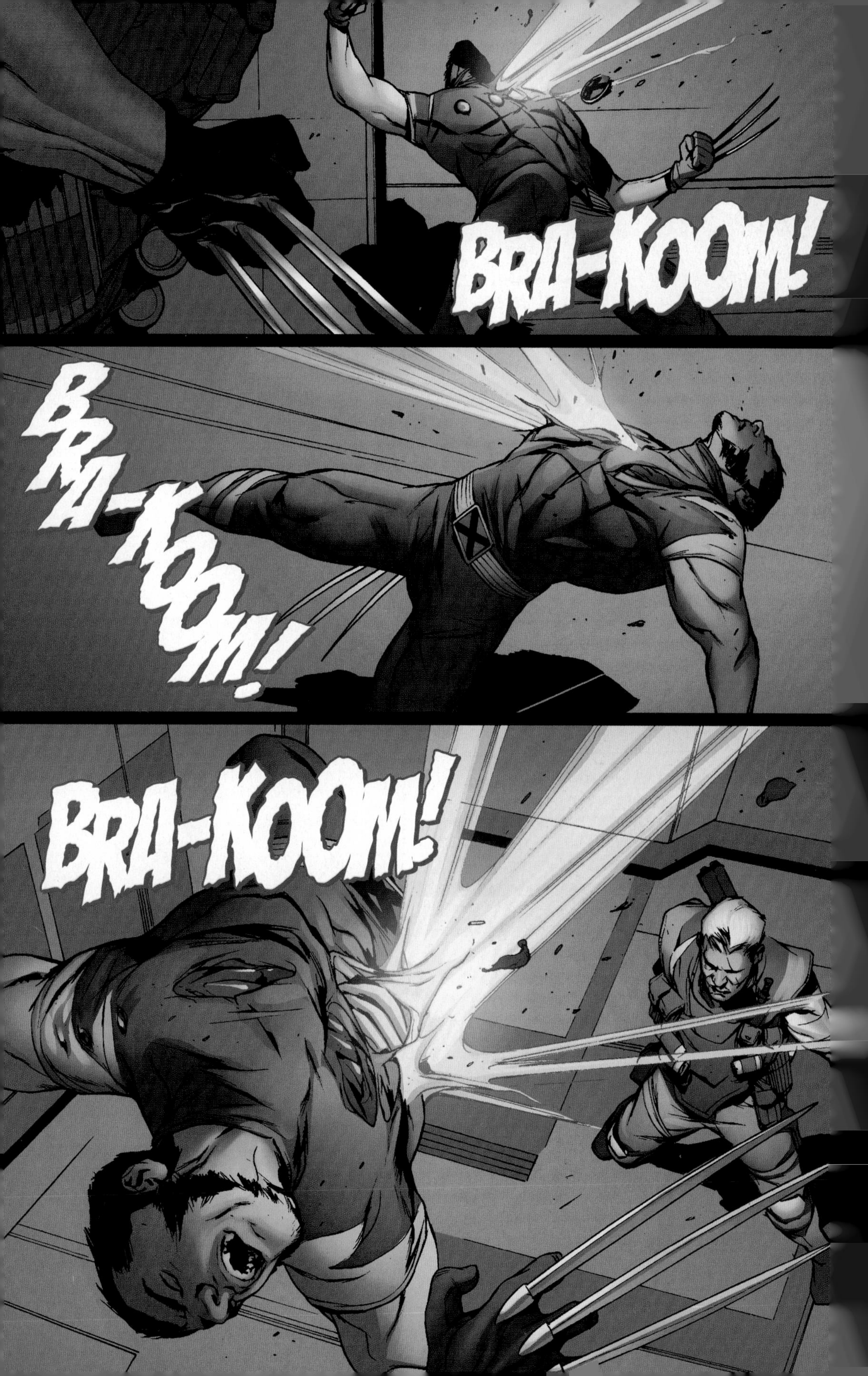
BRA-KOOM!
BRA-KOOM!
BRA-KOOM!

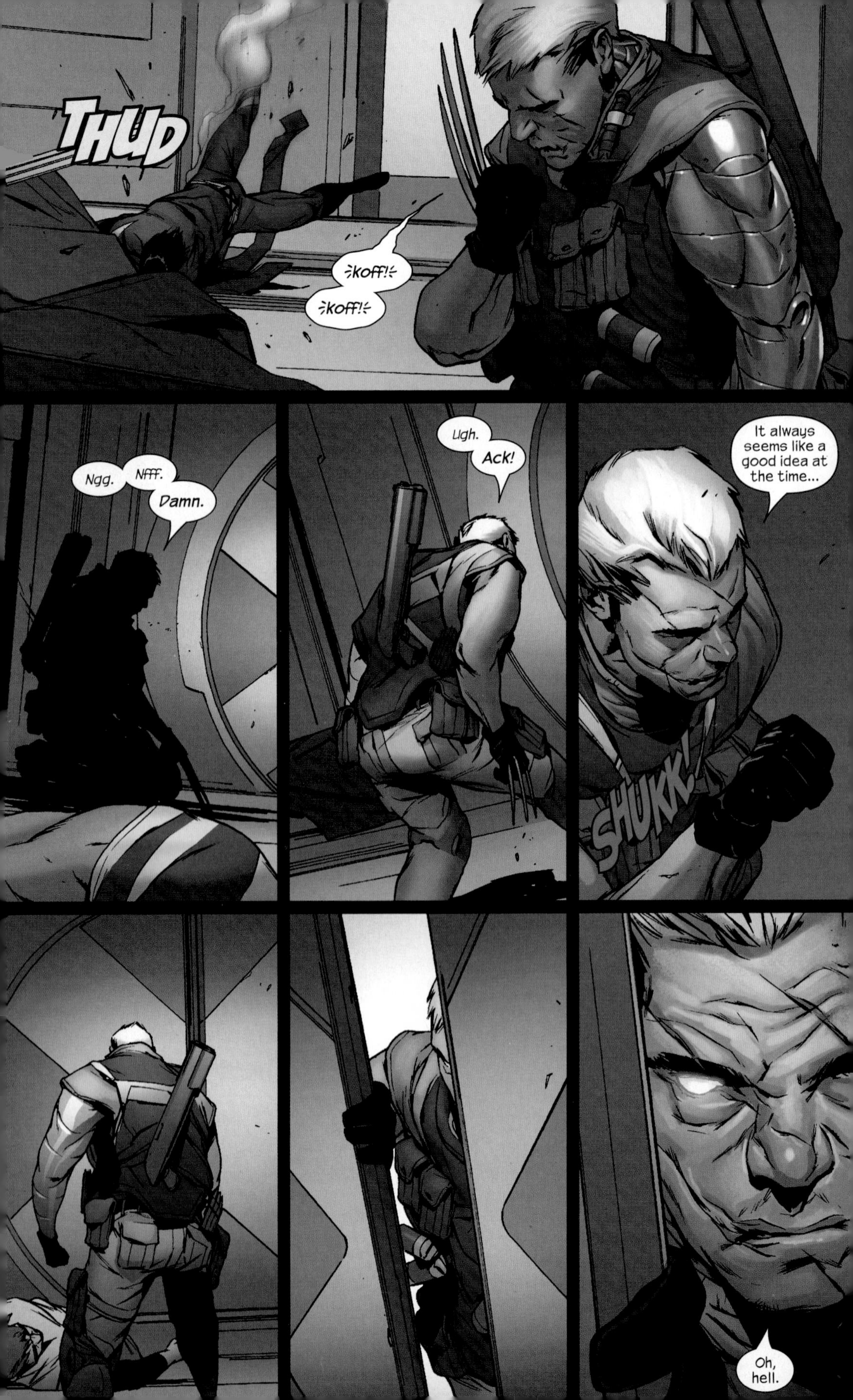
THUD
KOFF!
KOFF!
Ngg.
Nfff.
Damn.
Ugh.
Ack!
It always seems like a good idea at the time...
SHUKK!
Oh, hell.

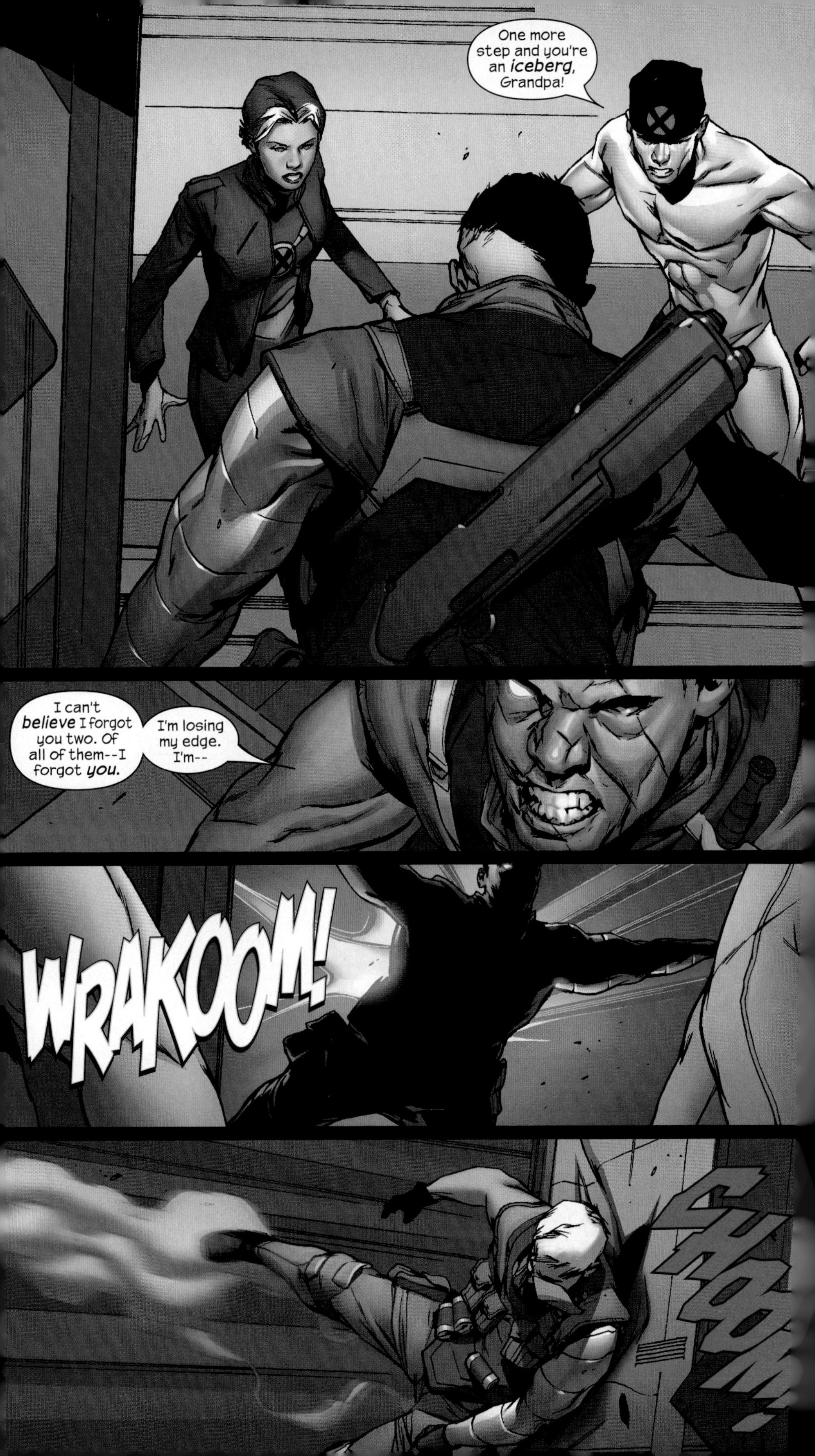

One more step and you're an iceberg, Grandpa!
I can't believe I forgot you two. Of all of them--I forgot you.
I'm losing my edge. I'm--
WRAKOOM!
CHOOM!

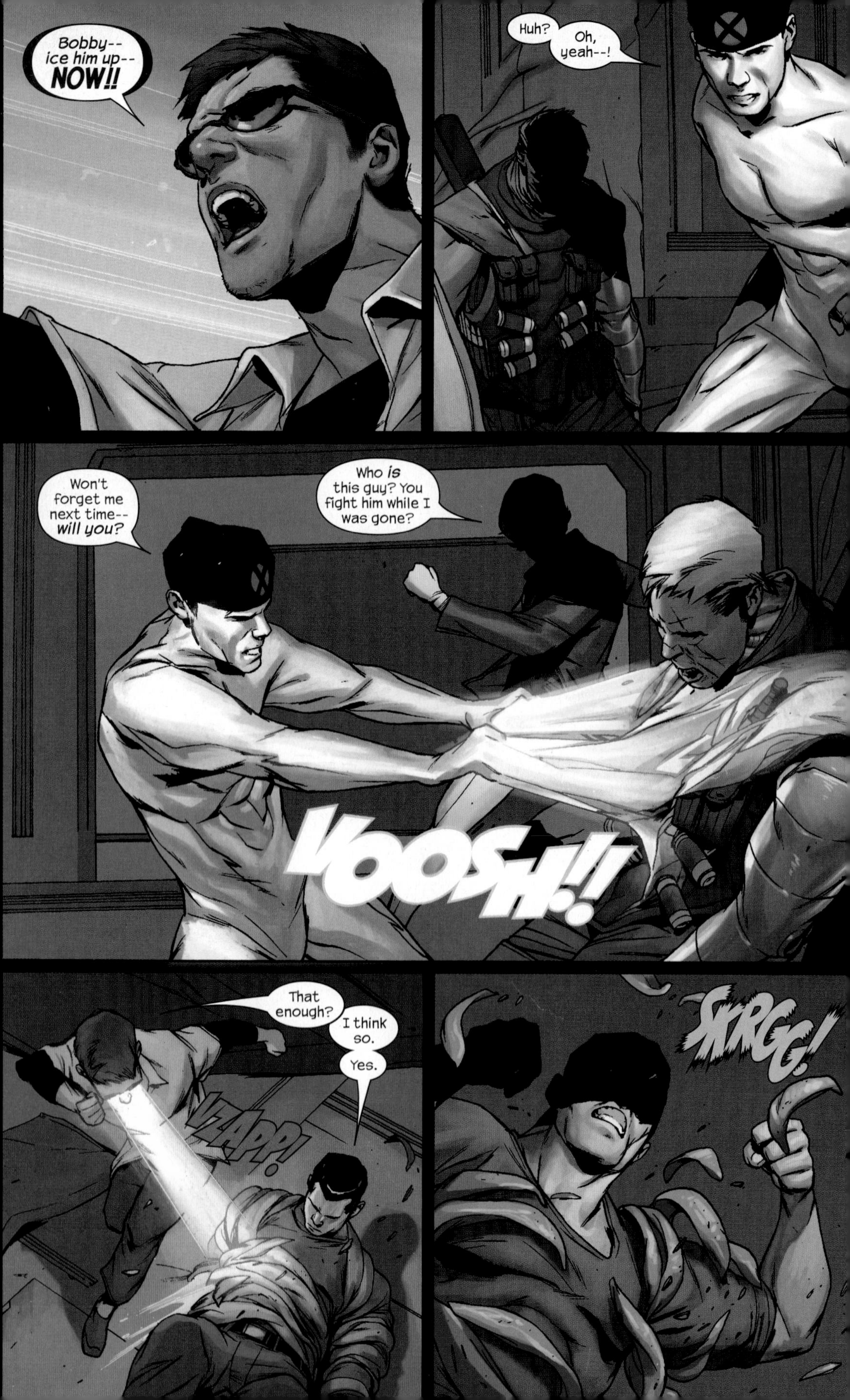
Bobby-- ice him up-- NOW!!
Huh?
Oh, yeah--!
Won't forget me next time-- will you?
Who is this guy? You fight him while I was gone?
VOOSH!!
That enough?
I think so.
Yes.
VZAPP!
SKRGG!

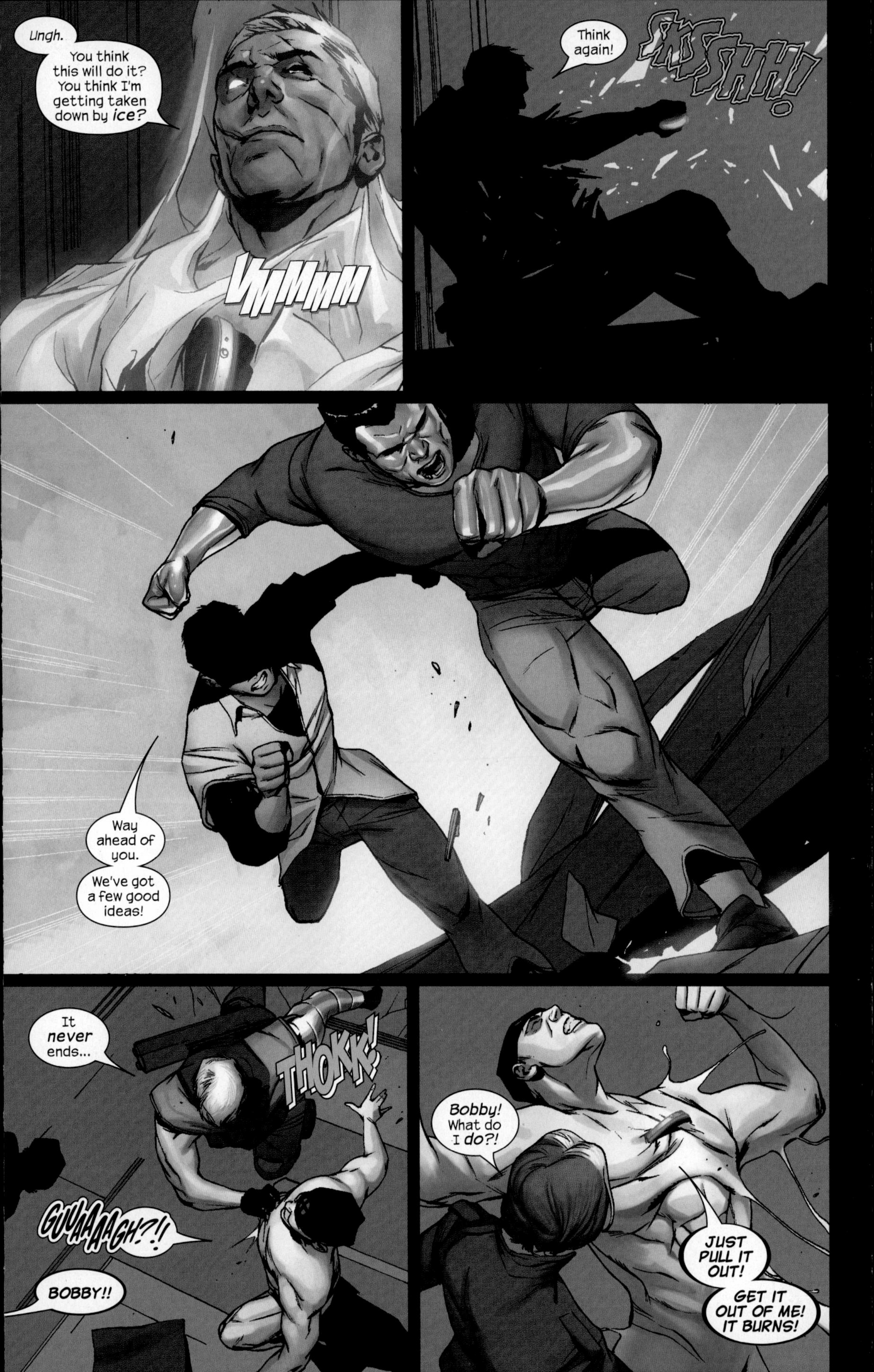

Ungh.
You think this will do it? You think I'm getting taken down by ice?
VMMMMM
Think again!
SKSSHH!
Way ahead of you.
We've got a few good ideas!
It never ends...
THOKK!
GUYAAAAGH?!!
BOBBY!!
Bobby! What do I do?!
JUST PULL IT OUT!
GET IT OUT OF ME! IT BURNS!

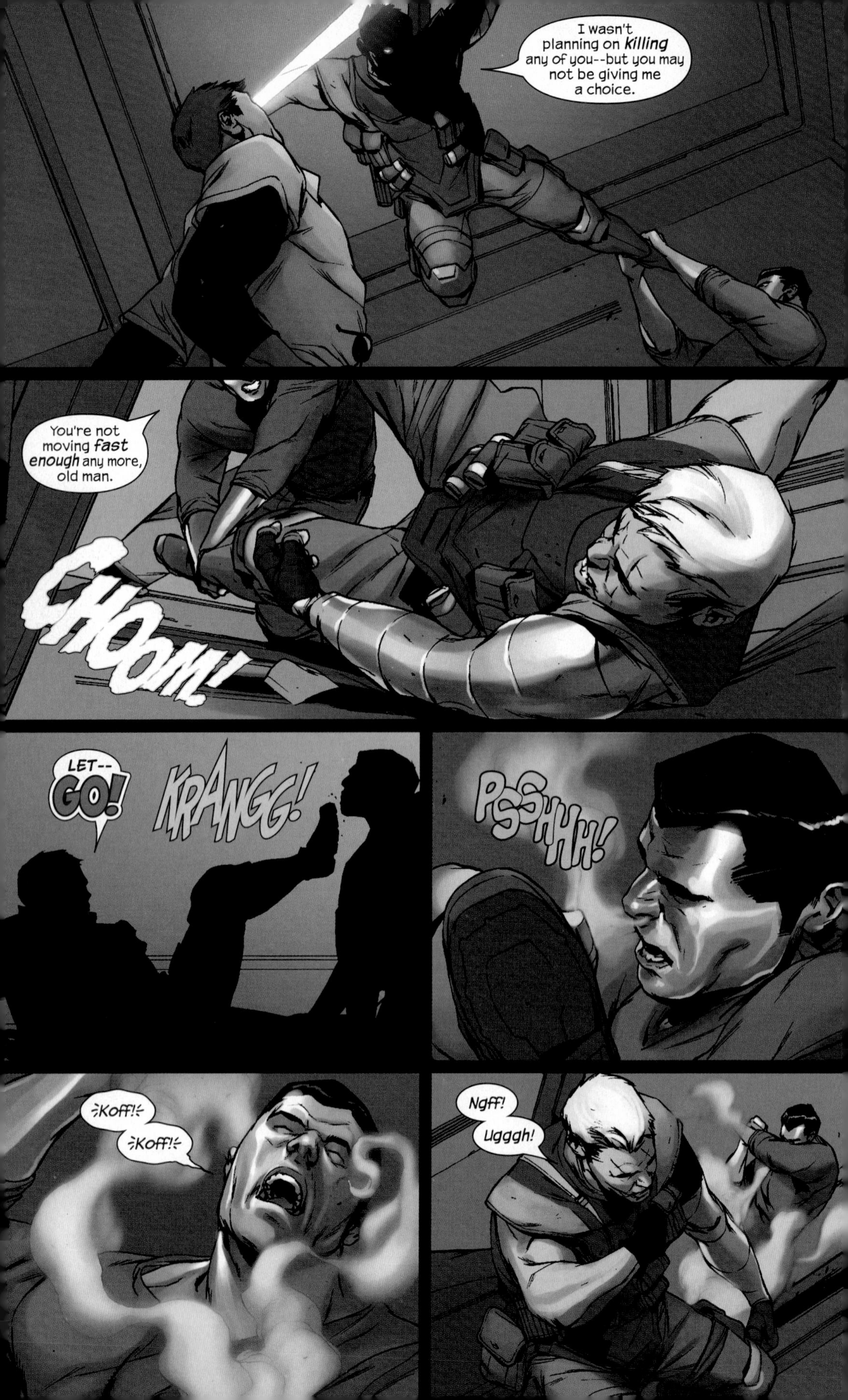

I wasn't planning on killing any of you--but you may not be giving me a choice.
You're not moving fast enough any more, old man.
CHOOM!
LET-- GO!
KRANGG!
PSSHHH!
Koff!
Koff!
Ngff!
Ugggh!

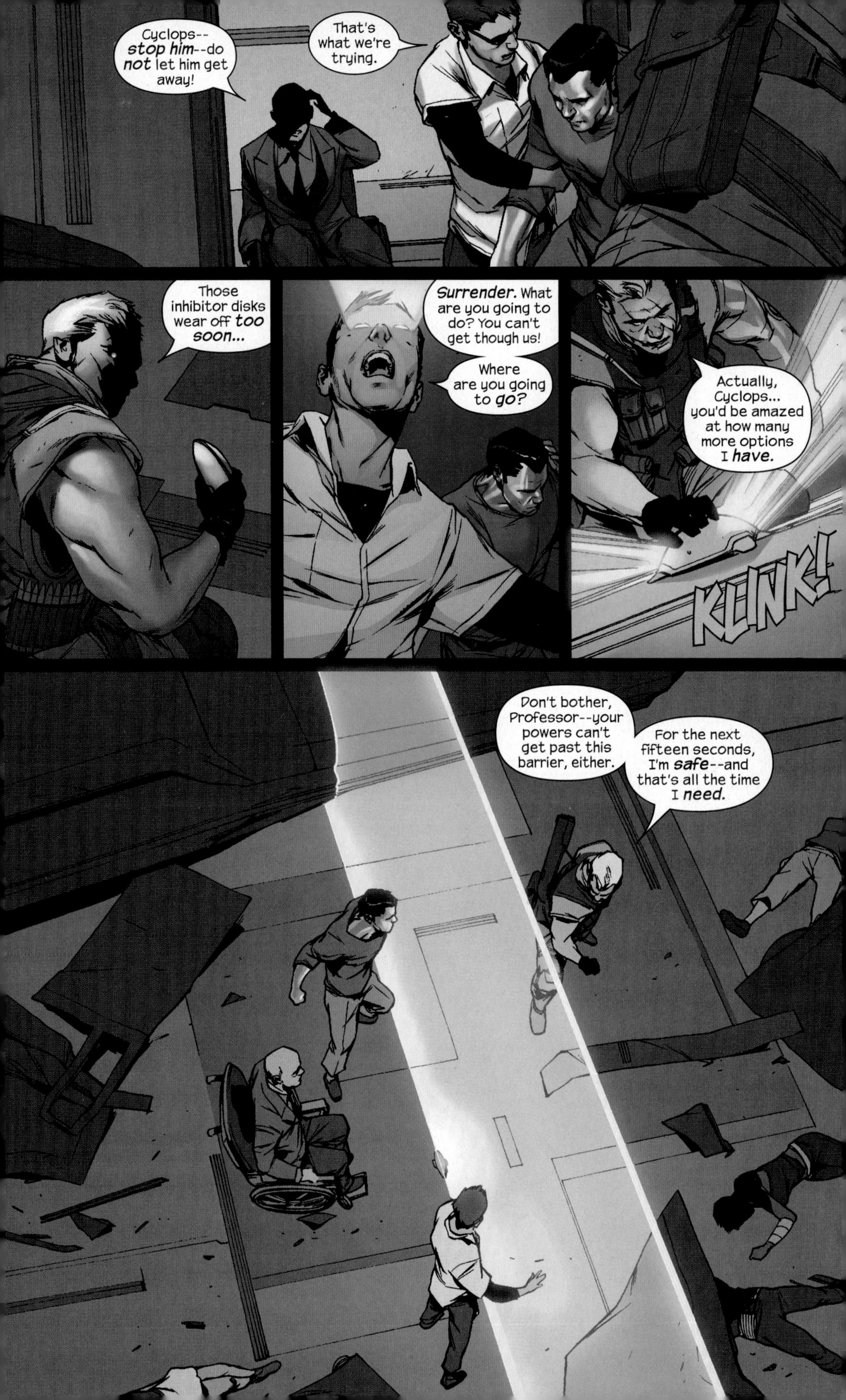

Cyclops--stop him--do not let him get away!
That's what we're trying.
Those inhibitor disks wear off too soon...
Surrender. What are you going to do? You can't get though us!
Where are you going to go?
Actually, Cyclops... you'd be amazed at how many more options I have.
KLINK!
Don't bother, Professor--your powers can't get past this barrier, either.
For the next fifteen seconds, I'm safe--and that's all the time I need.

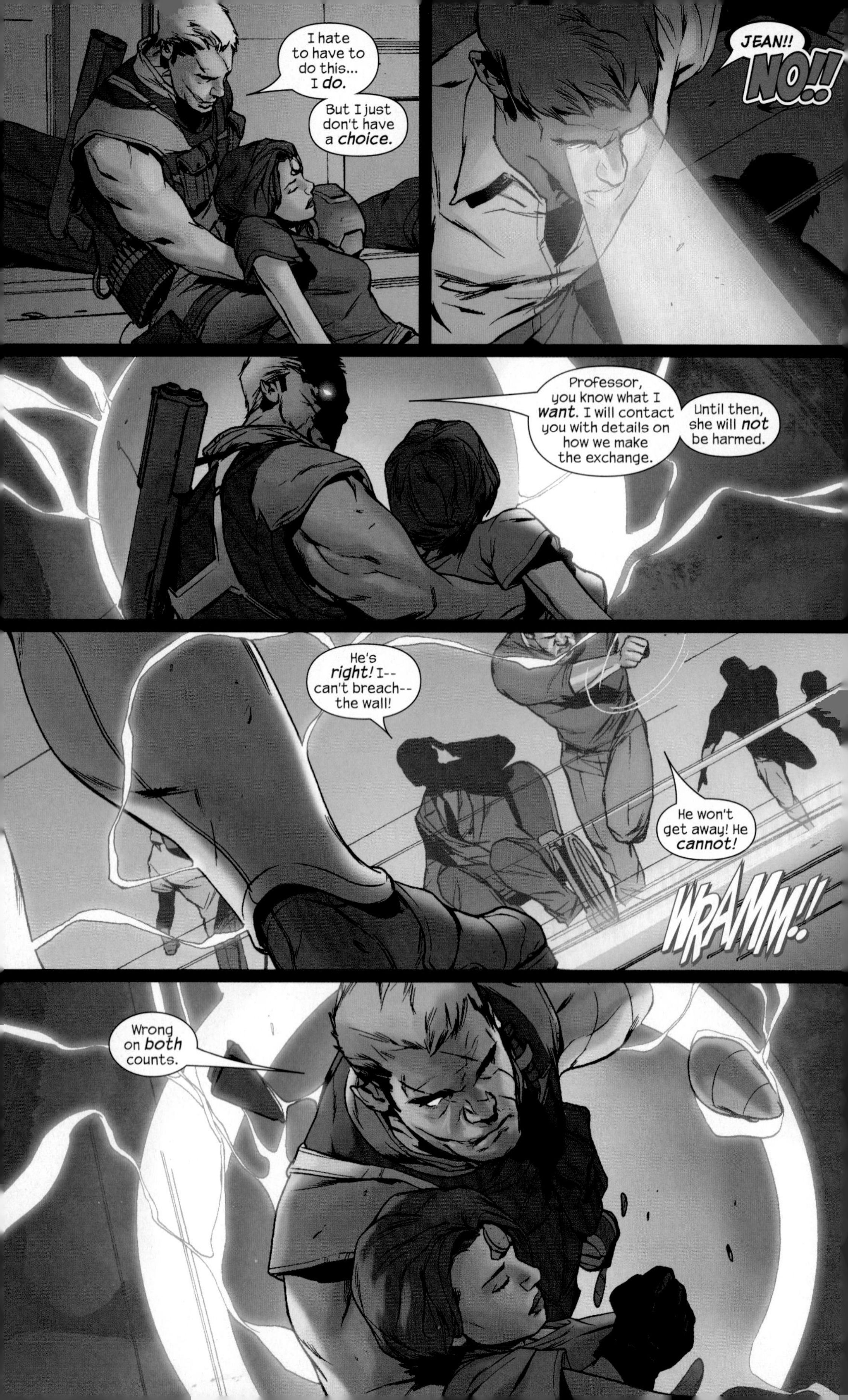

I hate to have to do this... I *do.*
But I just don't have a *choice.*
JEAN!! NO!!
Professor, you know what I *want.* I will contact you with details on how we make the exchange.
Until then, she will *not* be harmed.
He's *right!* I-- can't breach-- the wall!
He won't get away! He *cannot!*
WRAMM!!
Wrong on *both* counts.

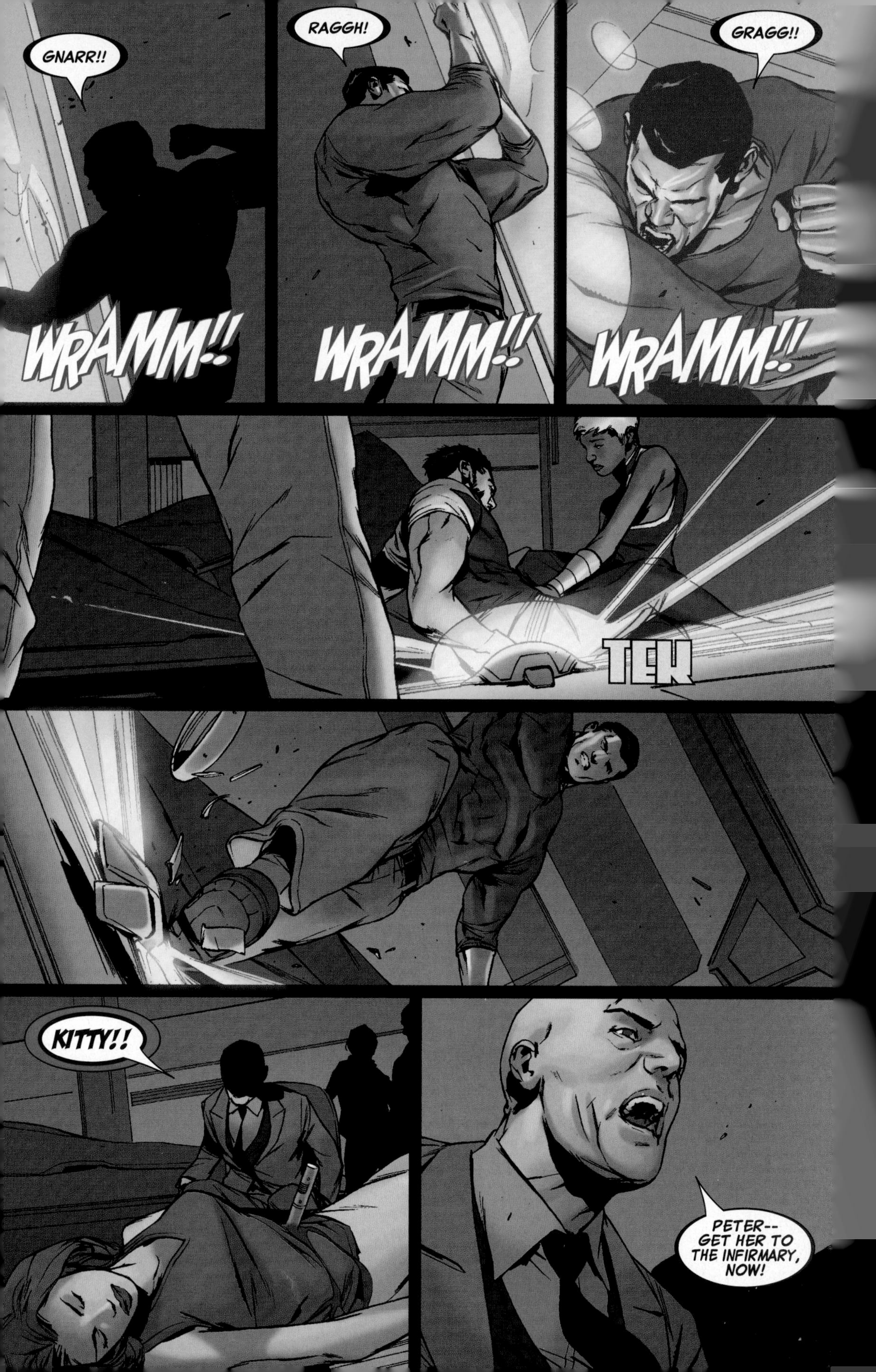
GNARR!!
WRAMM!!
RAGGH!
WRAMM!!
GRAGG!!
WRAMM!!
TEK
KITTY!!
PETER-- GET HER TO THE INFIRMARY, NOW!

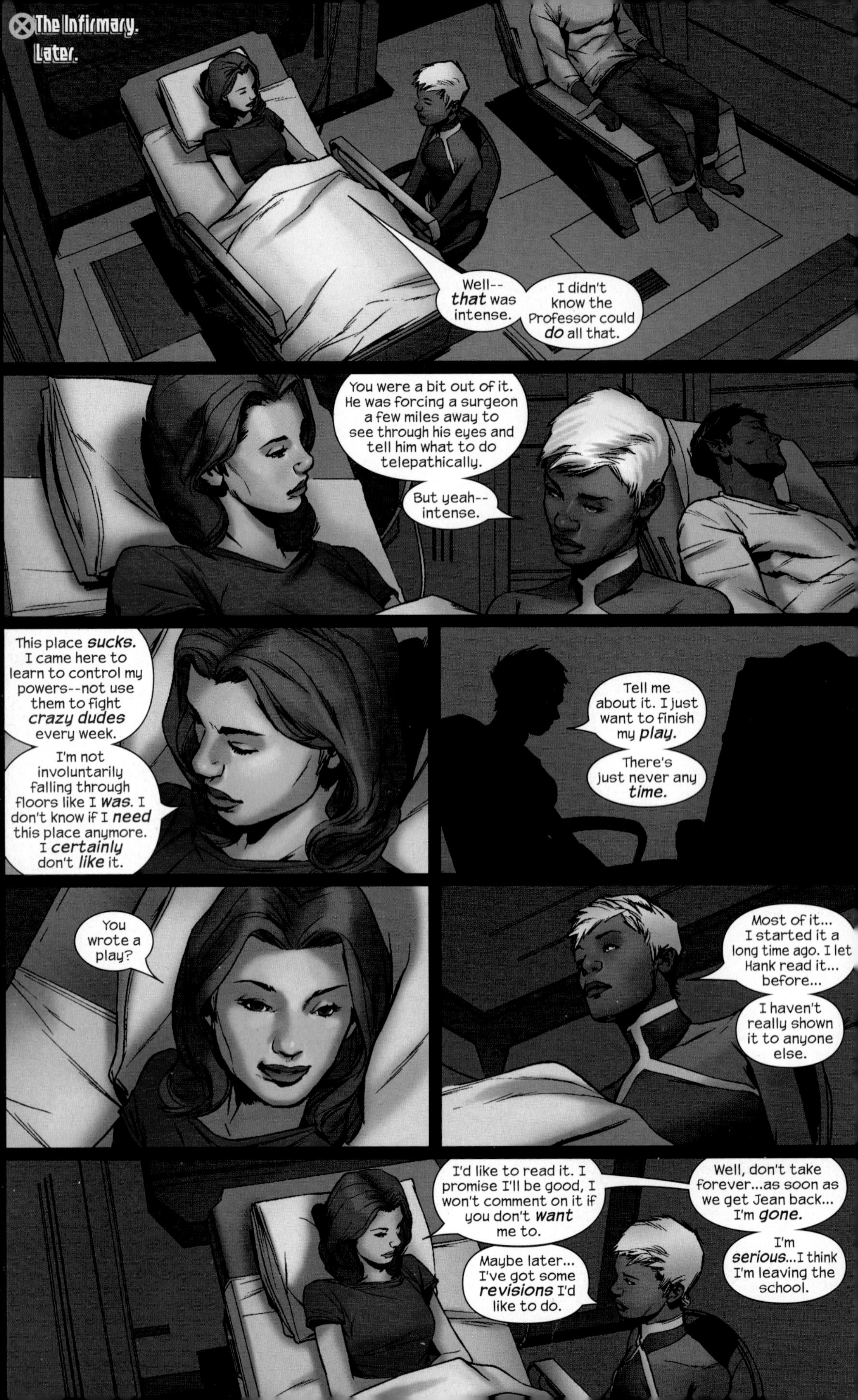
The Infirmary.
Later.
Well-- *that* was intense.
I didn't know the Professor could *do* all that.
You were a bit out of it. He was forcing a surgeon a few miles away to see through his eyes and tell him what to do telepathically.
But yeah-- intense.
This place *sucks.* I came here to learn to control my powers--not use them to fight *crazy dudes* every week.
I'm not involuntarily falling through floors like I *was.* I don't know if I *need* this place anymore. I *certainly* don't *like* it.
Tell me about it. I just want to finish my *play.*
There's just never any *time.*
You wrote a play?
Most of it... I started it a long time ago. I let Hank read it... before...
I haven't really shown it to anyone else.
I'd like to read it. I promise I'll be good, I won't comment on it if you don't *want* me to.
Maybe later... I've got some *revisions* I'd like to do.
Well, don't take forever...as soon as we get Jean back... I'm *gone.*
I'm *serious*...I think I'm leaving the school.

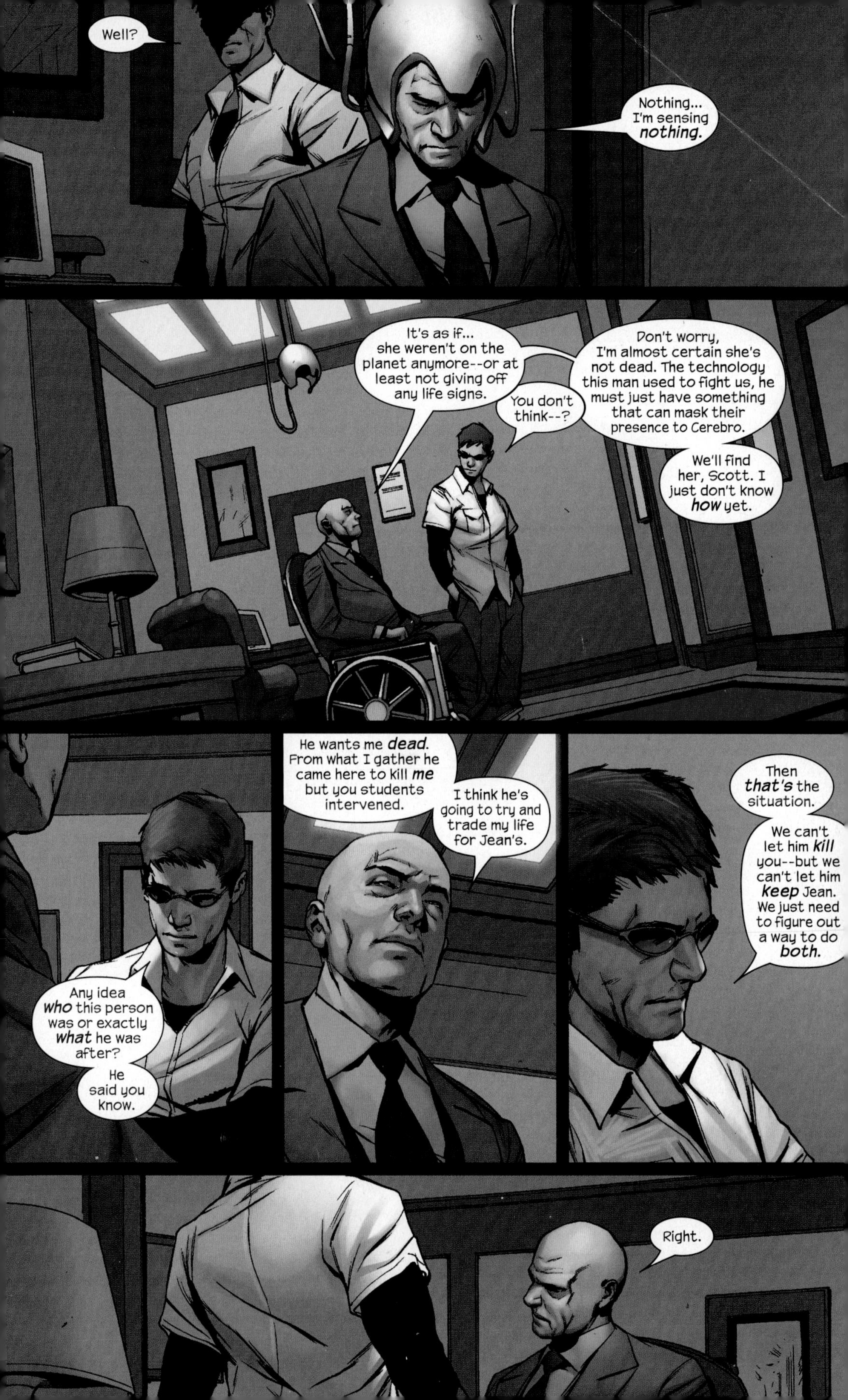
Well?
Nothing... I'm sensing *nothing.*
It's as if... she weren't on the planet anymore--or at least not giving off any life signs.
You don't think--?
Don't worry, I'm almost certain she's not dead. The technology this man used to fight us, he must just have something that can mask their presence to Cerebro.
We'll find her, Scott. I just don't know *how* yet.
Any idea *who* this person was or exactly *what* he was after?
He said you know.
He wants me *dead*. From what I gather he came here to kill *me* but you students intervened.
I think he's going to try and trade my life for Jean's.
Then *that's* the situation.
We can't let him *kill* you--but we can't let him *keep* Jean. We just need to figure out a way to do *both.*
Right.

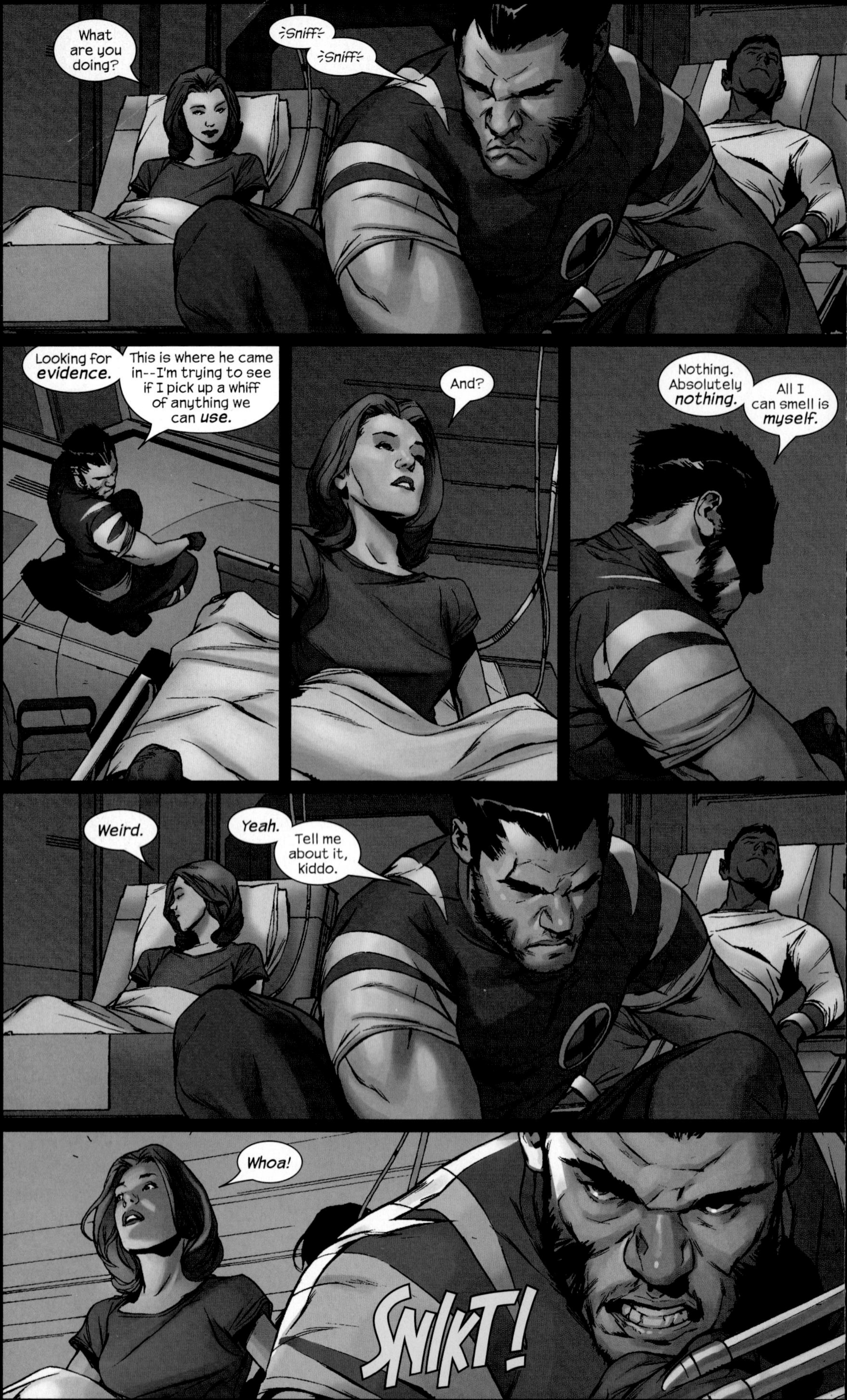
What are you doing?
Sniff
Sniff
Looking for evidence.
This is where he came in--I'm trying to see if I pick up a whiff of anything we can use.
And?
Nothing. Absolutely nothing.
All I can smell is myself.
Weird.
Yeah.
Tell me about it, kiddo.
Whoa!
SNIKT!

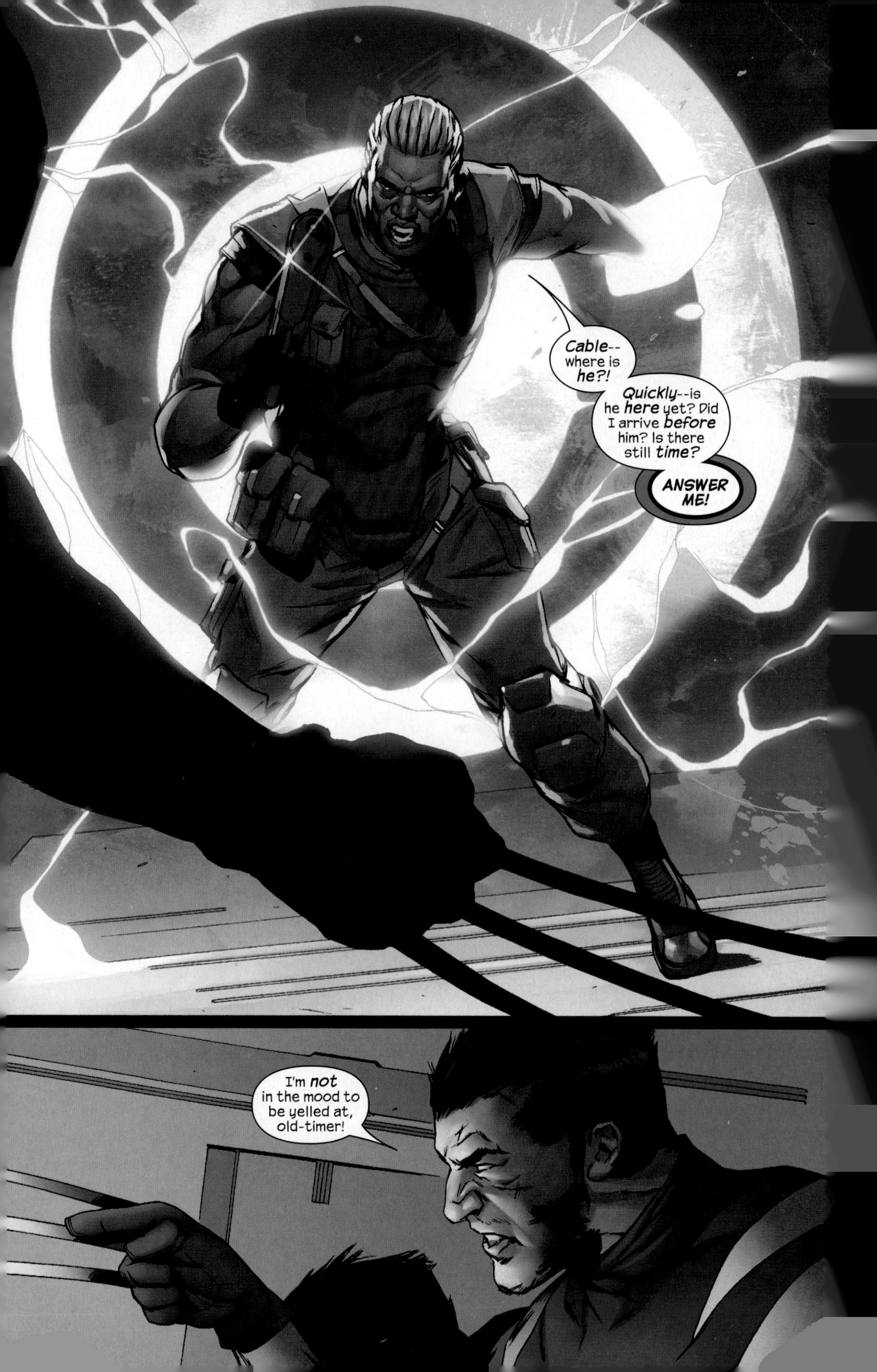
Cable--where is he?!
Quickly--is he here yet? Did I arrive before him? Is there still time?
ANSWER ME!
I'm not in the mood to be yelled at, old-timer!

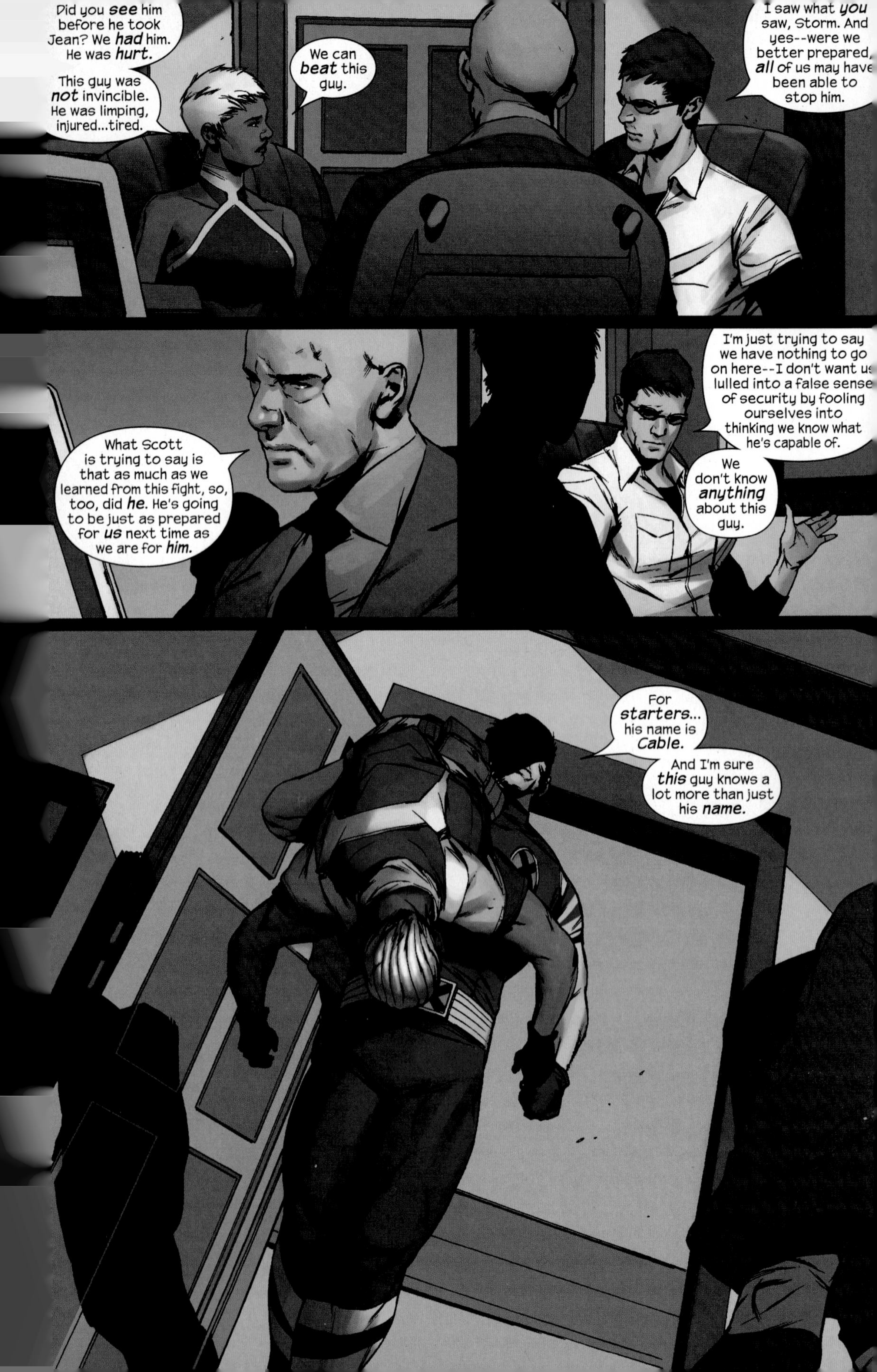
Did you see him before he took Jean? We had him. He was hurt.
This guy was not invincible. He was limping, injured...tired.
We can beat this guy.
I saw what you saw, Storm. And yes--were we better prepared, all of us may have been able to stop him.
What Scott is trying to say is that as much as we learned from this fight, so, too, did he. He's going to be just as prepared for us next time as we are for him.
I'm just trying to say we have nothing to go on here--I don't want us lulled into a false sense of security by fooling ourselves into thinking we know what he's capable of.
We don't know anything about this guy.
For starters... his name is Cable.
And I'm sure this guy knows a lot more than just his name.

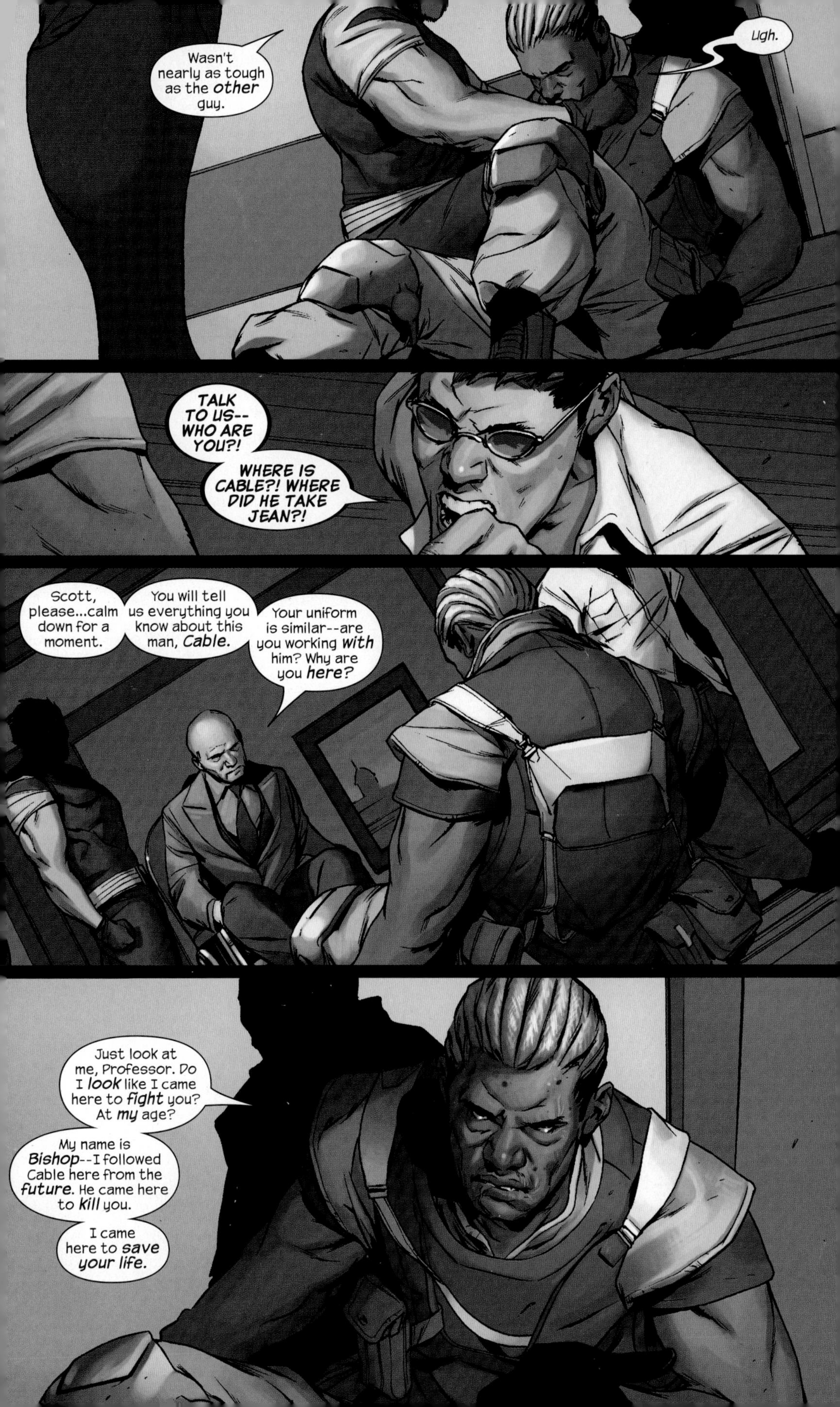
Wasn't nearly as tough as the *other* guy.
Ugh.
TALK TO US-- WHO ARE YOU?!
WHERE IS CABLE?! WHERE DID HE TAKE JEAN?!
Scott, please...calm down for a moment.
You will tell us everything you know about this man, *Cable.*
Your uniform is similar--are you working *with* him? Why are you *here?*
Just look at me, Professor. Do I *look* like I came here to *fight* you? At *my* age?
My name is *Bishop*--I followed Cable here from the *future.* He came here to *kill* you.
I came here to *save your life.*

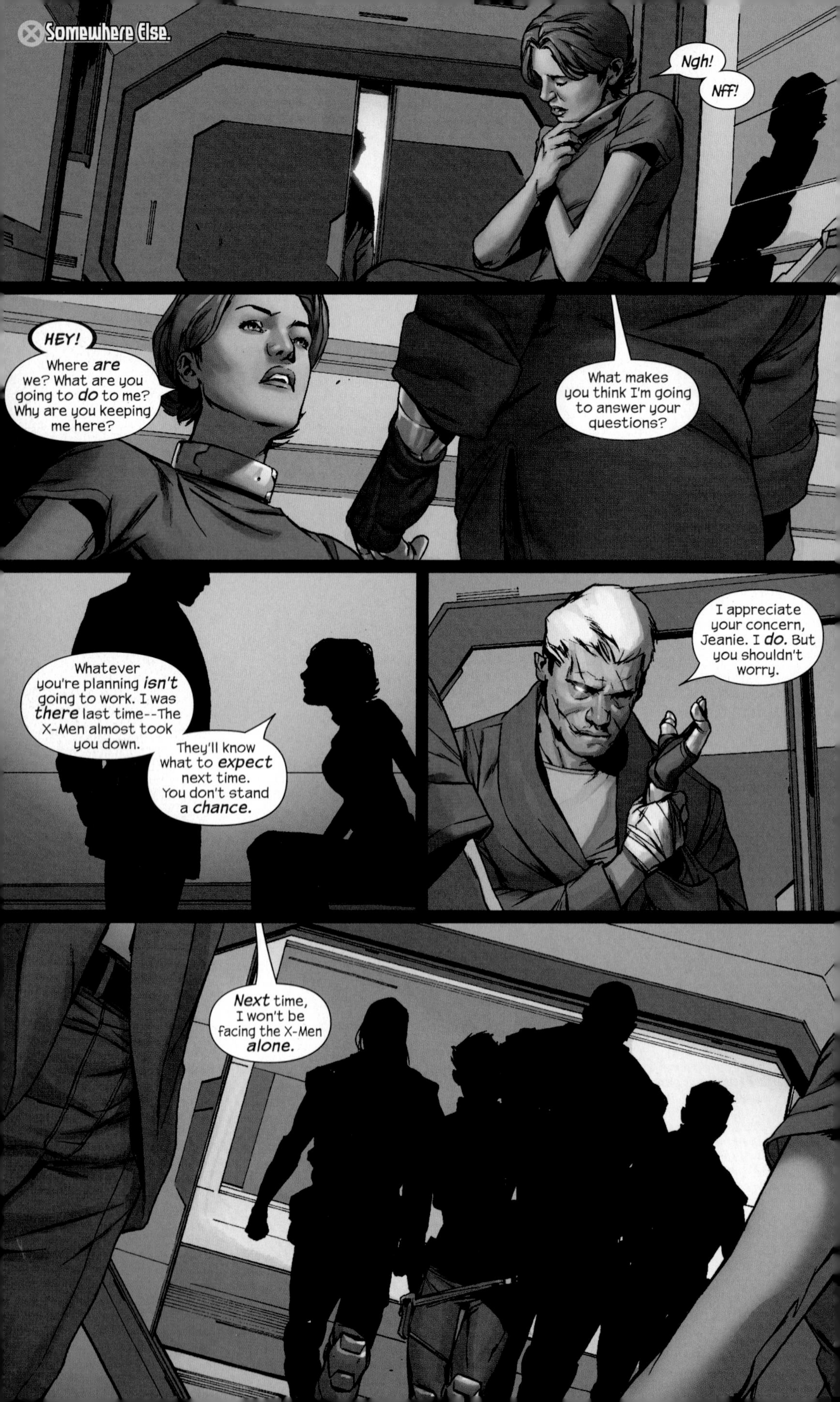
Somewhere Else.
Ngh!
Nff!
HEY!
Where are we? What are you going to do to me? Why are you keeping me here?
What makes you think I'm going to answer your questions?
Whatever you're planning isn't going to work. I was there last time--The X-Men almost took you down.
They'll know what to expect next time. You don't stand a chance.
I appreciate your concern, Jeanie. I do. But you shouldn't worry.
Next time, I won't be facing the X-Men alone.

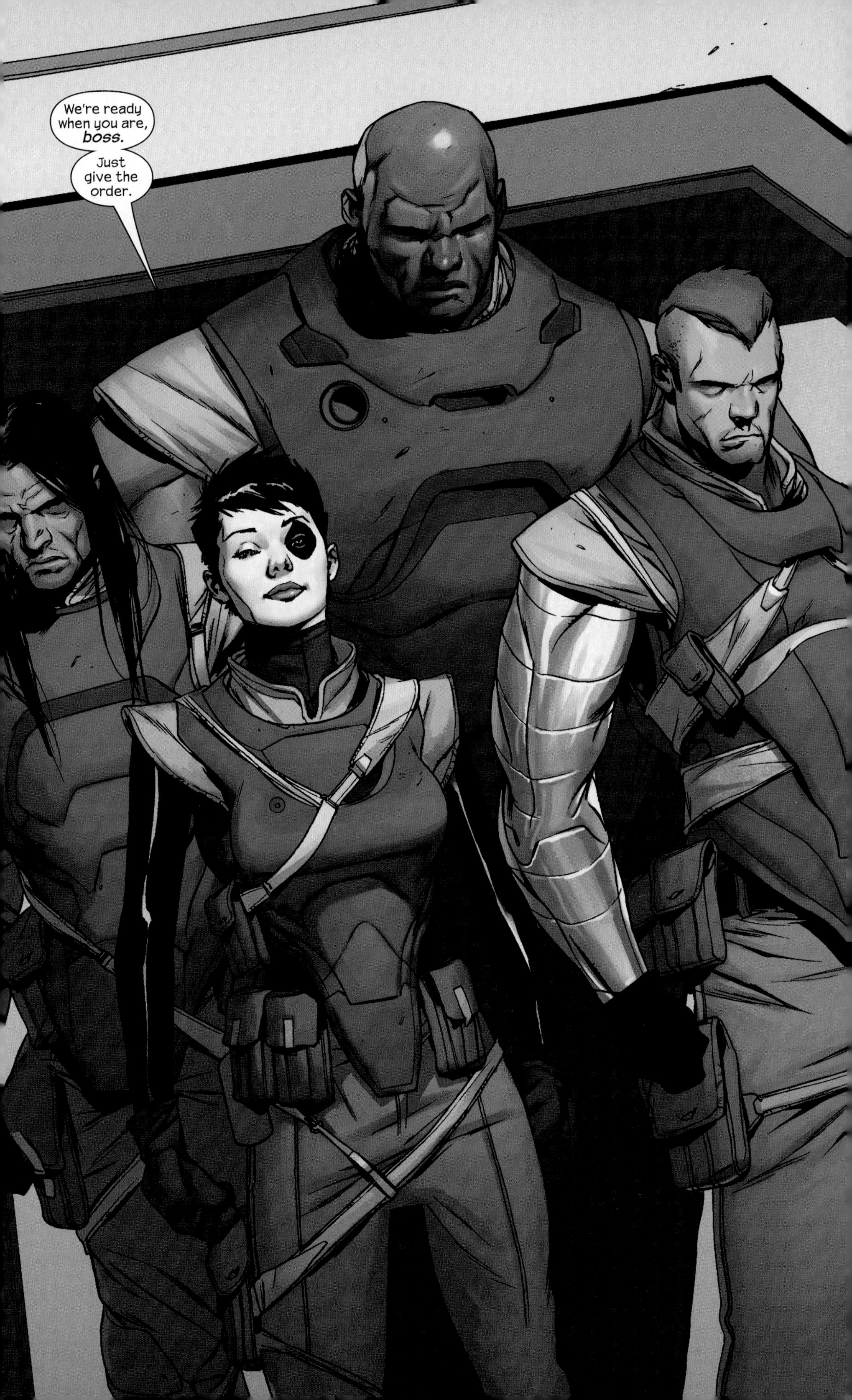
We're ready when you are, *boss.*
Just give the order.

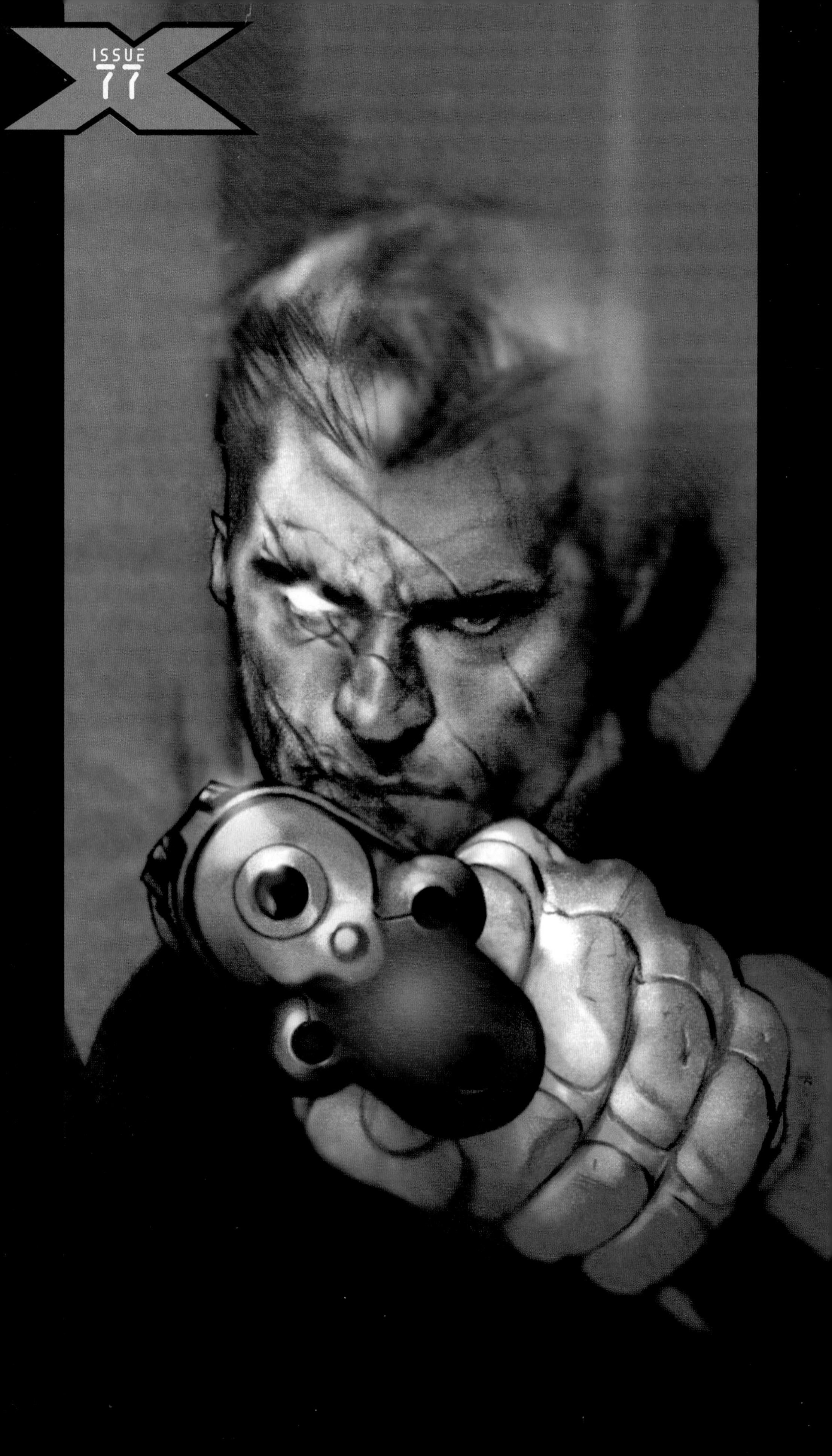
ISSUE
77

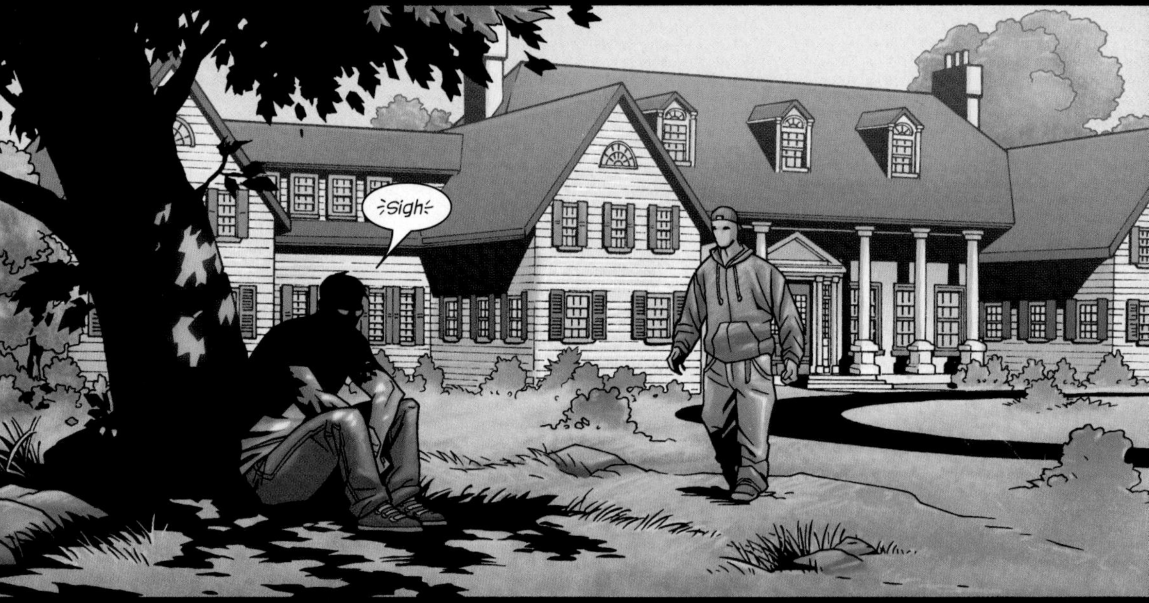
Sigh

CABLE
PART 3 (OF 4)

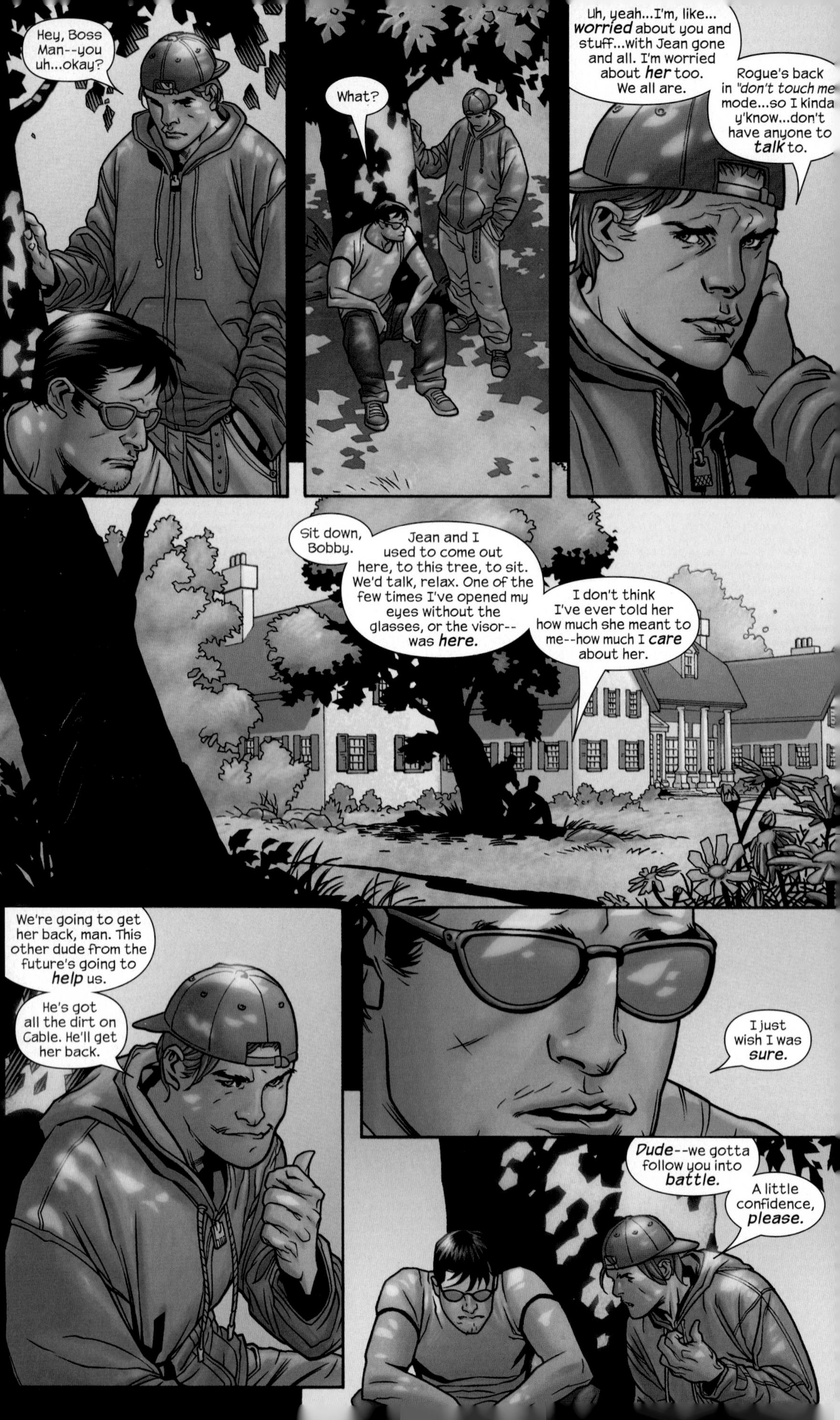
Hey, Boss Man--you uh...okay?
What?
Uh, yeah...I'm, like... worried about you and stuff...with Jean gone and all. I'm worried about her too. We all are.
Rogue's back in "don't touch me" mode...so I kinda y'know...don't have anyone to talk to.
Sit down, Bobby.
Jean and I used to come out here, to this tree, to sit. We'd talk, relax. One of the few times I've opened my eyes without the glasses, or the visor--was here.
I don't think I've ever told her how much she meant to me--how much I care about her.
We're going to get her back, man. This other dude from the future's going to help us.
He's got all the dirt on Cable. He'll get her back.
I just wish I was sure.
Dude--we gotta follow you into battle.
A little confidence, please.

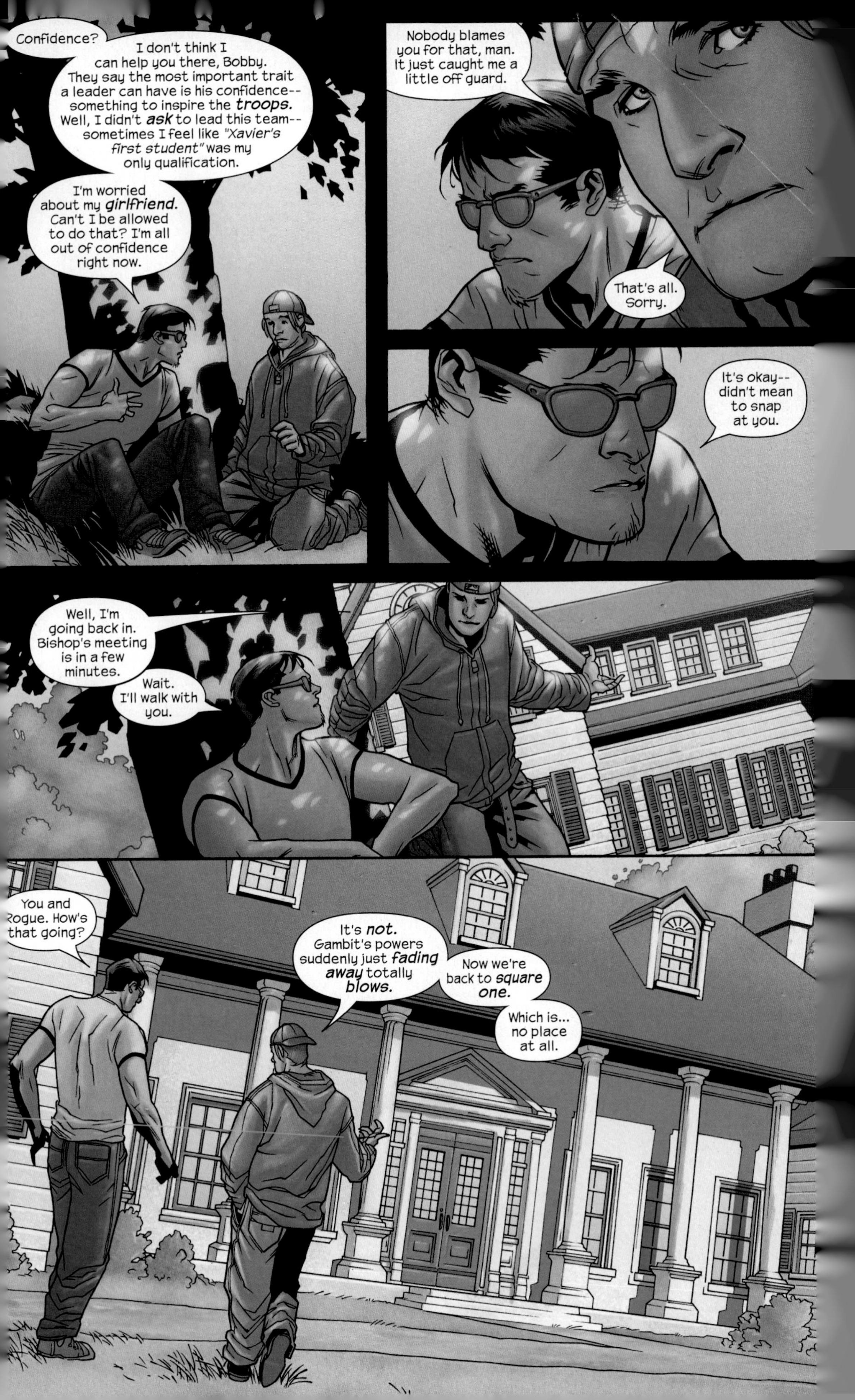
Confidence?
I don't think I can help you there, Bobby. They say the most important trait a leader can have is his confidence-- something to inspire the *troops.* Well, I didn't *ask* to lead this team-- sometimes I feel like *"Xavier's first student"* was my only qualification.
I'm worried about my *girlfriend.* Can't I be allowed to do that? I'm all out of confidence right now.
Nobody blames you for that, man. It just caught me a little off guard.
That's all. Sorry.
It's okay-- didn't mean to snap at you.
Well, I'm going back in. Bishop's meeting is in a few minutes.
Wait. I'll walk with you.
You and Rogue. How's that going?
It's *not.* Gambit's powers suddenly just *fading away* totally *blows.*
Now we're back to *square one.*
Which is... no place at all.

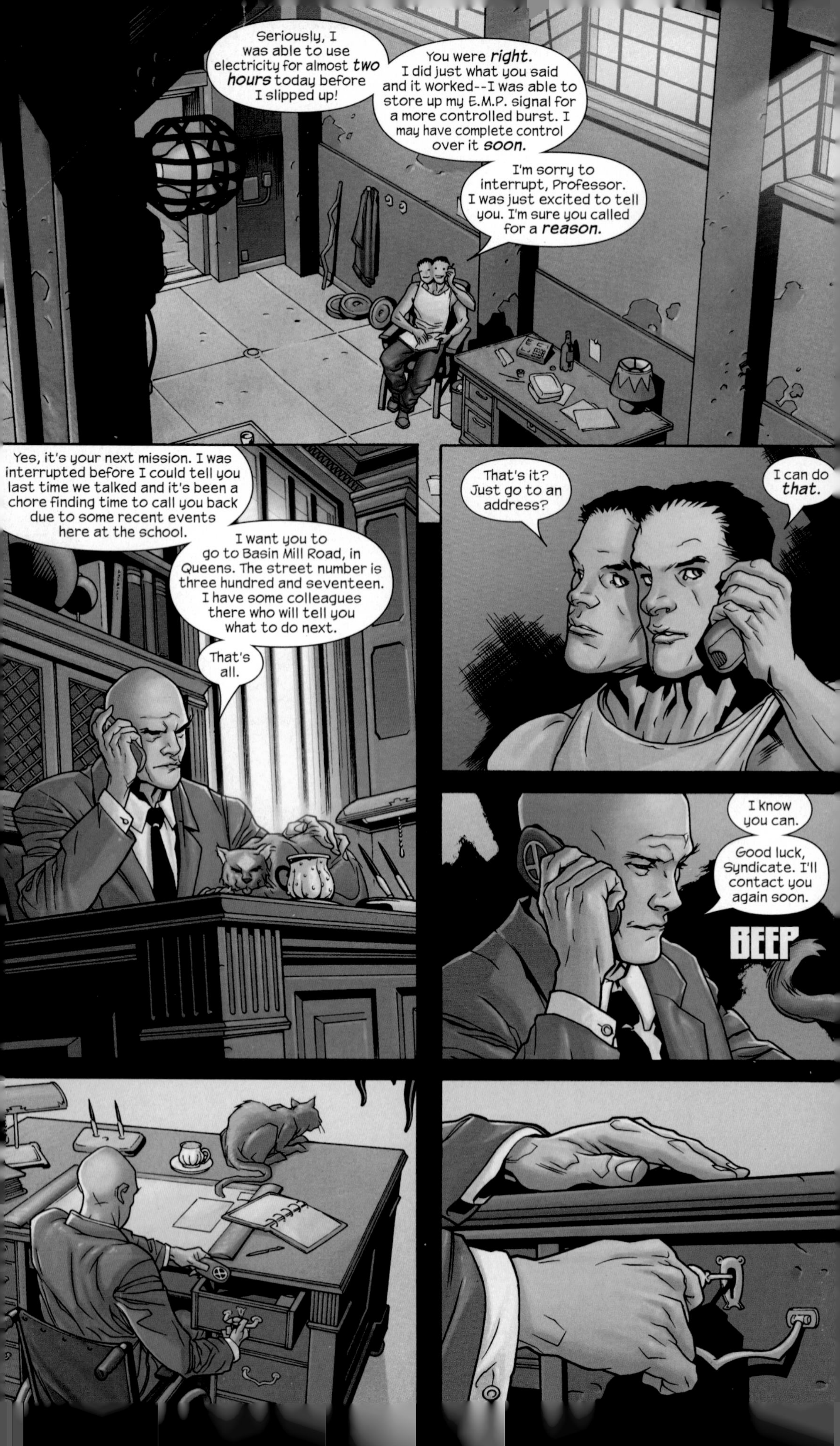
Seriously, I was able to use electricity for almost two hours today before I slipped up!
You were right. I did just what you said and it worked--I was able to store up my E.M.P. signal for a more controlled burst. I may have complete control over it soon.
I'm sorry to interrupt, Professor. I was just excited to tell you. I'm sure you called for a reason.
Yes, it's your next mission. I was interrupted before I could tell you last time we talked and it's been a chore finding time to call you back due to some recent events here at the school.
I want you to go to Basin Mill Road, in Queens. The street number is three hundred and seventeen. I have some colleagues there who will tell you what to do next.
That's all.
That's it? Just go to an address?
I can do that.
I know you can.
Good luck, Syndicate. I'll contact you again soon.
BEEP

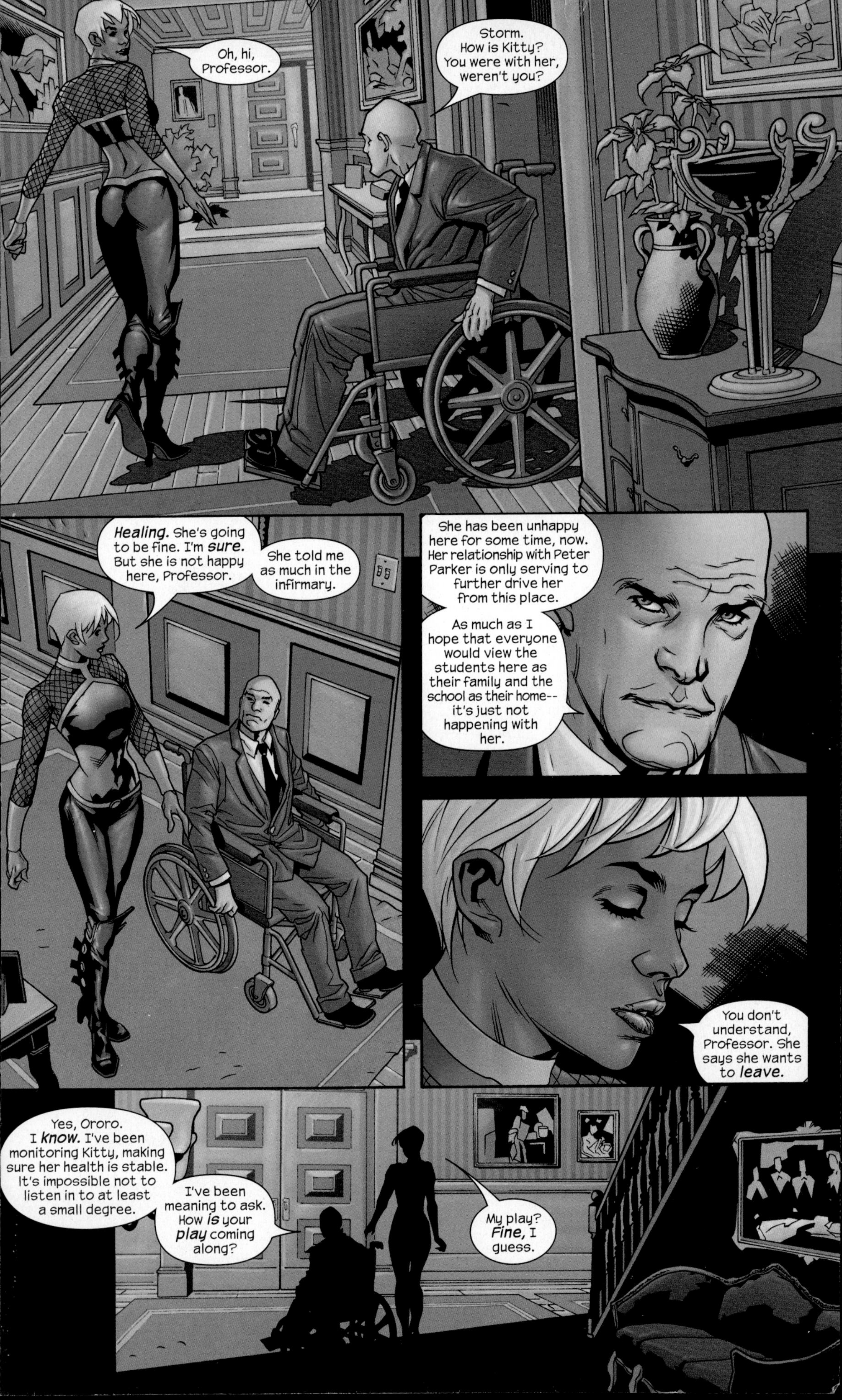
Oh, hi, Professor.
Storm. How is Kitty? You were with her, weren't you?
Healing. She's going to be fine. I'm sure. But she is not happy here, Professor.
She told me as much in the infirmary.
She has been unhappy here for some time, now. Her relationship with Peter Parker is only serving to further drive her from this place.
As much as I hope that everyone would view the students here as their family and the school as their home--it's just not happening with her.
You don't understand, Professor. She says she wants to leave.
Yes, Ororo. I know. I've been monitoring Kitty, making sure her health is stable. It's impossible not to listen in to at least a small degree.
I've been meaning to ask. How is your play coming along?
My play? Fine, I guess.

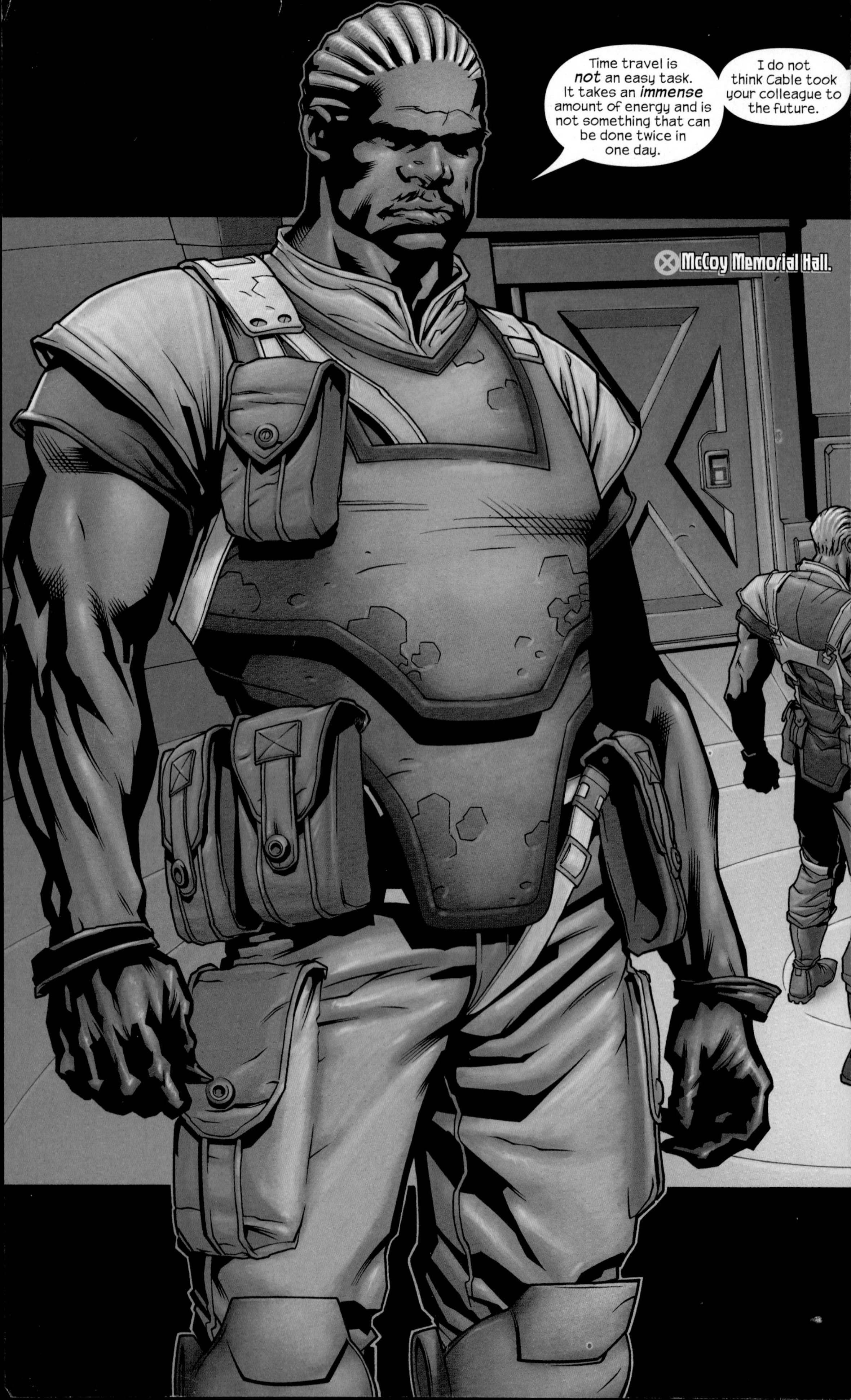
Time travel is *not* an easy task. It takes an *immense* amount of energy and is not something that can be done twice in one day.
I do not think Cable took your colleague to the future.
McCoy Memorial Hall.

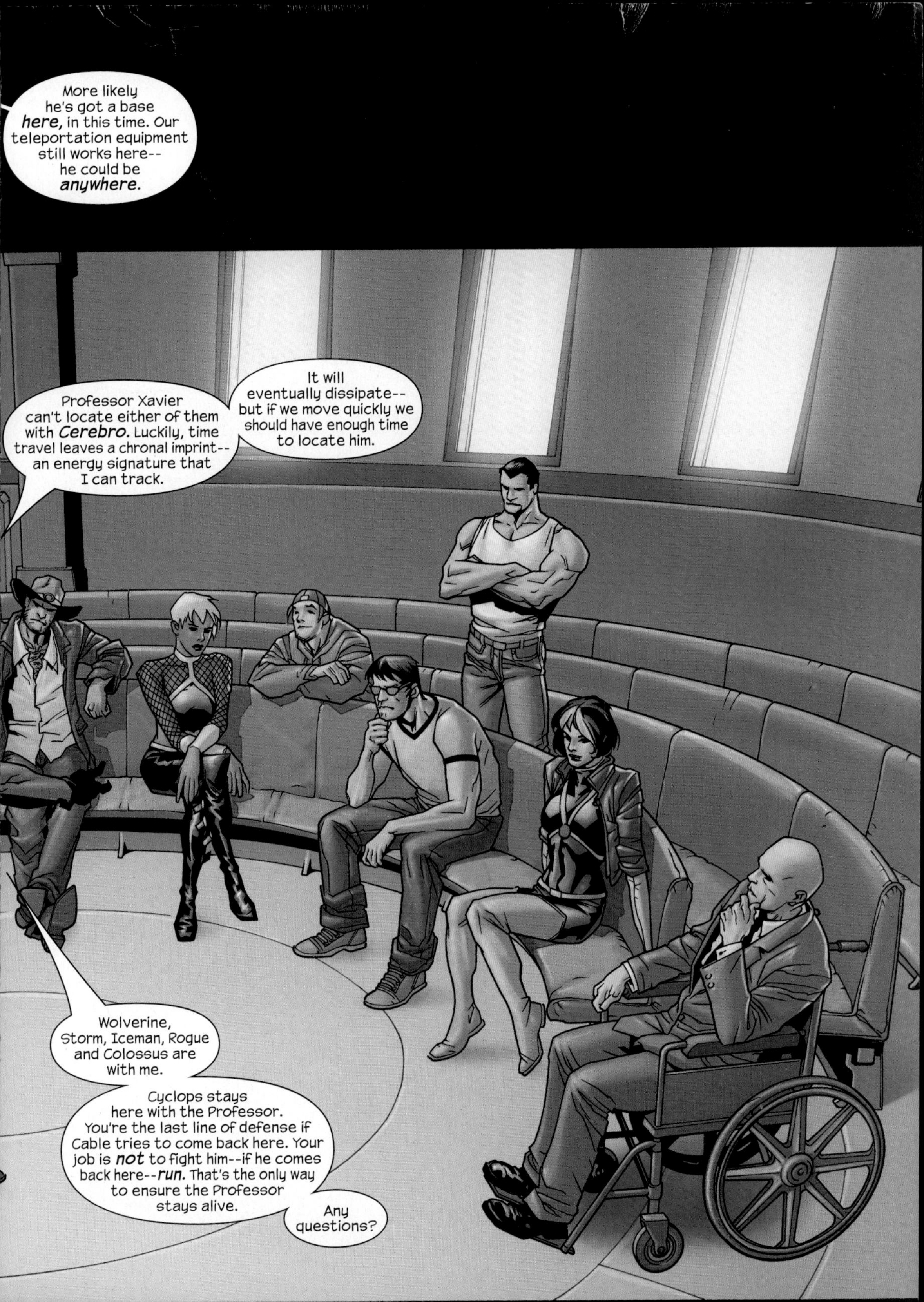
More likely he's got a base *here,* in this time. Our teleportation equipment still works here-- he could be *anywhere.*
Professor Xavier can't locate either of them with *Cerebro.* Luckily, time travel leaves a chronal imprint-- an energy signature that I can track.
It will eventually dissipate-- but if we move quickly we should have enough time to locate him.
Wolverine, Storm, Iceman, Rogue and Colossus are with me.
Cyclops stays here with the Professor. You're the last line of defense if Cable tries to come back here. Your job is *not* to fight him--if he comes back here--*run.* That's the only way to ensure the Professor stays alive.
Any questions?

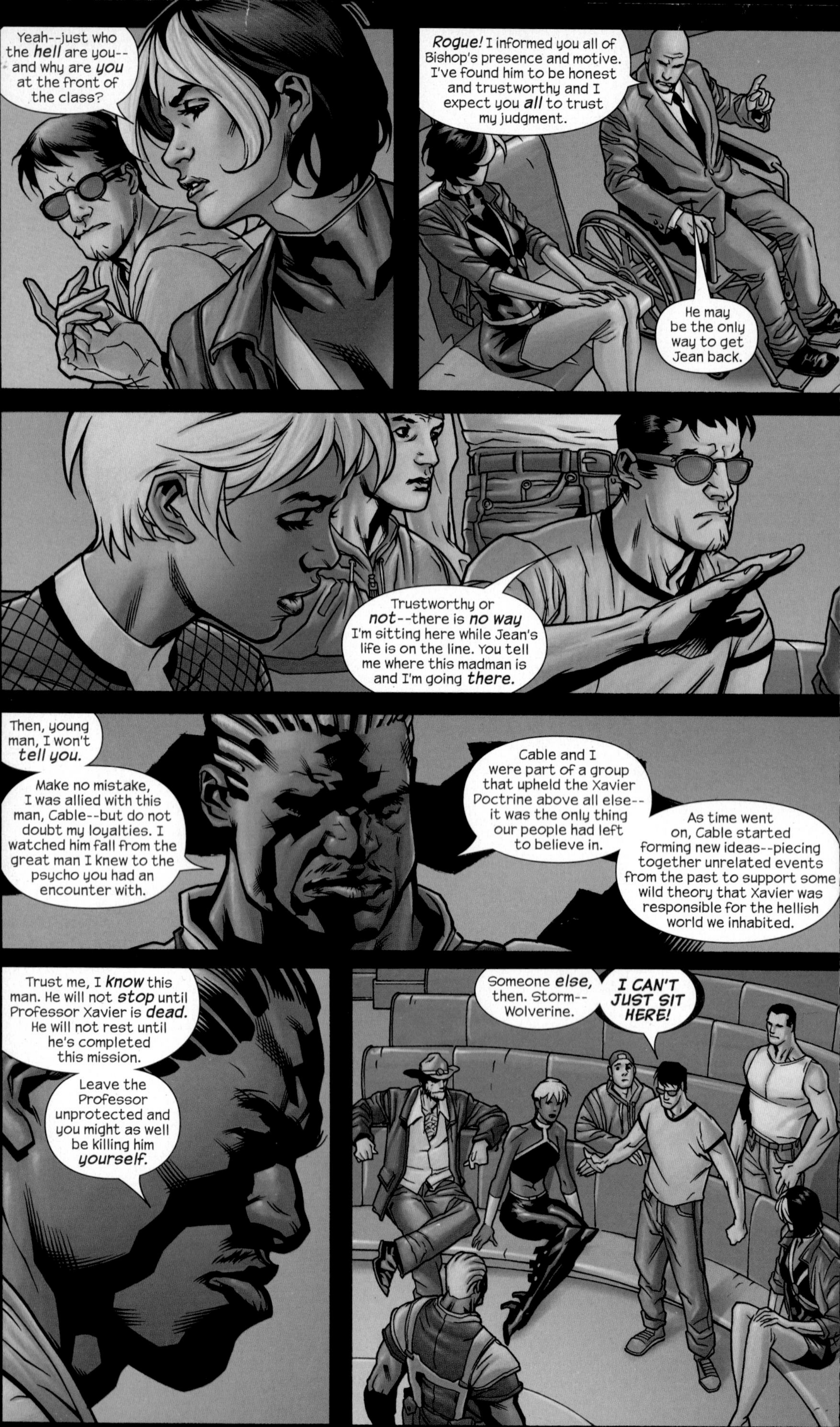

Yeah--just who the hell are you--and why are you at the front of the class?
Rogue! I informed you all of Bishop's presence and motive. I've found him to be honest and trustworthy and I expect you all to trust my judgment.
He may be the only way to get Jean back.
Trustworthy or not--there is no way I'm sitting here while Jean's life is on the line. You tell me where this madman is and I'm going there.
Then, young man, I won't tell you.
Make no mistake, I was allied with this man, Cable--but do not doubt my loyalties. I watched him fall from the great man I knew to the psycho you had an encounter with.
Cable and I were part of a group that upheld the Xavier Doctrine above all else--it was the only thing our people had left to believe in.
As time went on, Cable started forming new ideas--piecing together unrelated events from the past to support some wild theory that Xavier was responsible for the hellish world we inhabited.
Trust me, I know this man. He will not stop until Professor Xavier is dead. He will not rest until he's completed this mission.
Leave the Professor unprotected and you might as well be killing him yourself.
Someone else, then. Storm--Wolverine.
I CAN'T JUST SIT HERE!

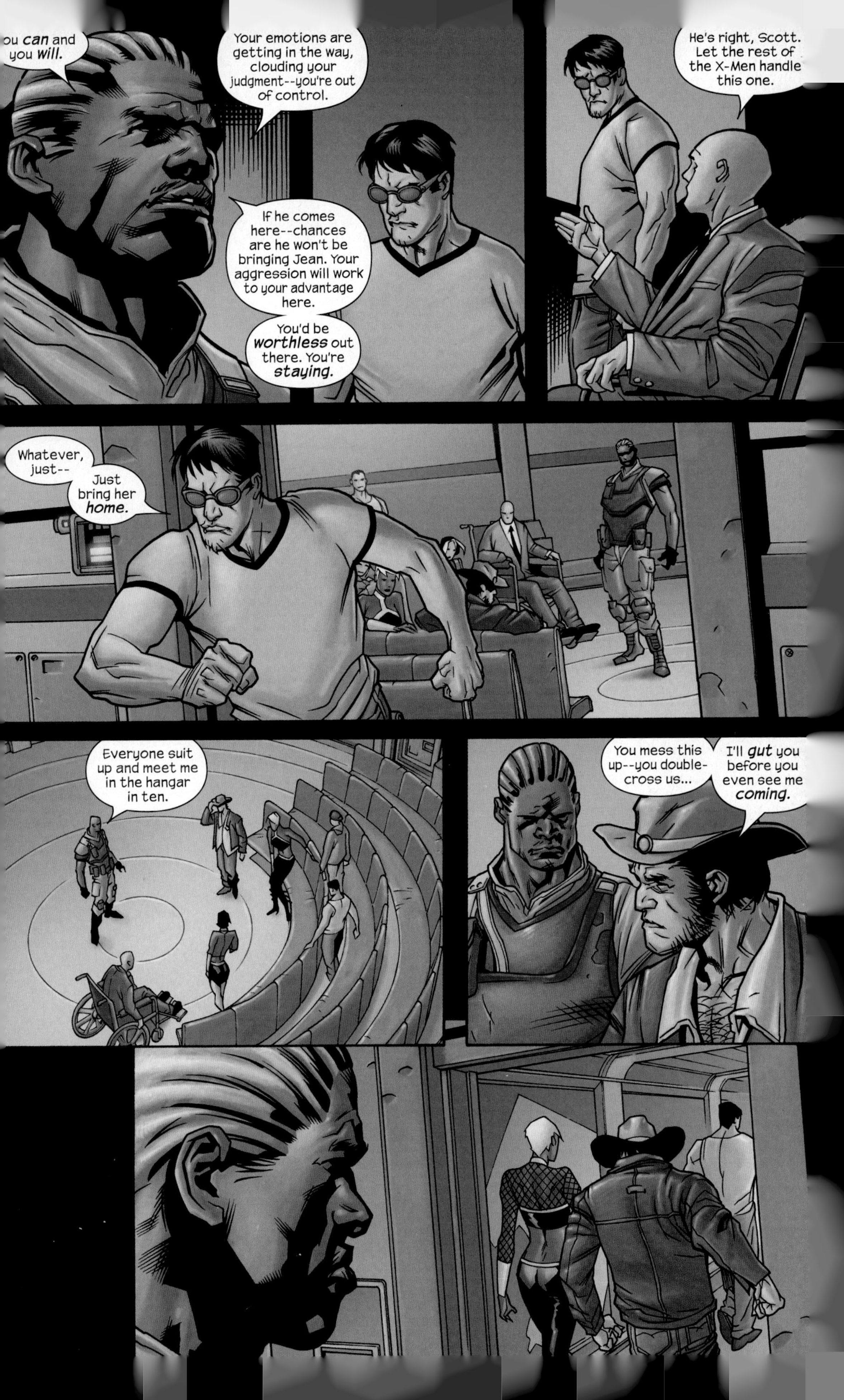

ou can and you will.
Your emotions are getting in the way, clouding your judgment--you're out of control.
If he comes here--chances are he won't be bringing Jean. Your aggression will work to your advantage here.
You'd be worthless out there. You're staying.
He's right, Scott. Let the rest of the X-Men handle this one.
Whatever, just--
Just bring her home.
Everyone suit up and meet me in the hangar in ten.
You mess this up--you double-cross us...
I'll gut you before you even see me coming.

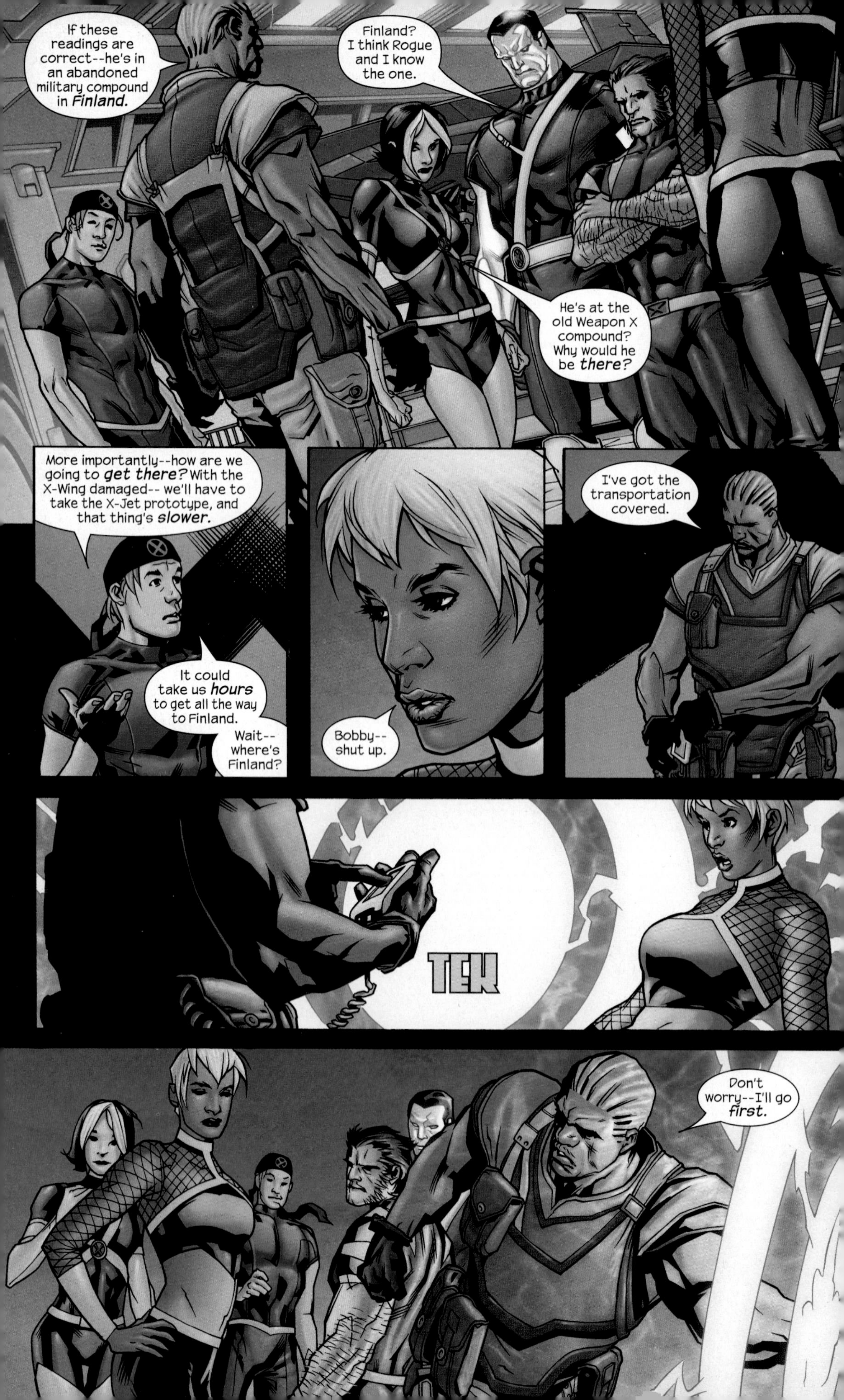
If these readings are correct--he's in an abandoned military compound in *Finland.*
Finland? I think Rogue and I know the one.
He's at the old Weapon X compound? Why would he be *there?*
More importantly--how are we going to *get there?* With the X-Wing damaged-- we'll have to take the X-Jet prototype, and that thing's *slower.*
It could take us *hours* to get all the way to Finland.
Wait-- where's Finland?
Bobby-- shut up.
I've got the transportation covered.
TEK
Don't worry--I'll go *first.*

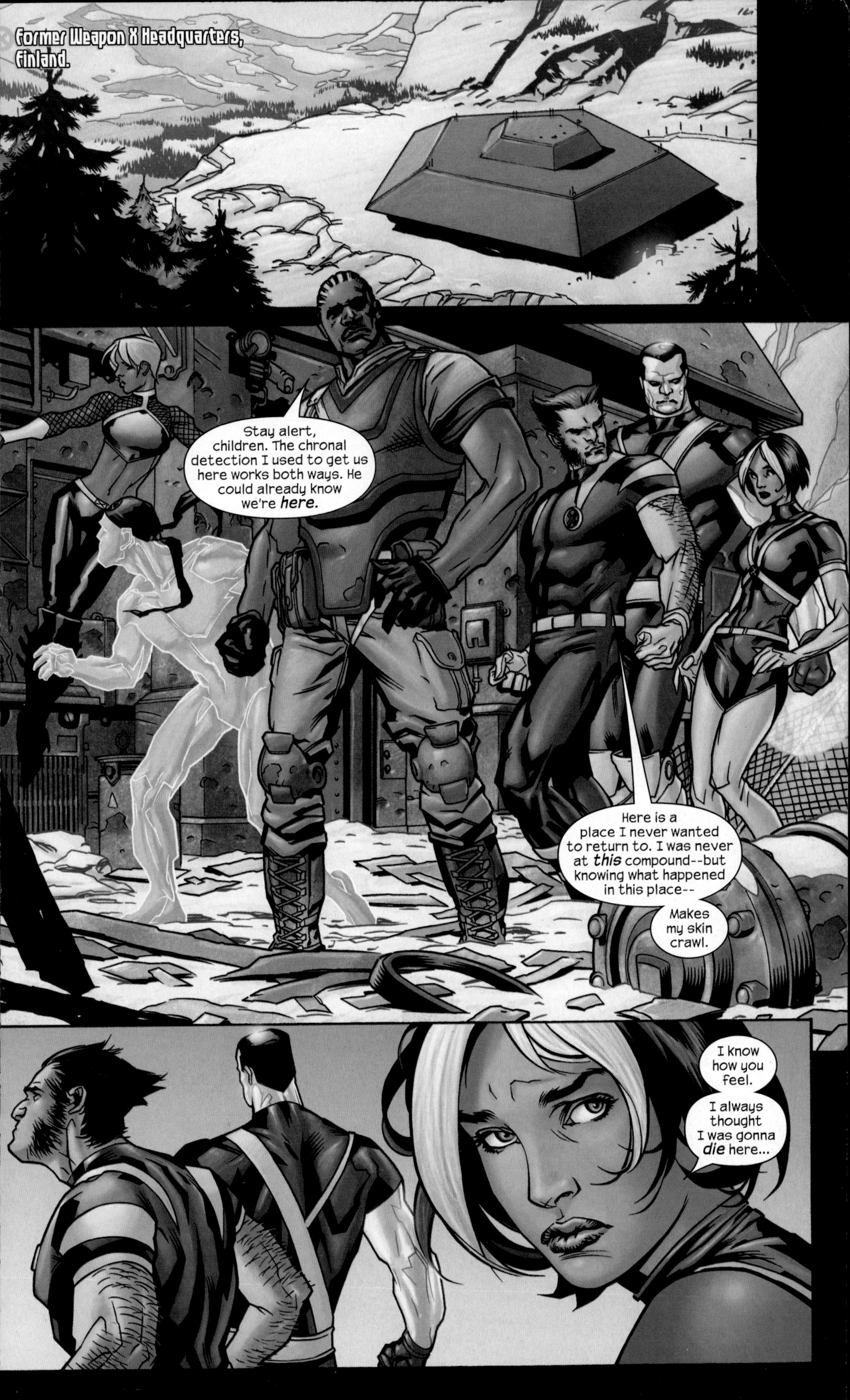
Former Weapon X Headquarters, Finland.
Stay alert, children. The chronal detection I used to get us here works both ways. He could already know we're *here.*
Here is a place I never wanted to return to. I was never at *this* compound--but knowing what happened in this place--
Makes my skin crawl.
I know how you feel.
I always thought I was gonna *die* here...

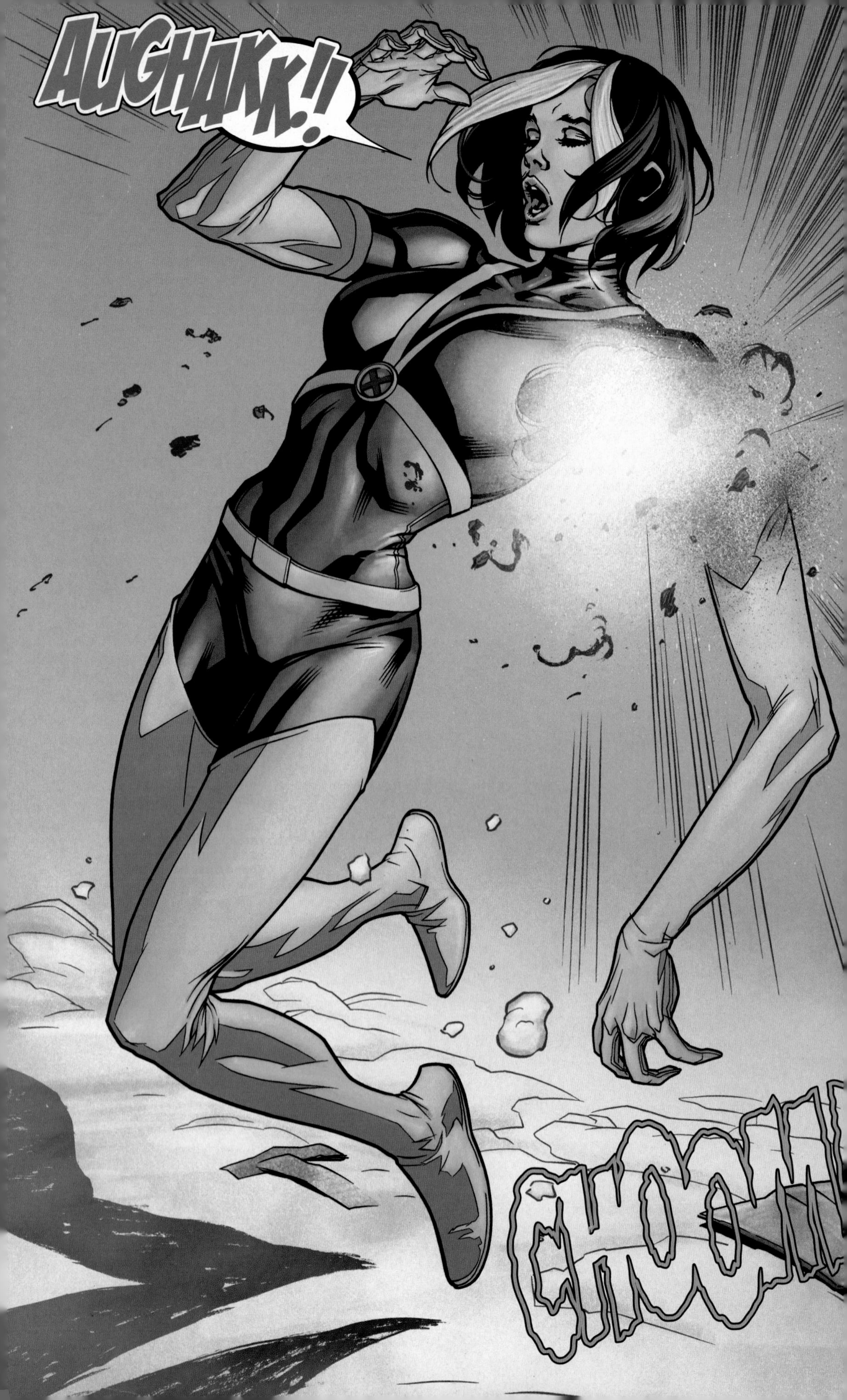
AUGHAKK!!
CHOOM

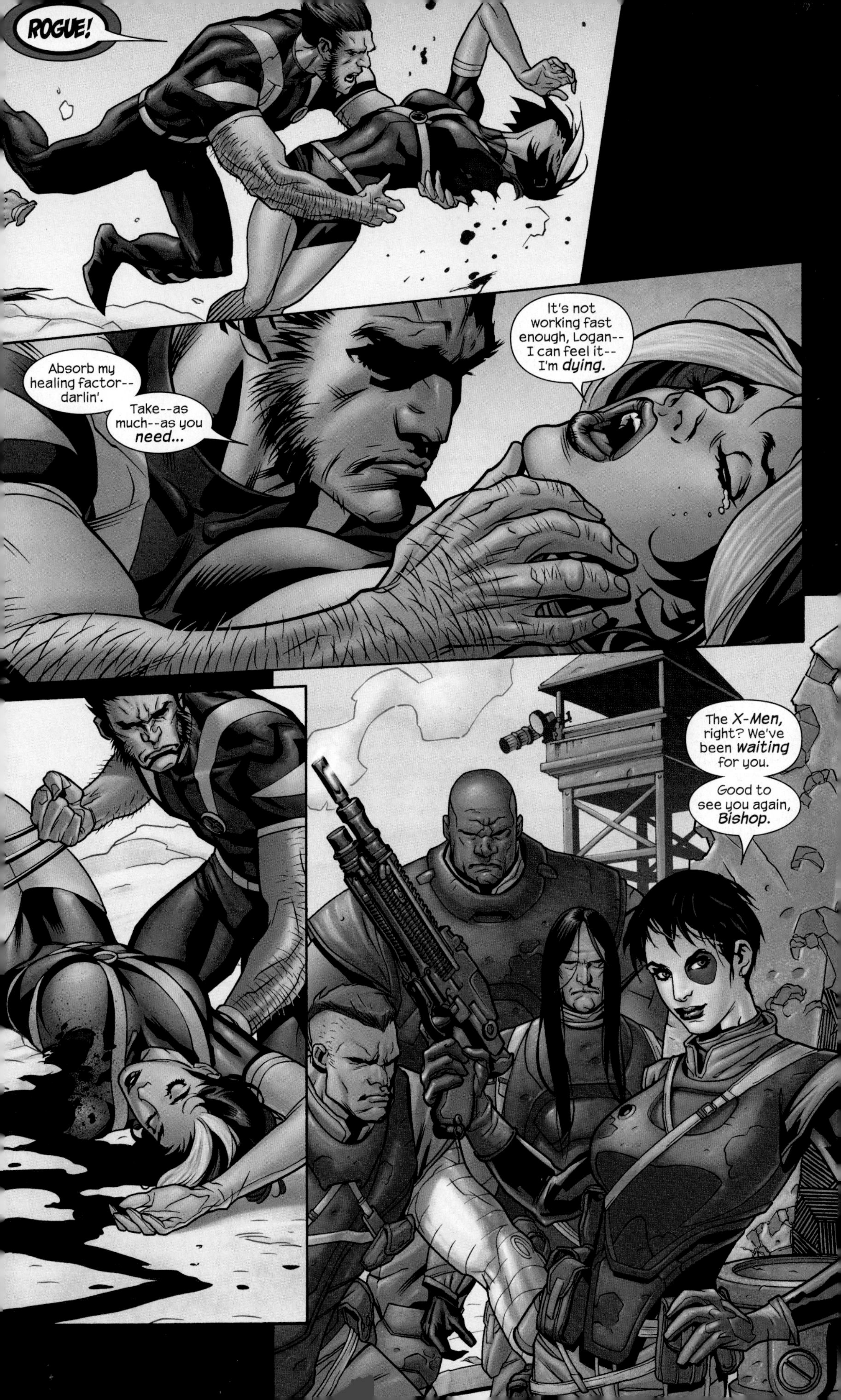
ROGUE!
Absorb my healing factor--darlin'.
Take--as much--as you need...
It's not working fast enough, Logan-- I can feel it-- I'm dying.
The X-Men, right? We've been waiting for you.
Good to see you again, Bishop.

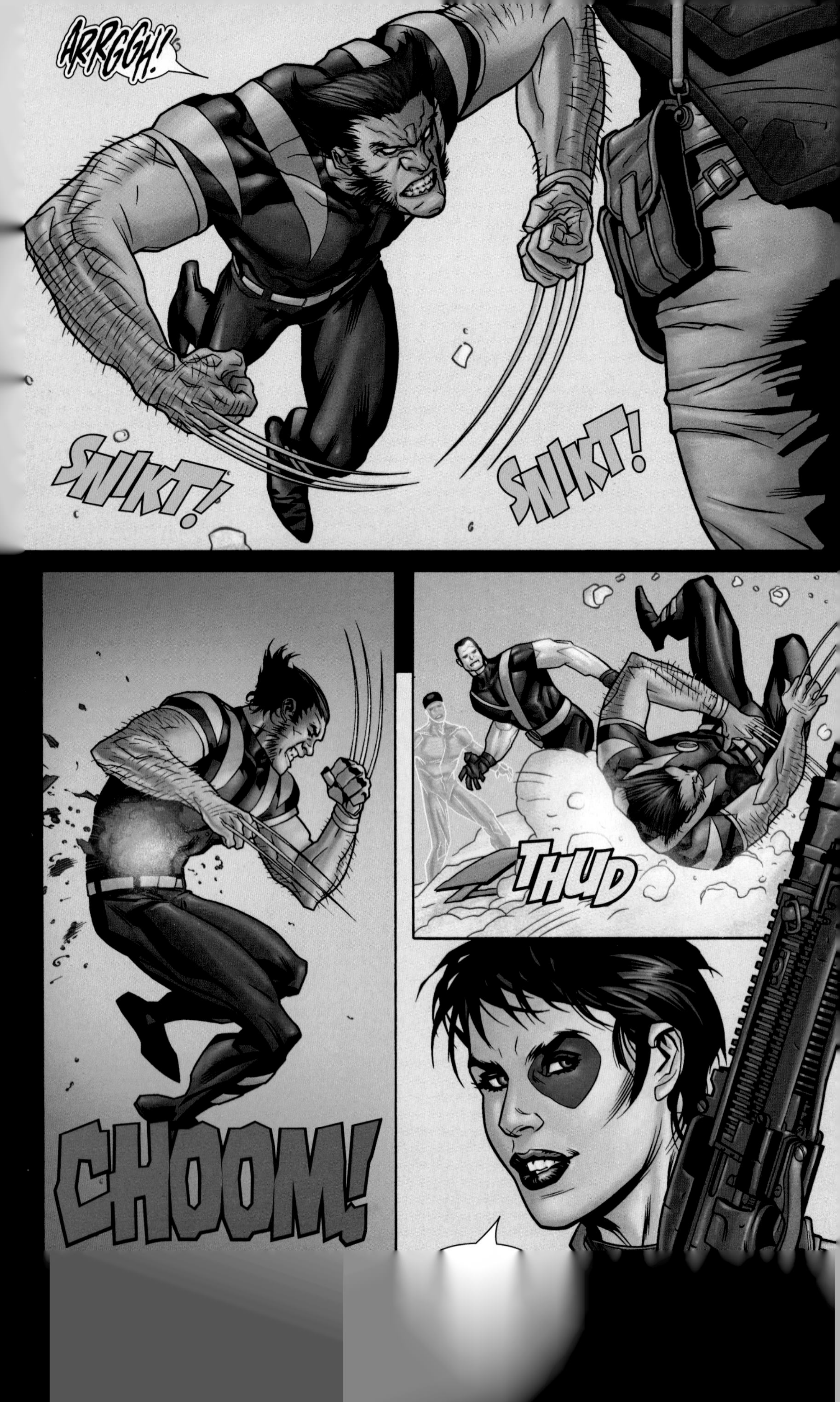
ARRGGH!
SNIKT!
SNIKT!
CHOOM!
THUD

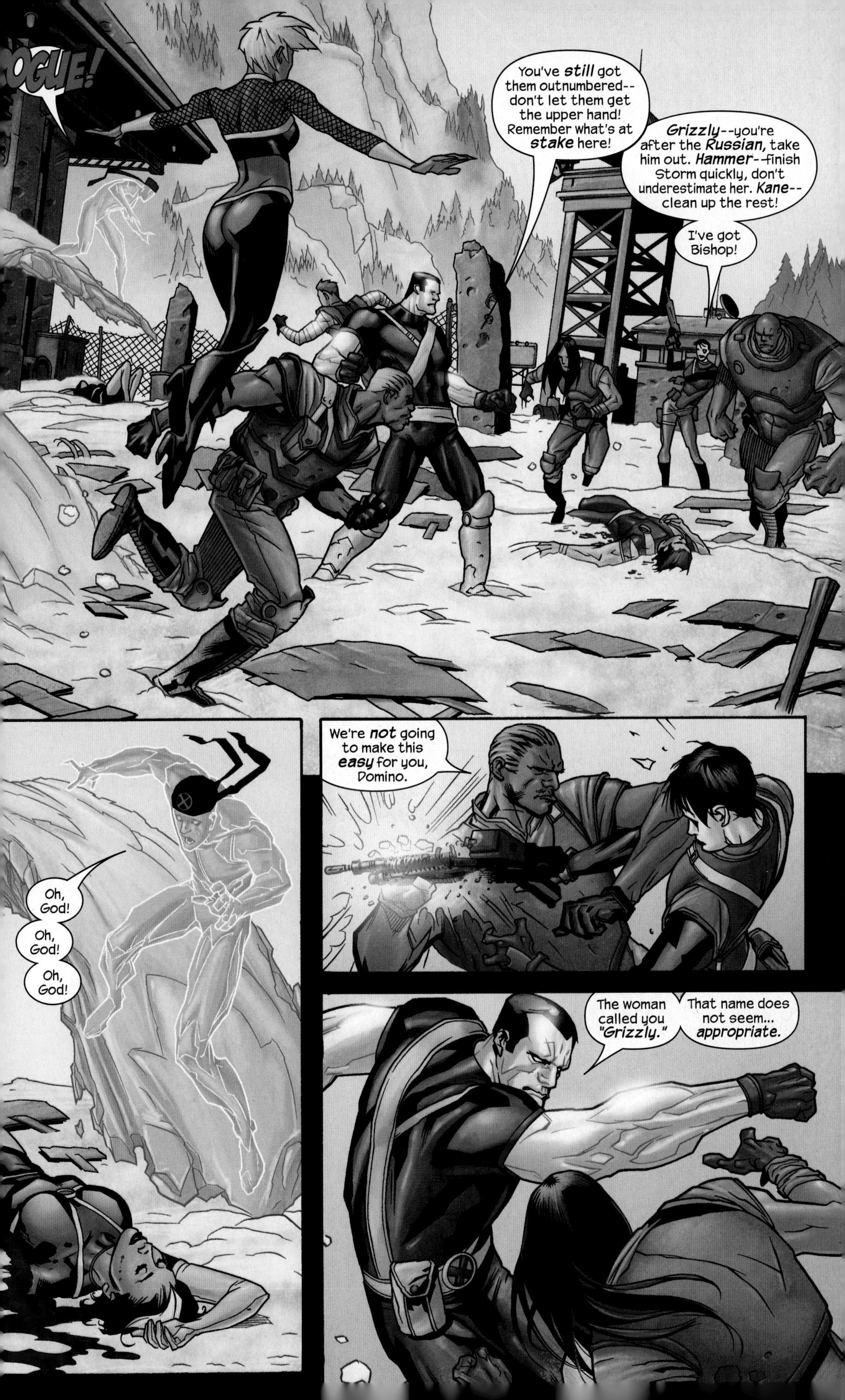
OGUE!
You've still got them outnumbered--don't let them get the upper hand! Remember what's at stake here!
Grizzly--you're after the Russian, take him out. Hammer--finish Storm quickly, don't underestimate her. Kane--clean up the rest!
I've got Bishop!
Oh, God!
Oh, God!
Oh, God!
We're not going to make this easy for you, Domino.
The woman called you "Grizzly."
That name does not seem... appropriate.

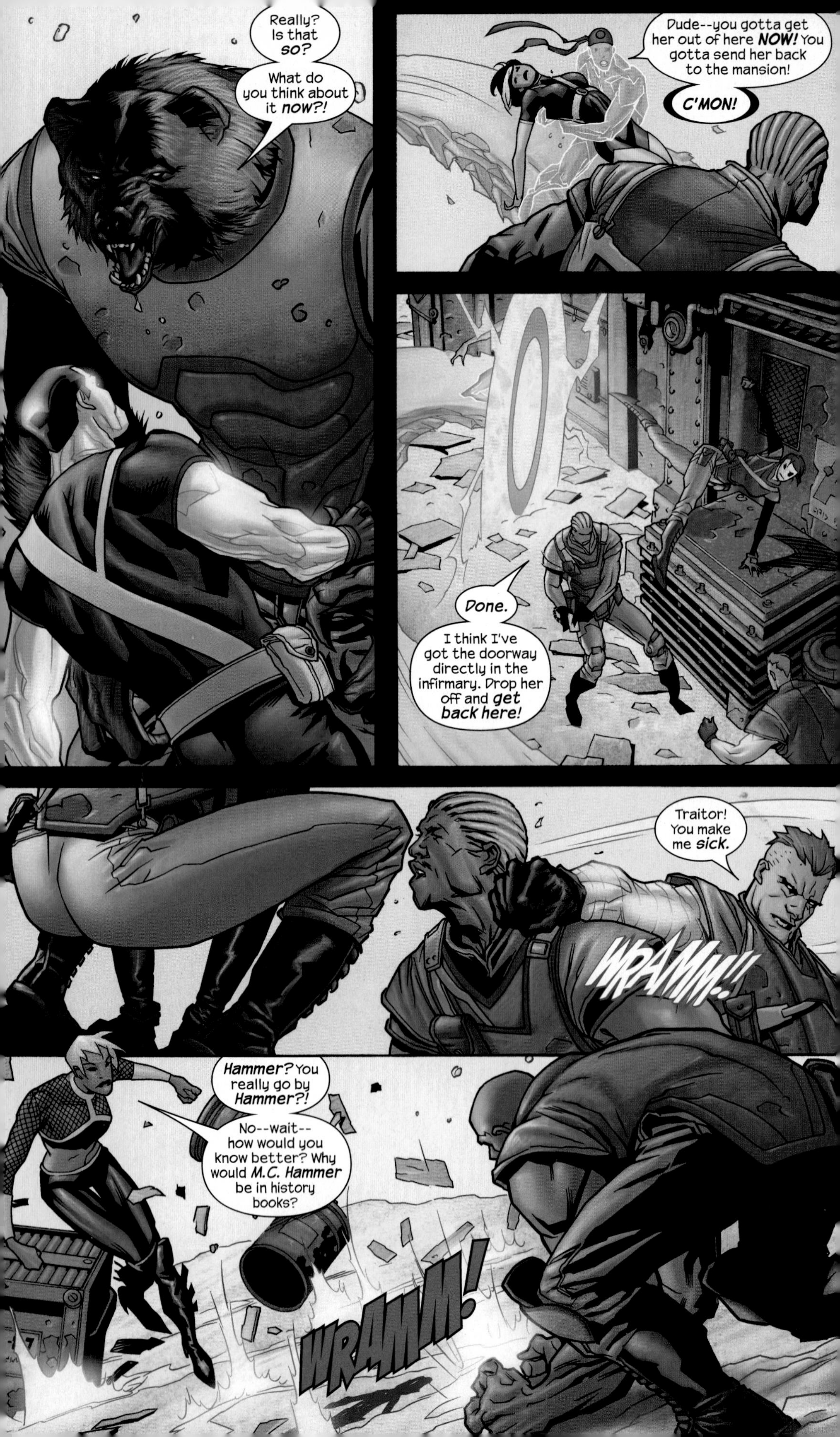

Really? Is that so?
What do you think about it now?!
Dude--you gotta get her out of here NOW! You gotta send her back to the mansion!
C'MON!
Done.
I think I've got the doorway directly in the infirmary. Drop her off and get back here!
Traitor! You make me sick.
WRAMM!!
Hammer? You really go by Hammer?!
No--wait--how would you know better? Why would M.C. Hammer be in history books?
WRAMM!

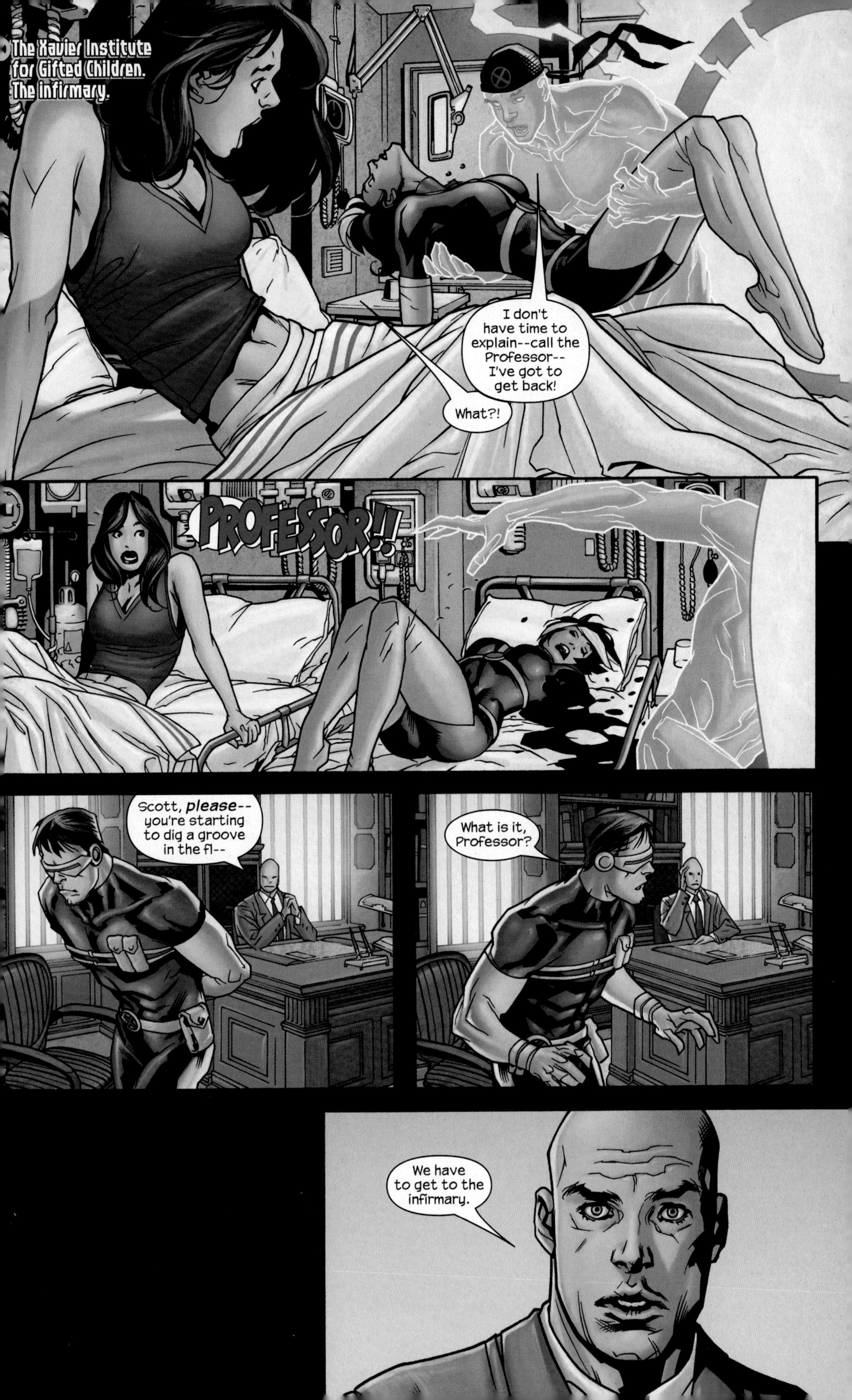

The Xavier Institute for Gifted Children. The infirmary.
I don't have time to explain--call the Professor--I've got to get back!
What?!
PROFESSOR!!
Scott, *please*--you're starting to dig a groove in the fl--
What is it, Professor?
We have to get to the infirmary.

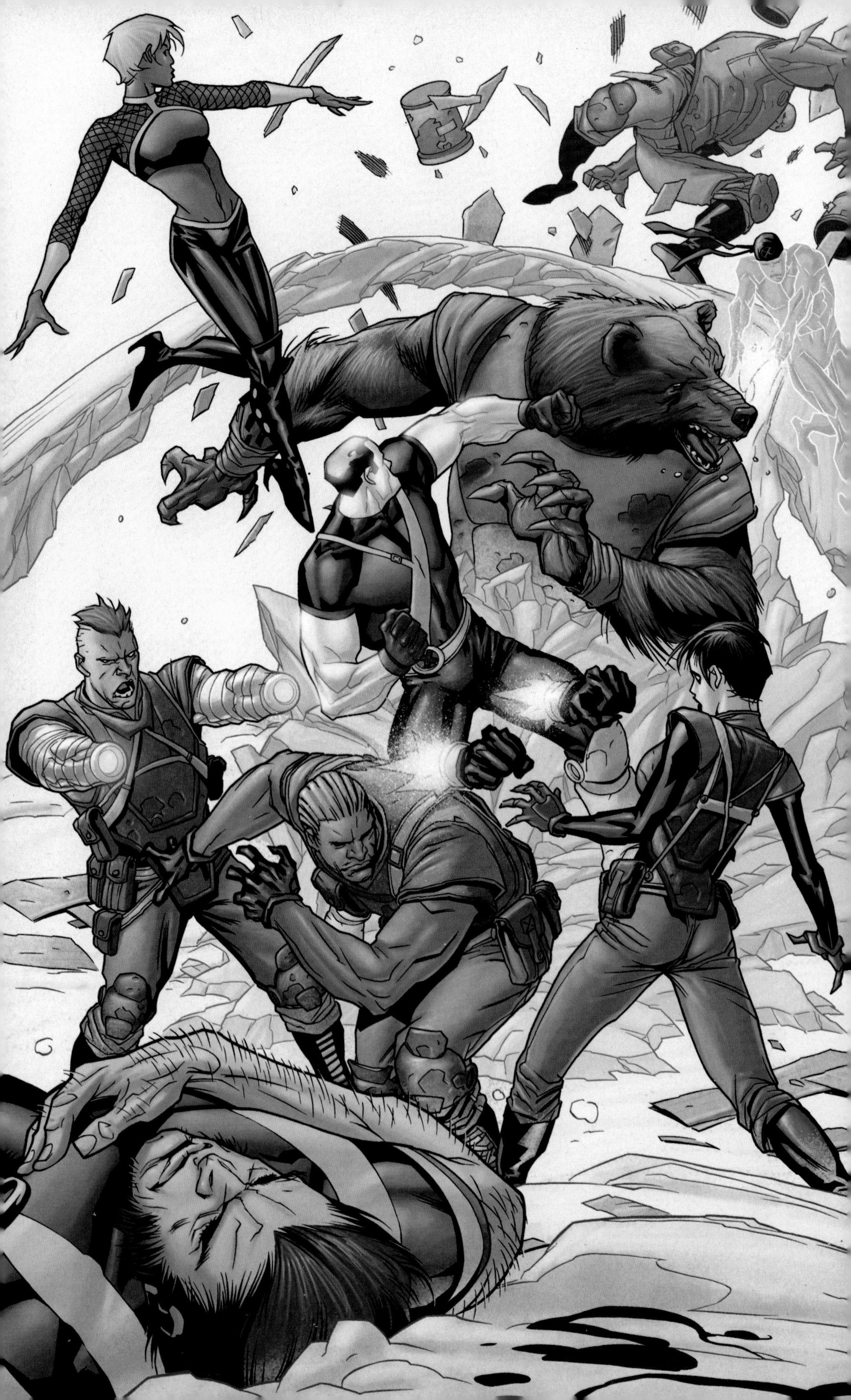

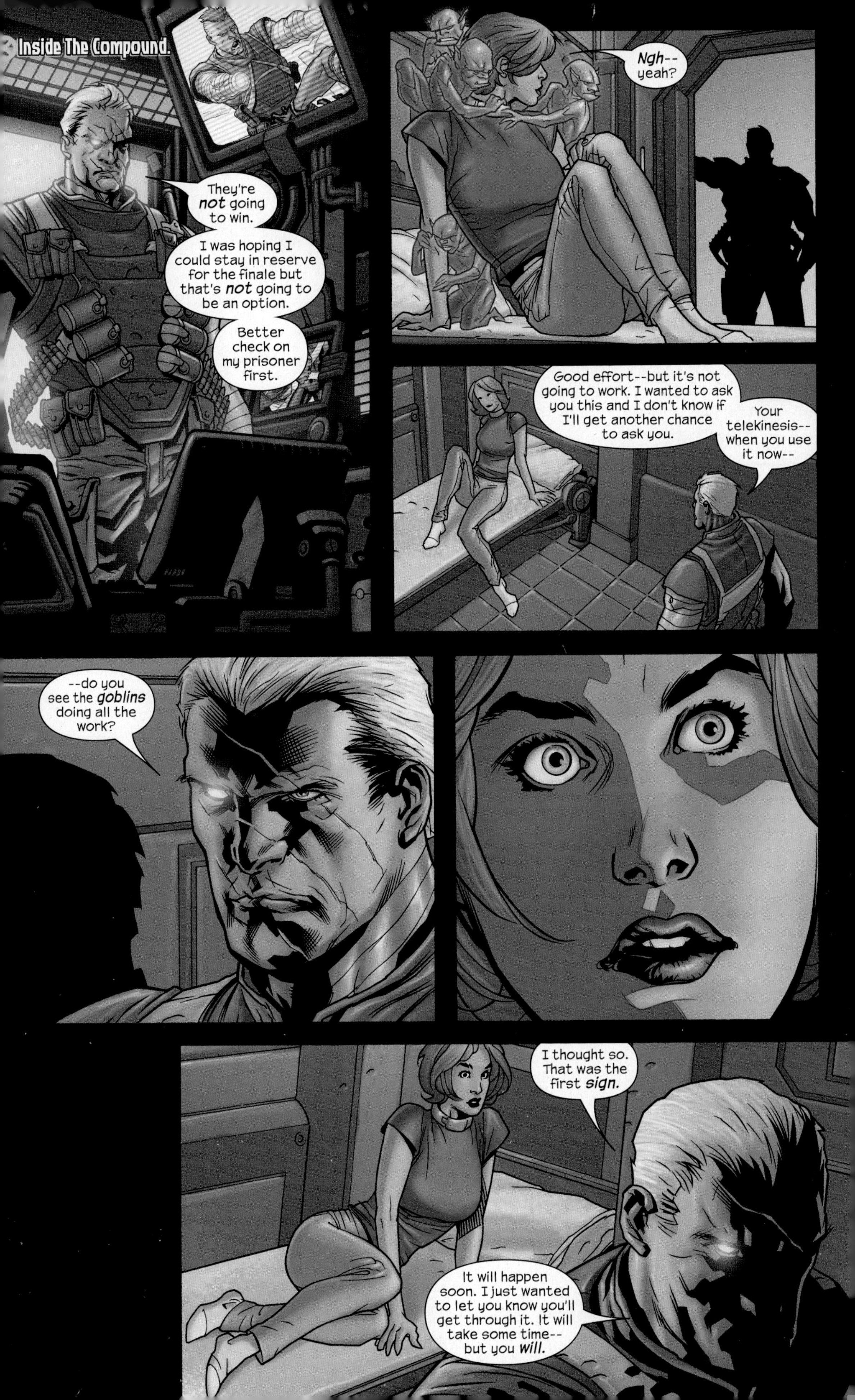
Inside The Compound.
They're *not* going to win.
I was hoping I could stay in reserve for the finale but that's *not* going to be an option.
Better check on my prisoner first.
Ngh--yeah?
Good effort--but it's not going to work. I wanted to ask you this and I don't know if I'll get another chance to ask you.
Your telekinesis--when you use it now--
--do you see the *goblins* doing all the work?
I thought so. That was the first *sign*.
It will happen soon. I just wanted to let you know you'll get through it. It will take some time--but you *will*.

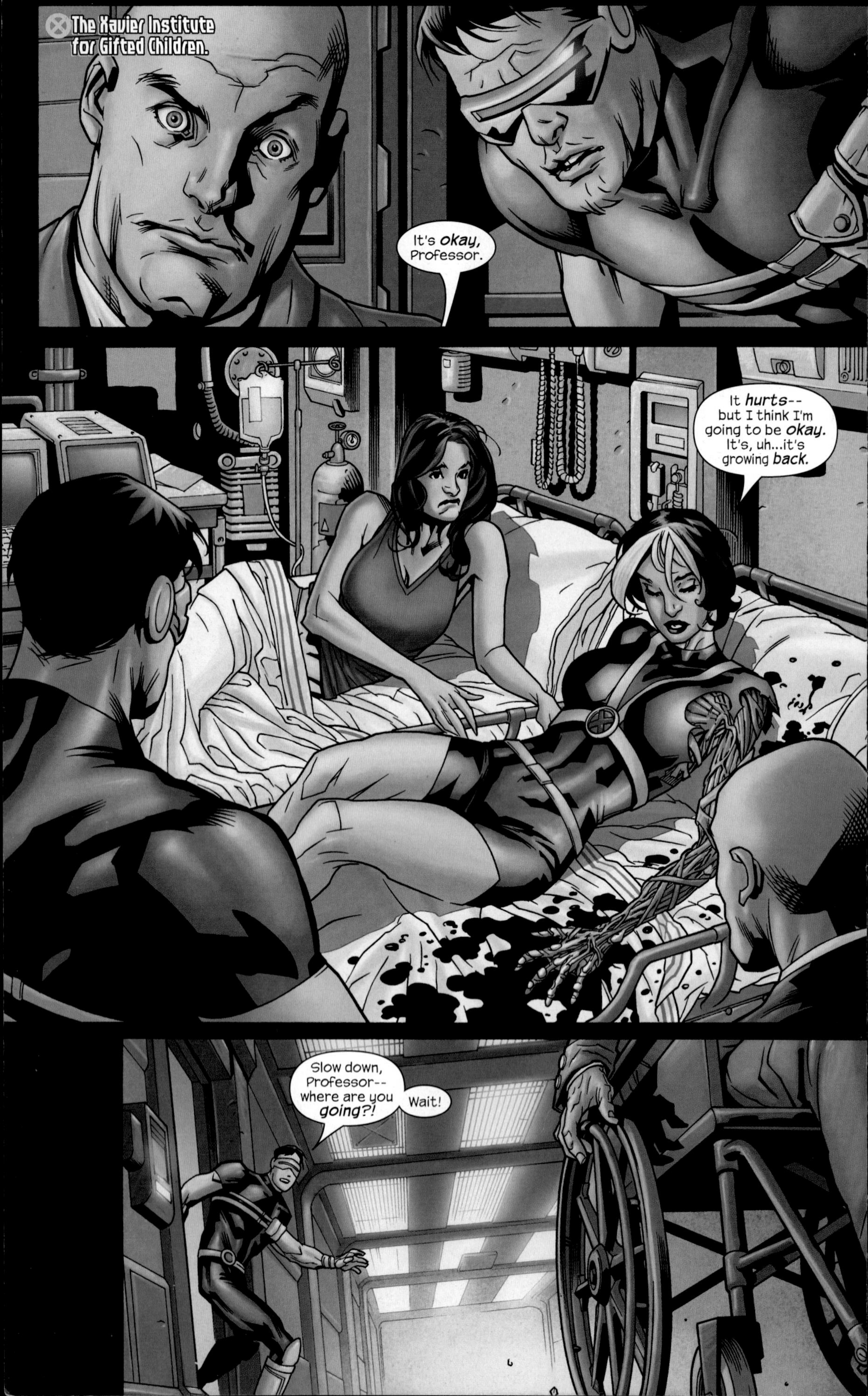
The Xavier Institute for Gifted Children.
It's *okay,* Professor.
It *hurts*-- but I think I'm going to be *okay.* It's, uh...it's growing *back.*
Slow down, Professor-- where are you *going?!*
Wait!

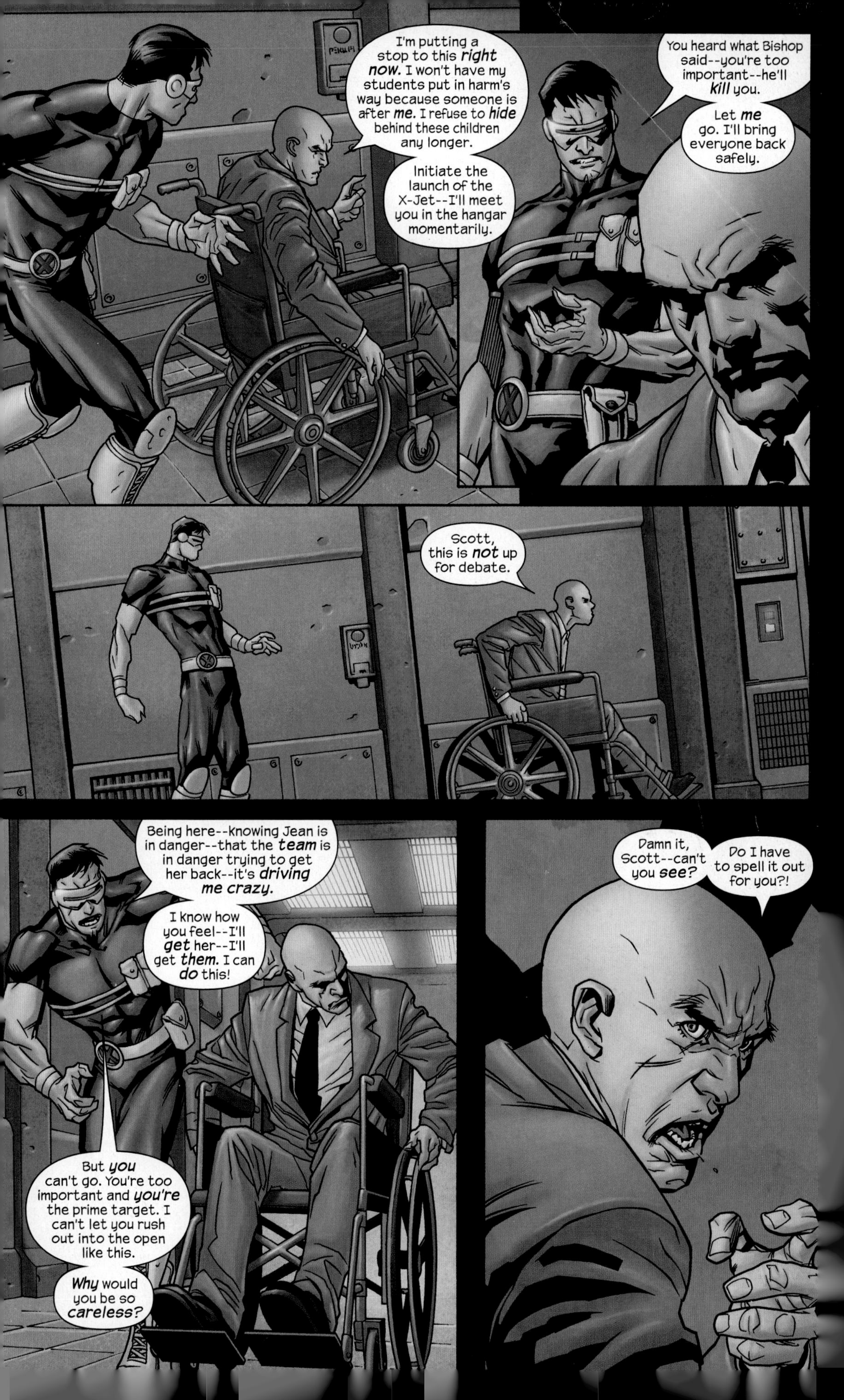

I'm putting a stop to this right now. I won't have my students put in harm's way because someone is after me. I refuse to hide behind these children any longer.
Initiate the launch of the X-Jet--I'll meet you in the hangar momentarily.
You heard what Bishop said--you're too important--he'll kill you.
Let me go. I'll bring everyone back safely.
Scott, this is not up for debate.
Being here--knowing Jean is in danger--that the team is in danger trying to get her back--it's driving me crazy.
I know how you feel--I'll get her--I'll get them. I can do this!
But you can't go. You're too important and you're the prime target. I can't let you rush out into the open like this.
Why would you be so careless?
Damn it, Scott--can't you see?
Do I have to spell it out for you?!

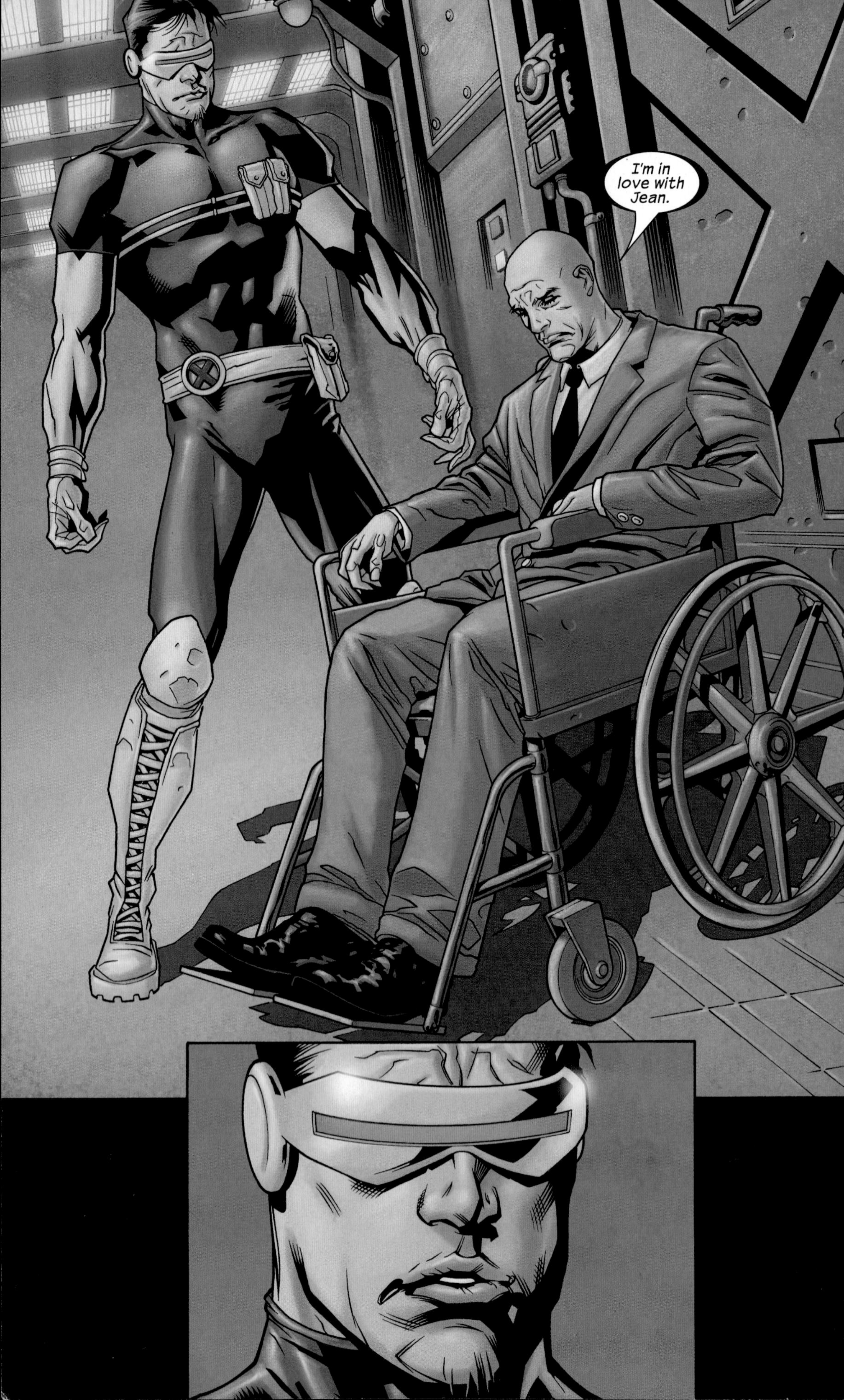
I'm in love with Jean.

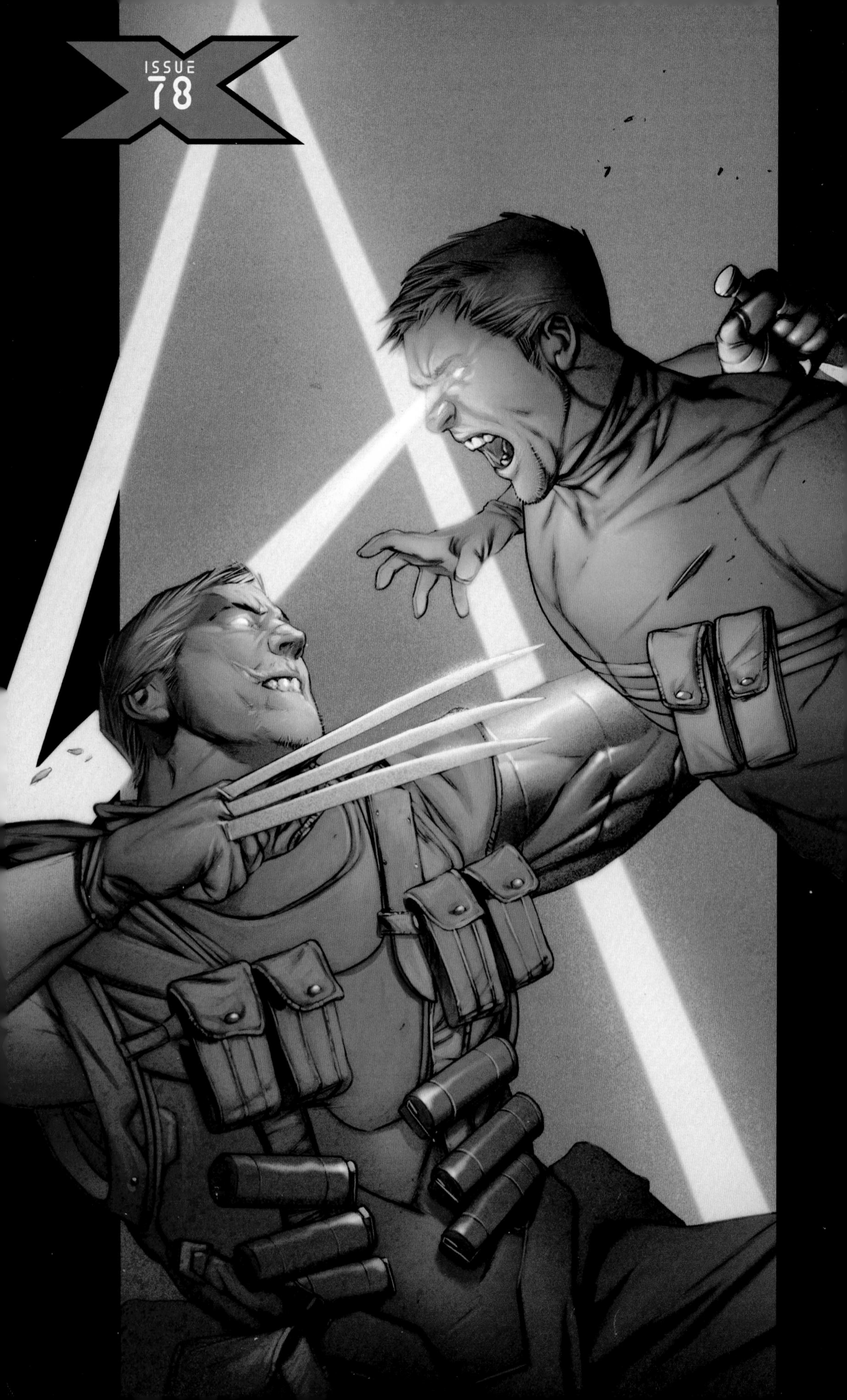
ISSUE 78

CABLE: CONCLUSION

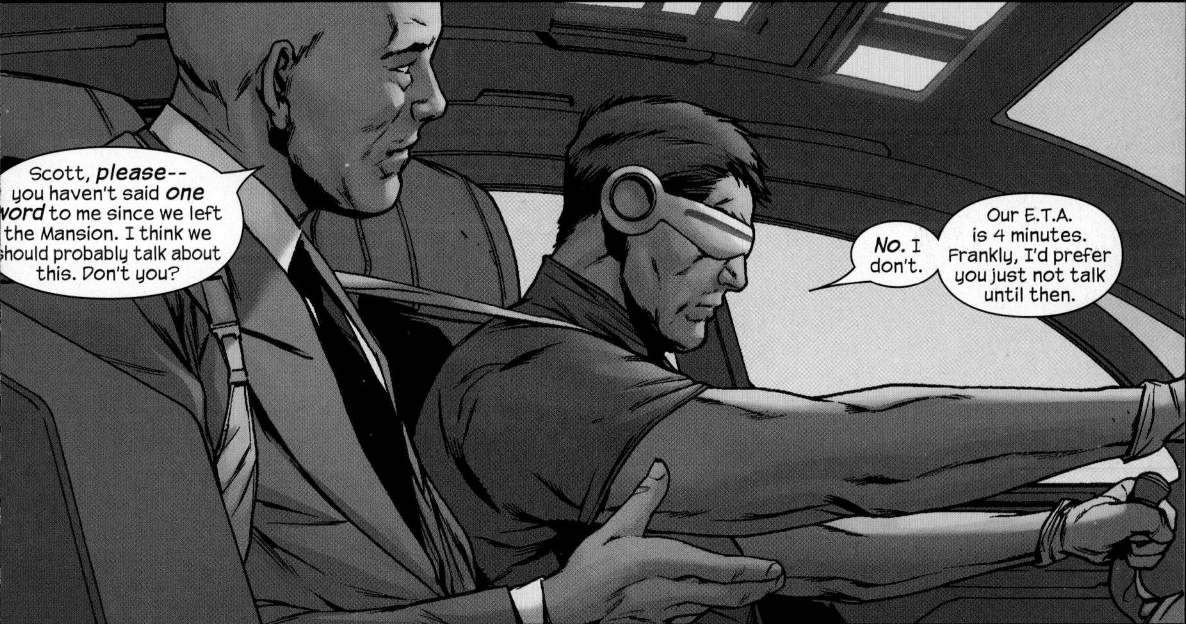
Scott, *please*-- you haven't said *one* *vord* to me since we left the Mansion. I think we hould probably talk about this. Don't you?
No. I don't.
Our E.T.A. is 4 minutes. Frankly, I'd prefer you just not talk until then.

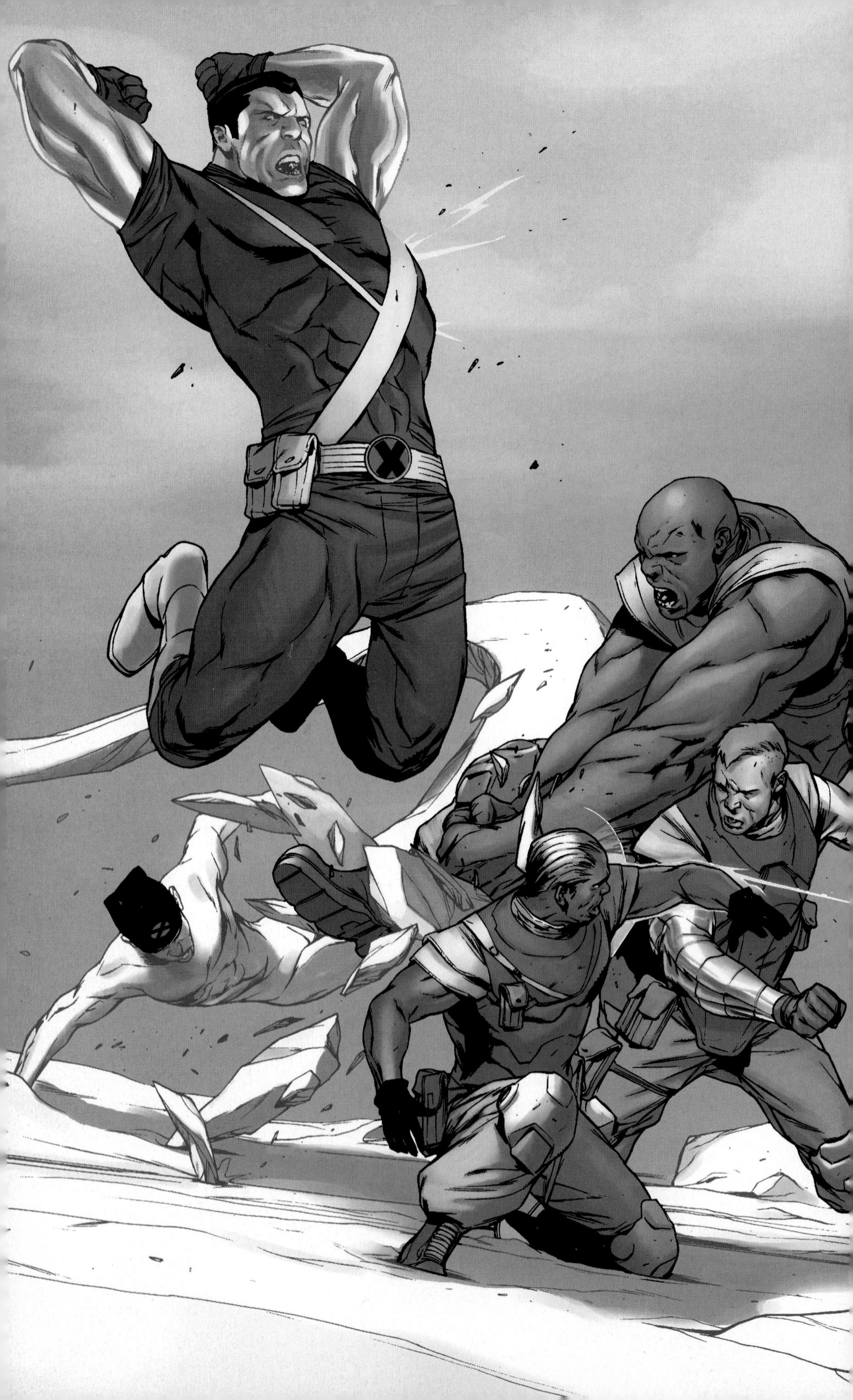

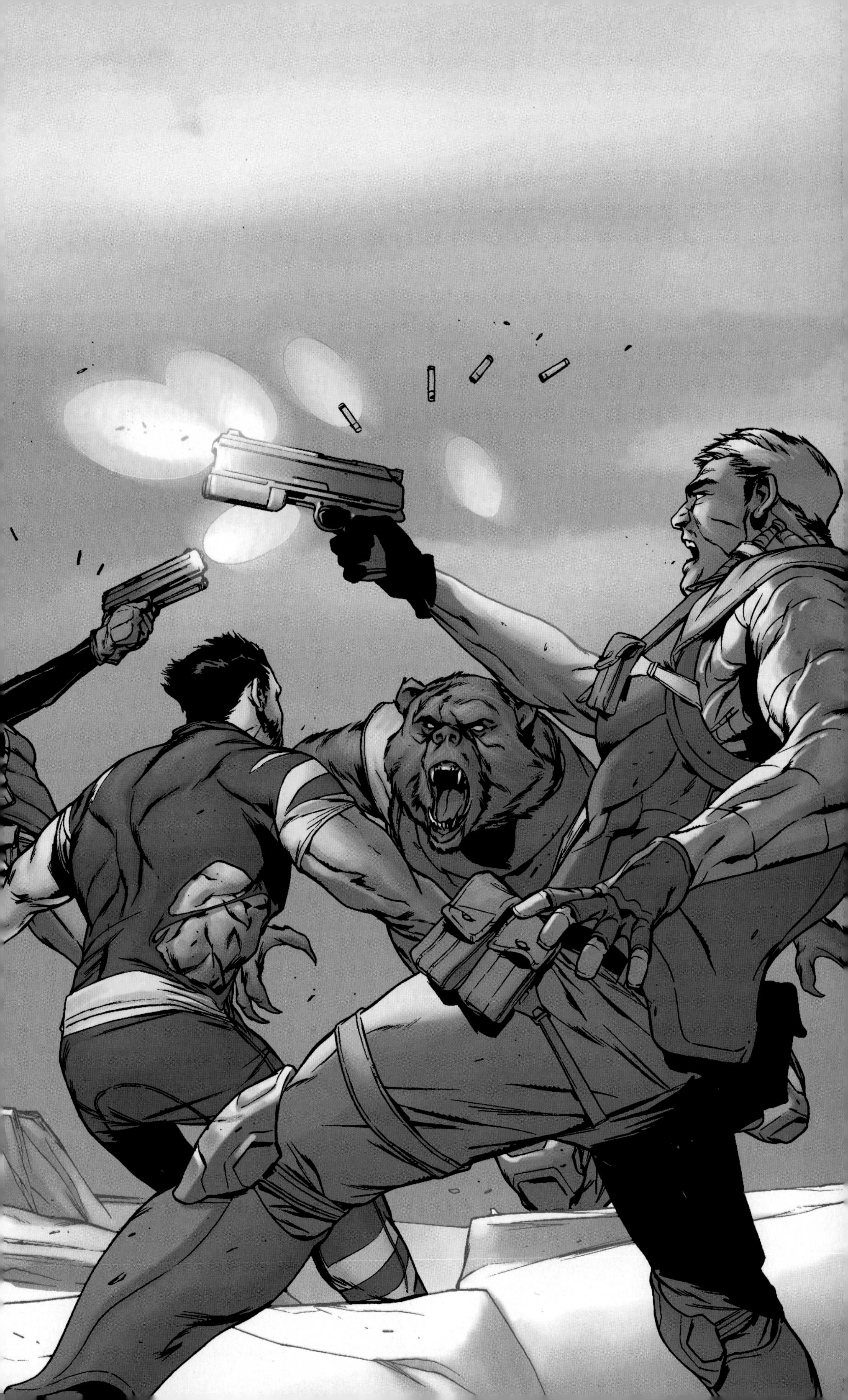

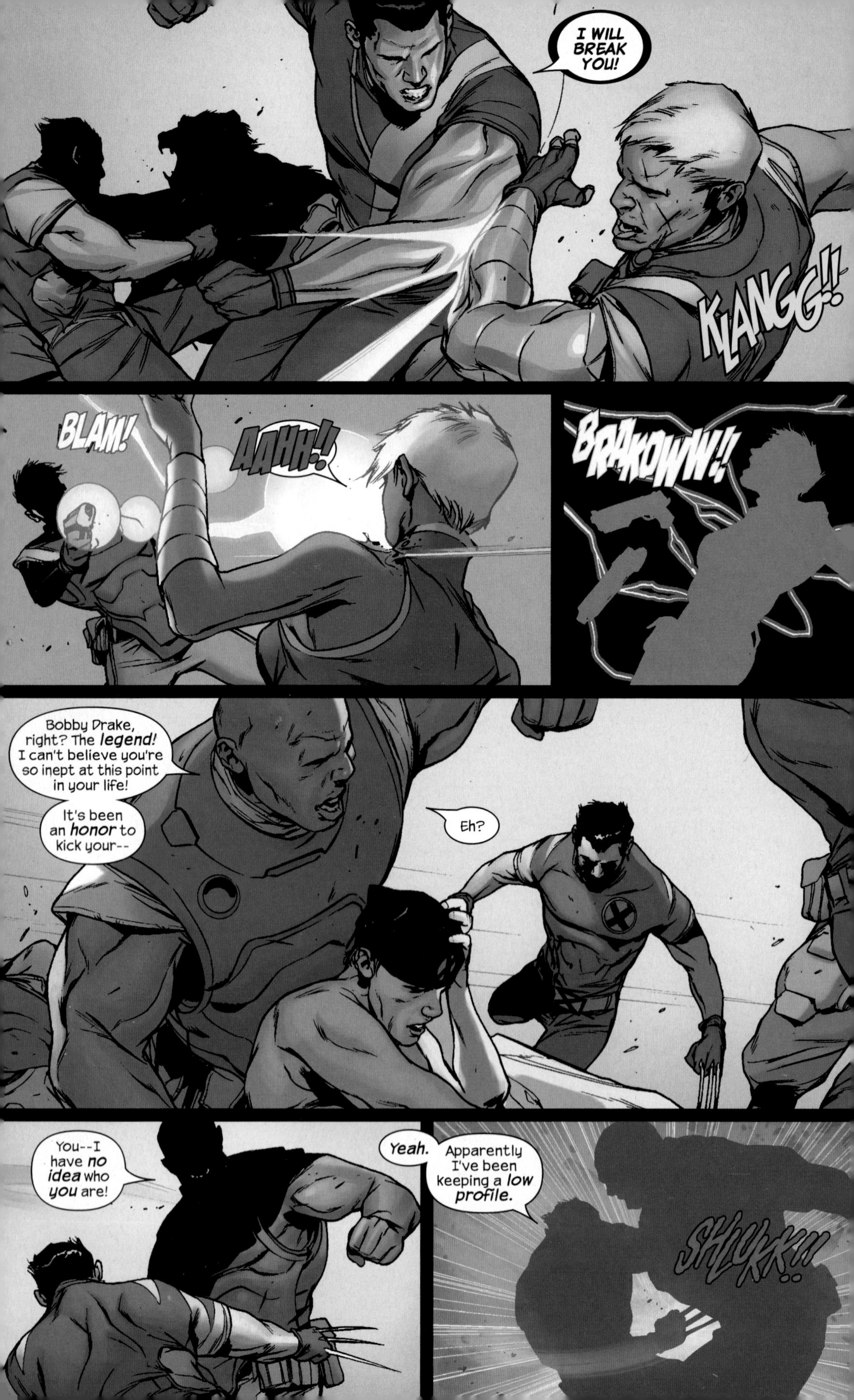
I WILL BREAK YOU!
KLANGG!!
BLAM!
AAHH!!
BRAKOWW!!
Bobby Drake, right? The legend! I can't believe you're so inept at this point in your life!
It's been an honor to kick your--
Eh?
You--I have no idea who you are!
Yeah.
Apparently I've been keeping a low profile.
SHLUKK!!

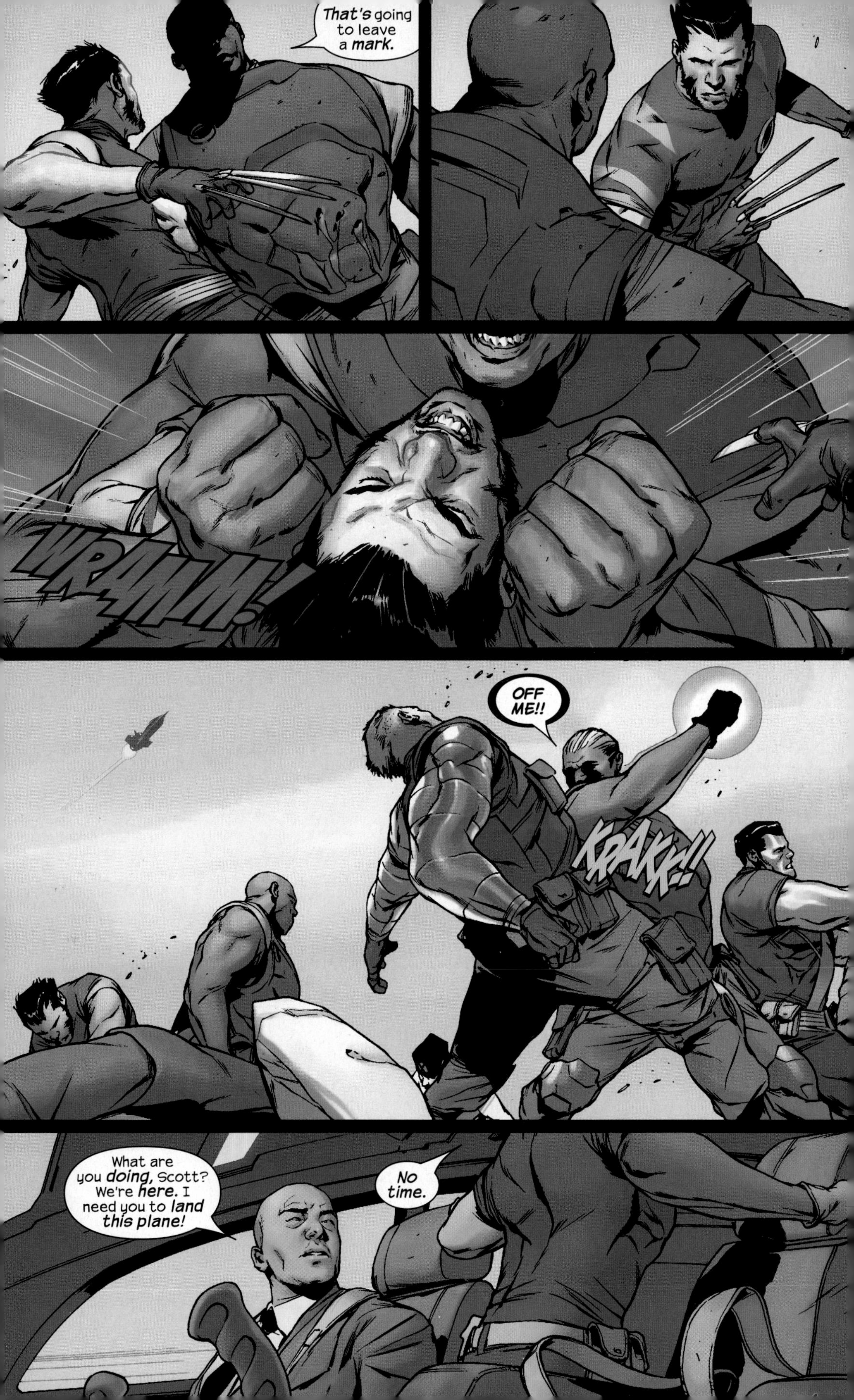
That's going to leave a mark.
WRAMM!!
OFF ME!!
KRAKK!!
What are you doing, Scott? We're here. I need you to land this plane!
No time.

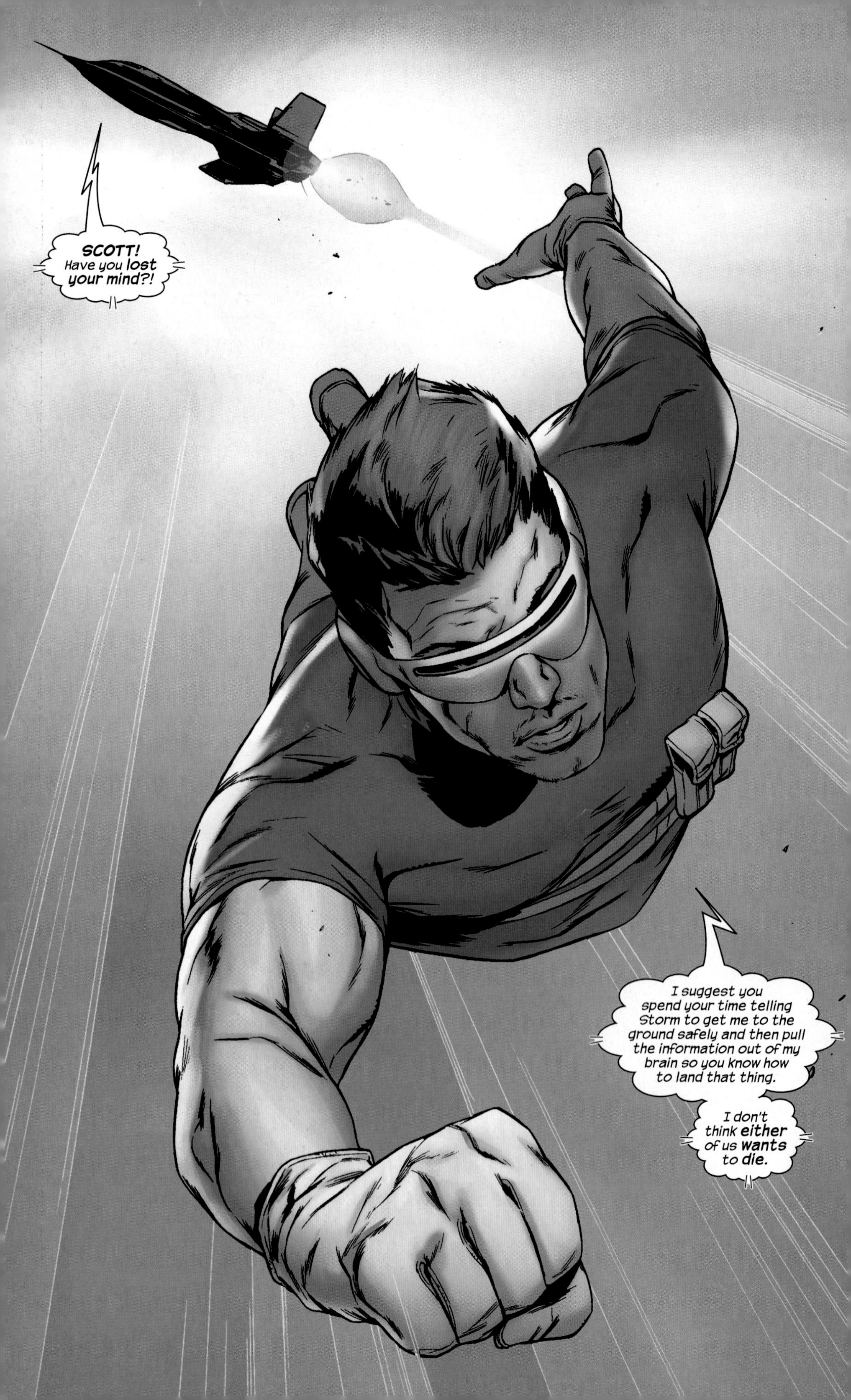
SCOTT! Have you lost your mind?!
I suggest you spend your time telling Storm to get me to the ground safely and then pull the information out of my brain so you know how to land that thing.
I don't think either of us wants to die.

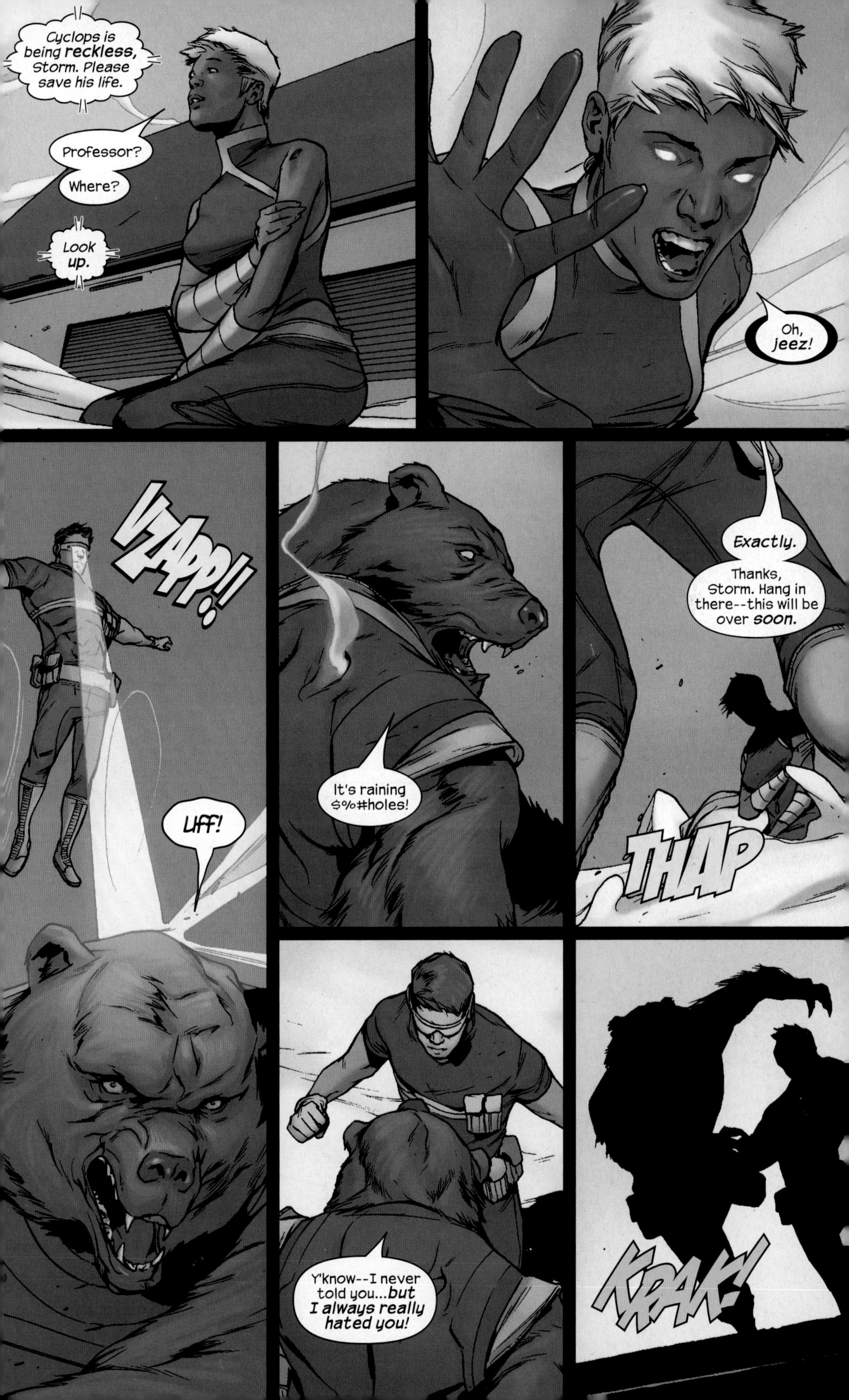

Cyclops is being reckless, Storm. Please save his life.
Professor?
Where?
Look up.
Oh, jeez!
VZAPP!!
UFF!
It's raining $%#holes!
Exactly.
Thanks, Storm. Hang in there--this will be over soon.
THAP
Y'know--I never told you...but I always really hated you!
KRAK!

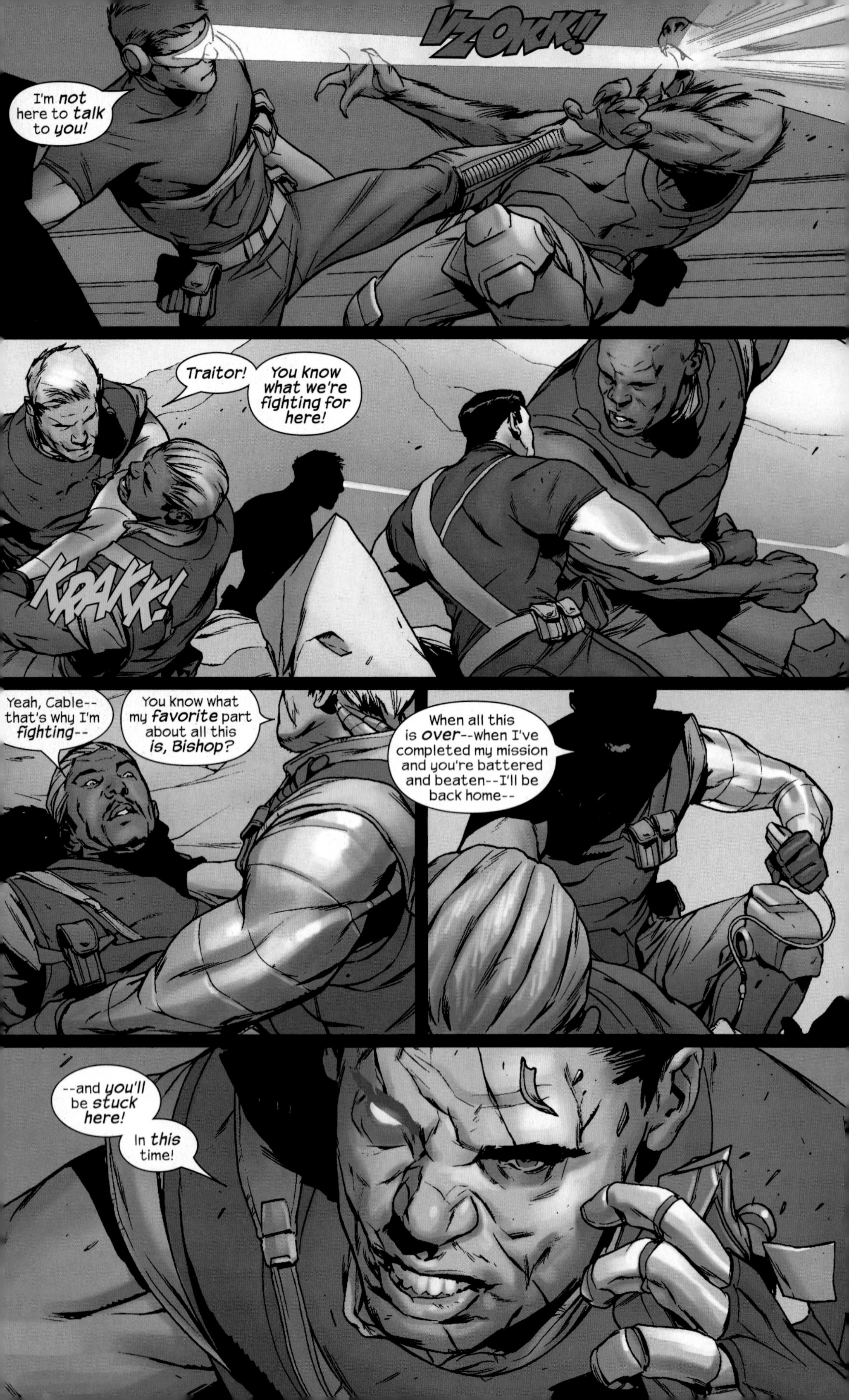
VZOKK!!
I'm not here to talk to you!
Traitor!
You know what we're fighting for here!
KRAKK!
Yeah, Cable-- that's why I'm fighting--
You know what my favorite part about all this is, Bishop?
When all this is over--when I've completed my mission and you're battered and beaten--I'll be back home--
--and you'll be stuck here!
In this time!

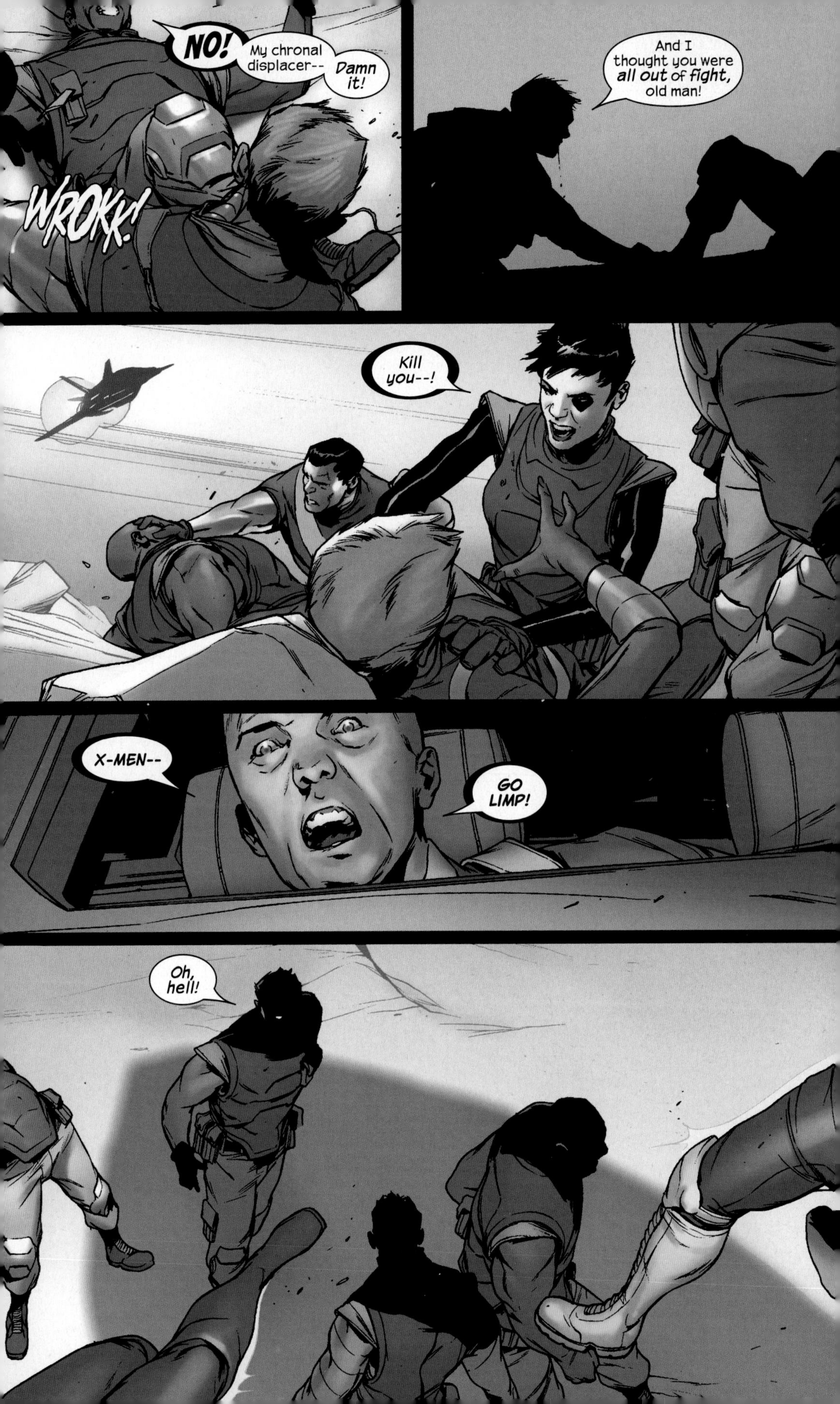
NO!
My chronal displacer--
Damn it!
WROKK!
And I thought you were all out of fight, old man!
Kill you--!
X-MEN--
GO LIMP!
Oh, hell!

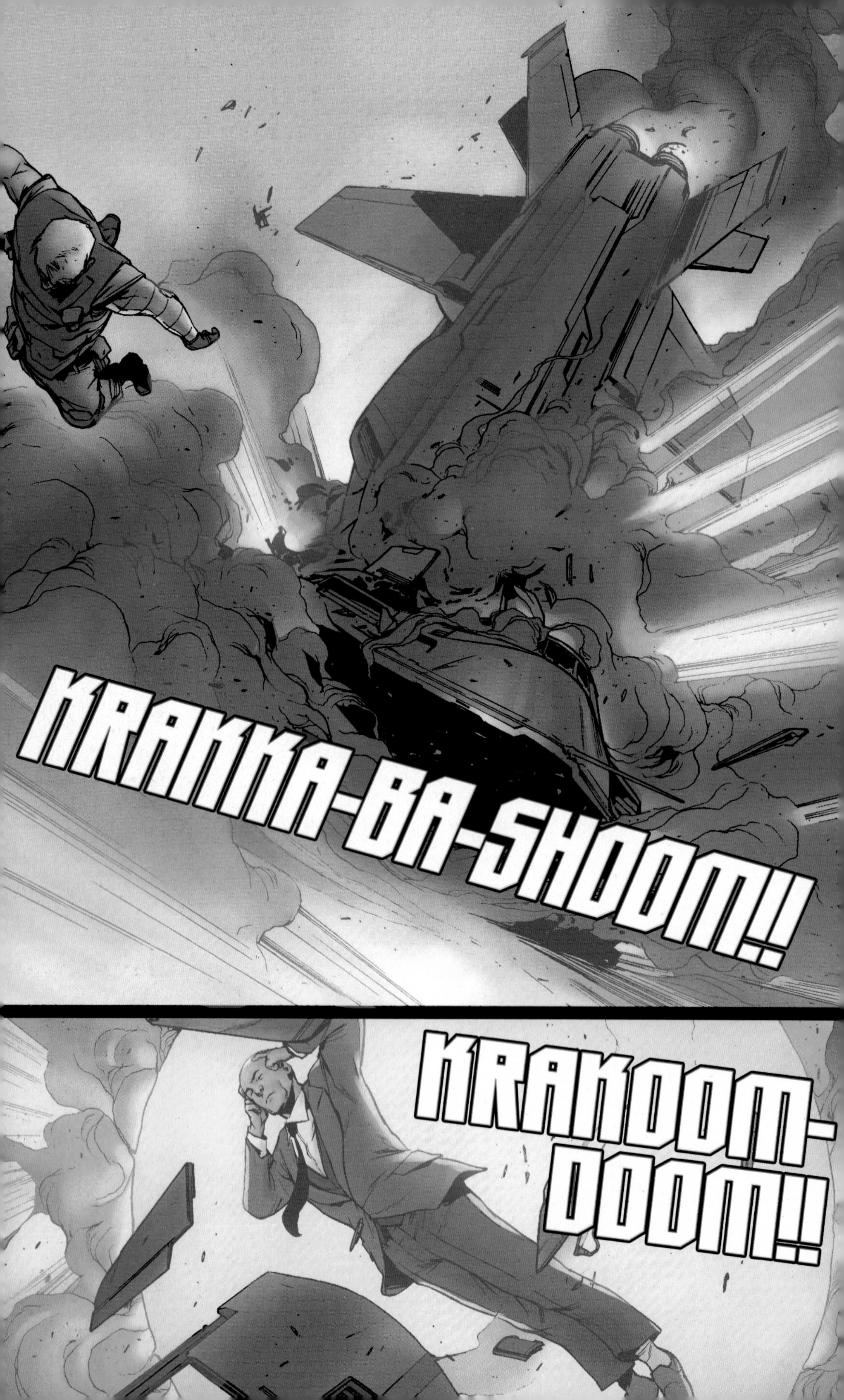
KRAKKA-BA-SHOOM!!
KRAKOOM-DOOM!!

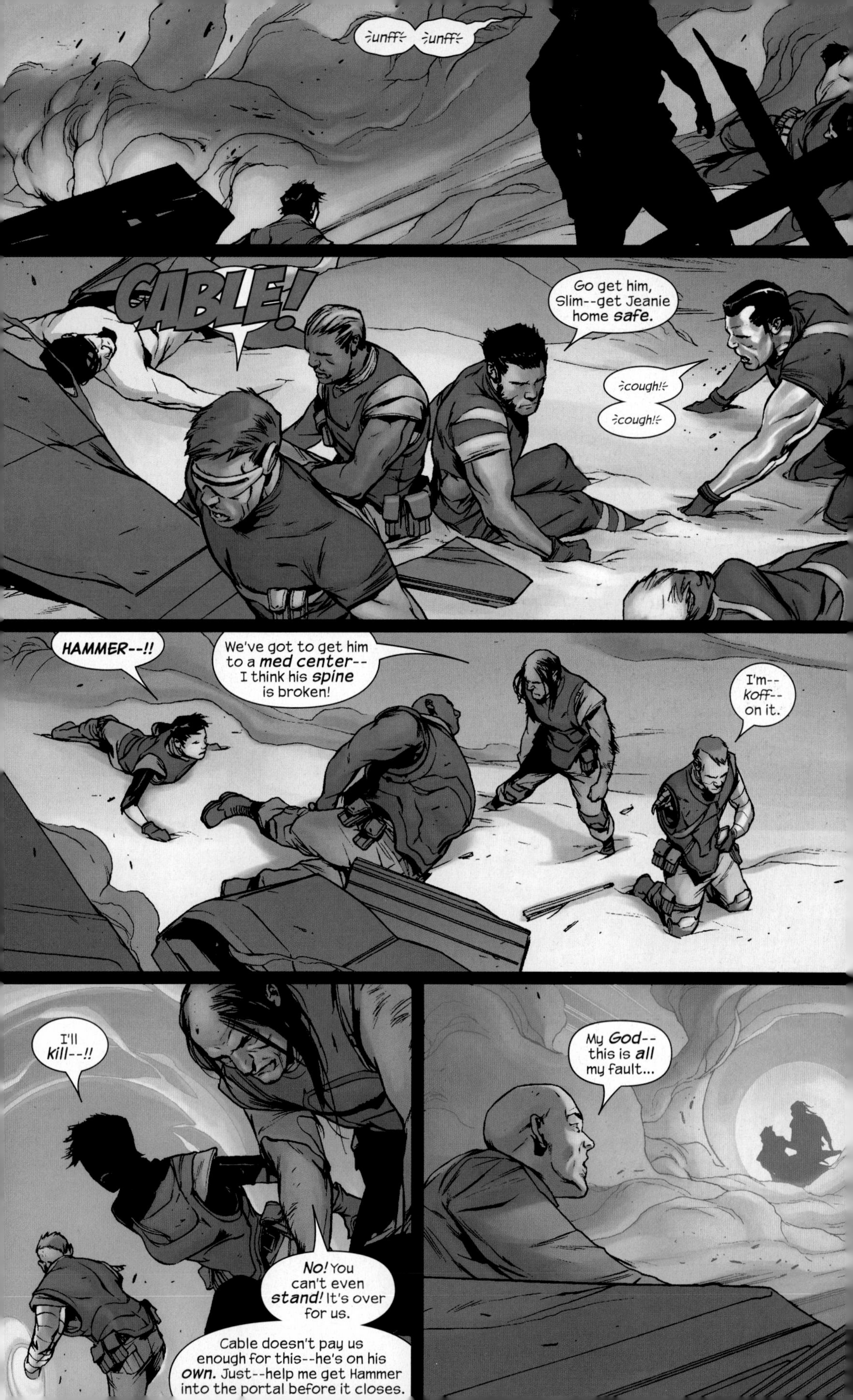
unff
unff
CABLE!
Go get him, Slim--get Jeanie home safe.
cough!
cough!
HAMMER--!!
We've got to get him to a med center-- I think his spine is broken!
I'm-- koff-- on it.
I'll kill--!!
No! You can't even stand! It's over for us.
Cable doesn't pay us enough for this--he's on his own. Just--help me get Hammer into the portal before it closes.
My God-- this is all my fault...

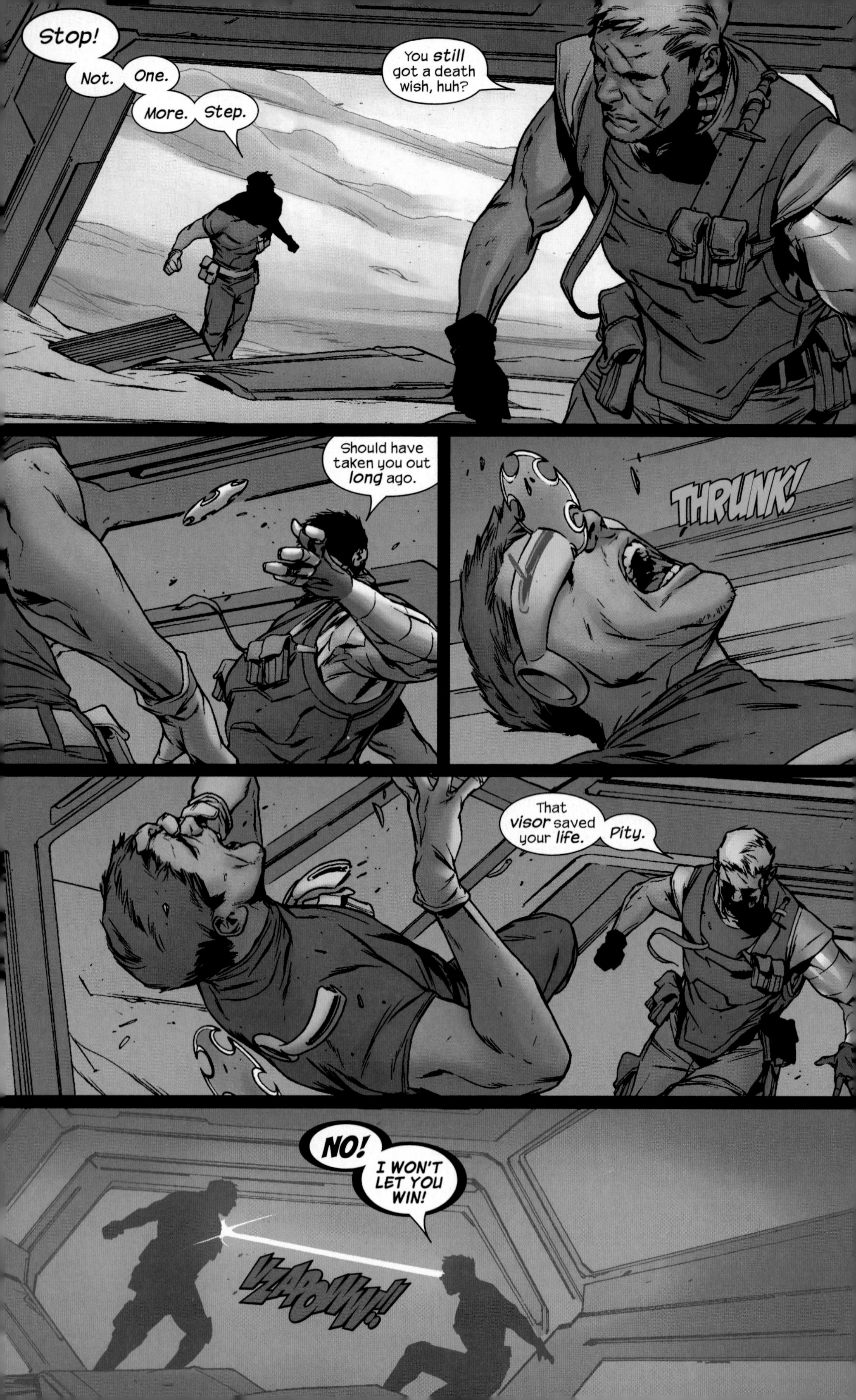
Stop!
Not. One.
More. Step.
You still got a death wish, huh?
Should have taken you out long ago.
THRUNK!
That visor saved your life.
Pity.
NO!
I WON'T LET YOU WIN!
VZARONNN!

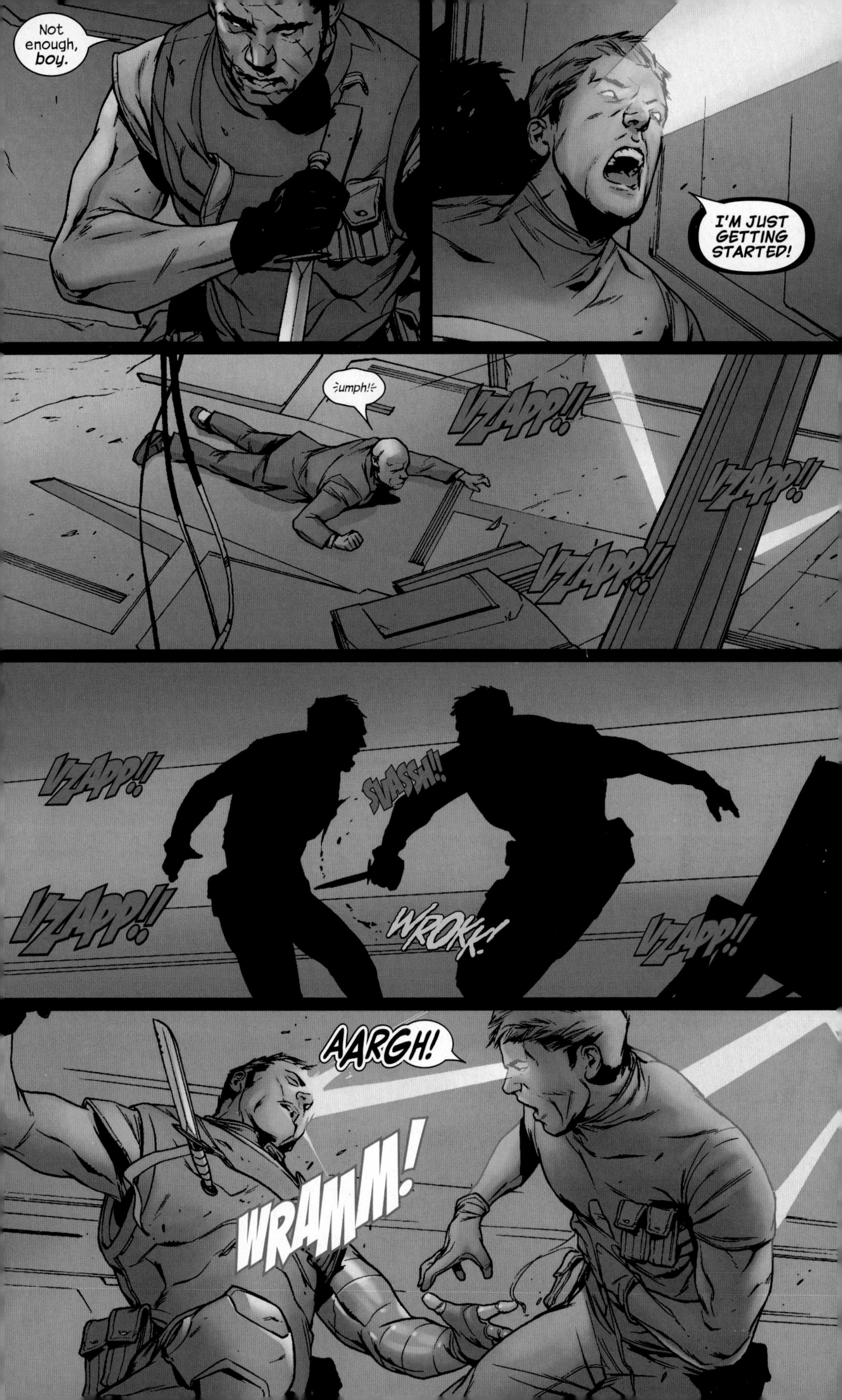

Not enough, boy.
I'M JUST GETTING STARTED!
umph!
VZAPP!!
VZAPP!!
VZAPP!!
VZAPP!!
SLASSH!!
VZAPP!!
WROKK!
VZAPP!!
AARGH!
WRAMM!

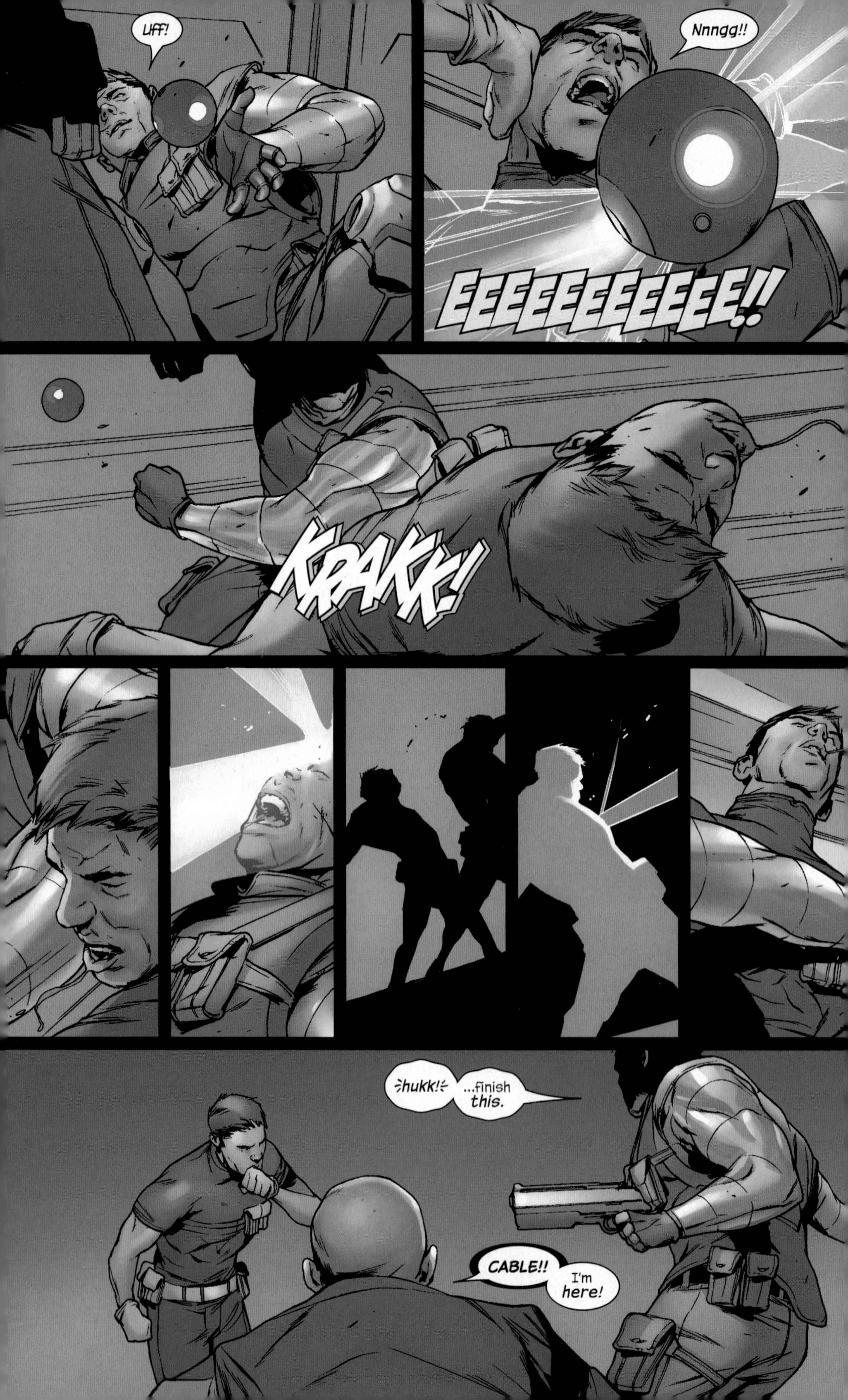
Uff!
Nnngg!!
EEEEEEEEEEEE!!
KRAKK!
hukk!
...finish this.
CABLE!!
I'm here!

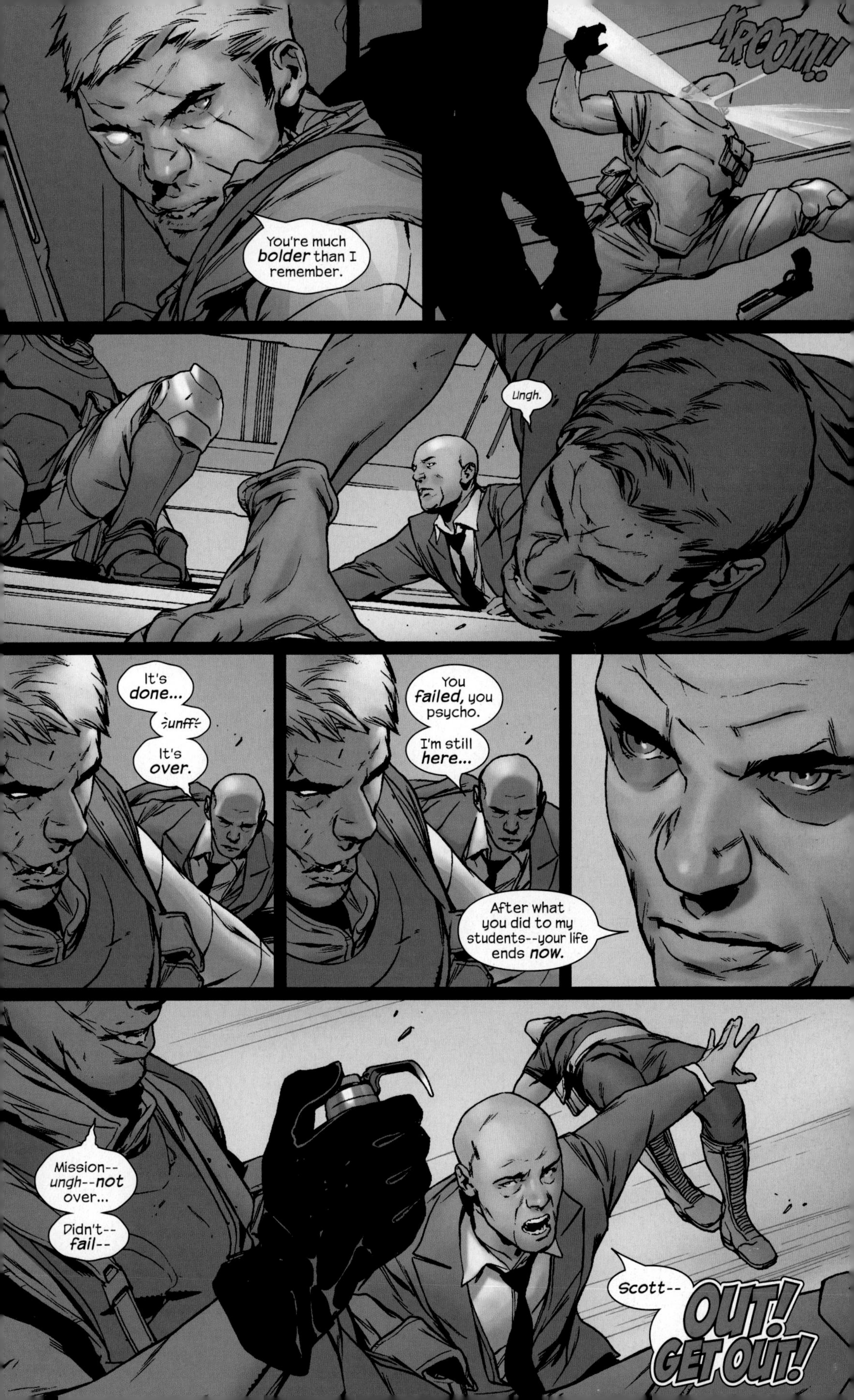
KROOM!!
You're much bolder than I remember.
Ungh.
It's done...
unff
It's over.
You failed, you psycho.
I'm still here...
After what you did to my students--your life ends now.
Mission--ungh--not over...
Didn't--fail--
Scott--
OUT! GET OUT!

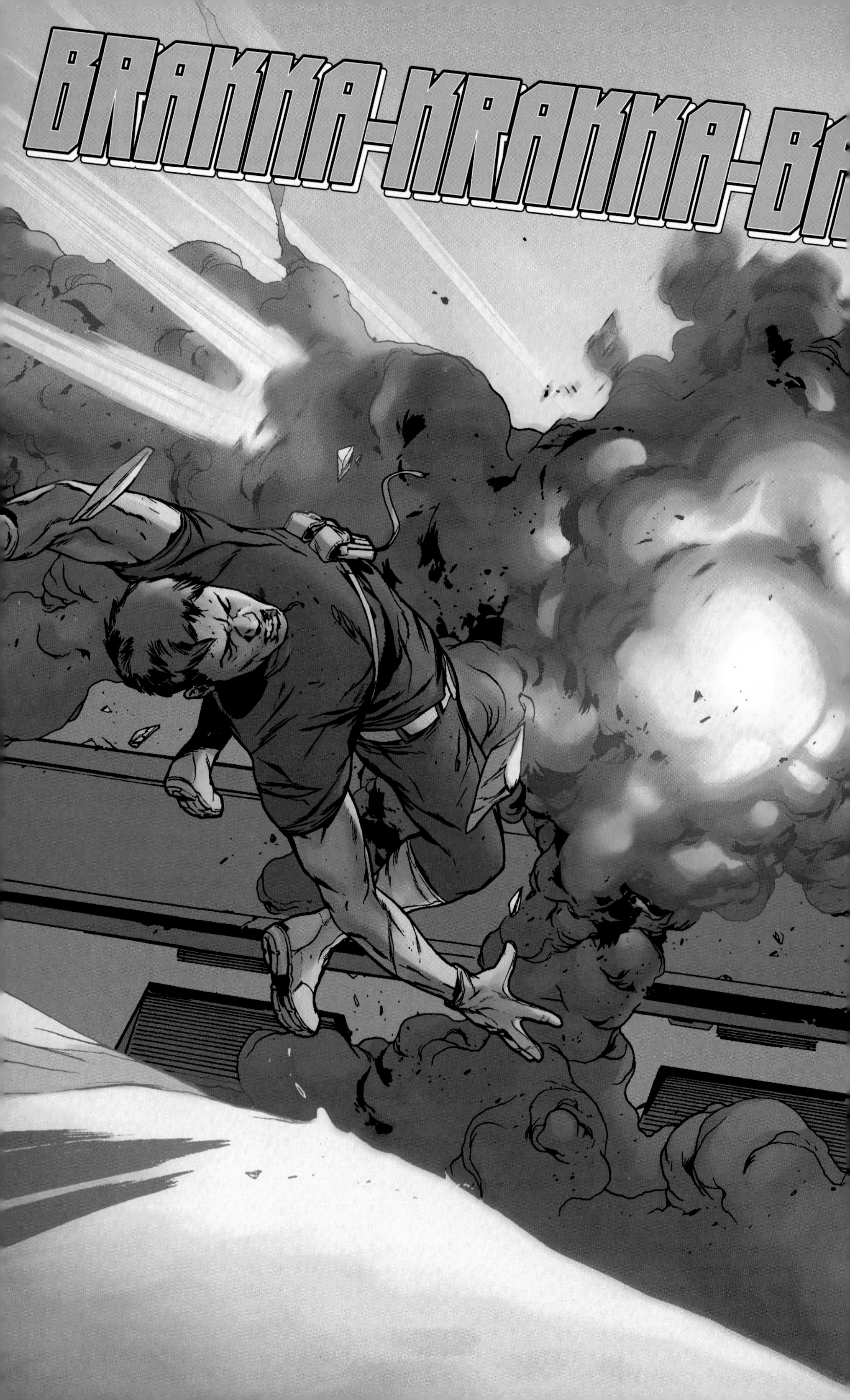
BRAKKA-KRAKKA-BA

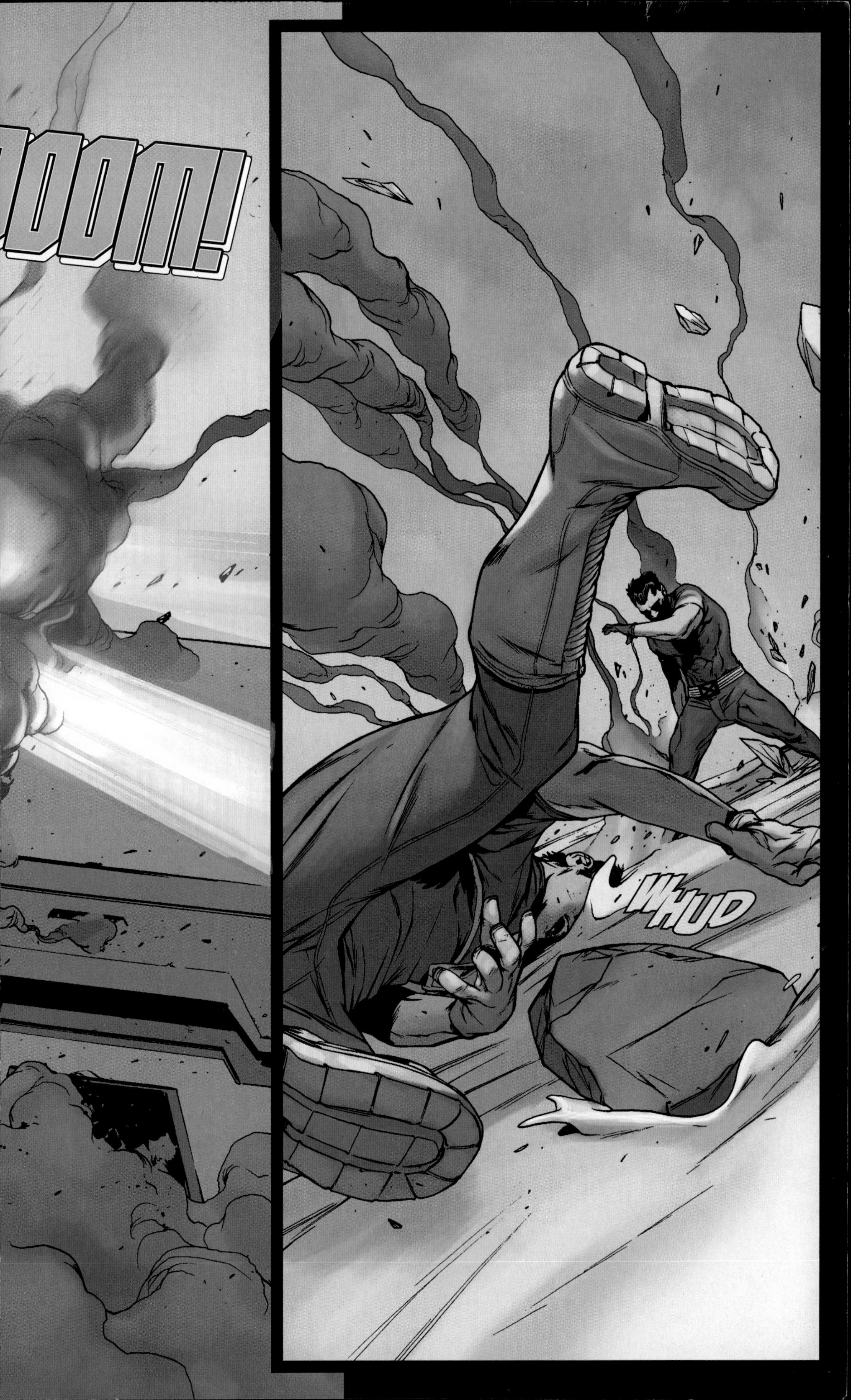
WHUD

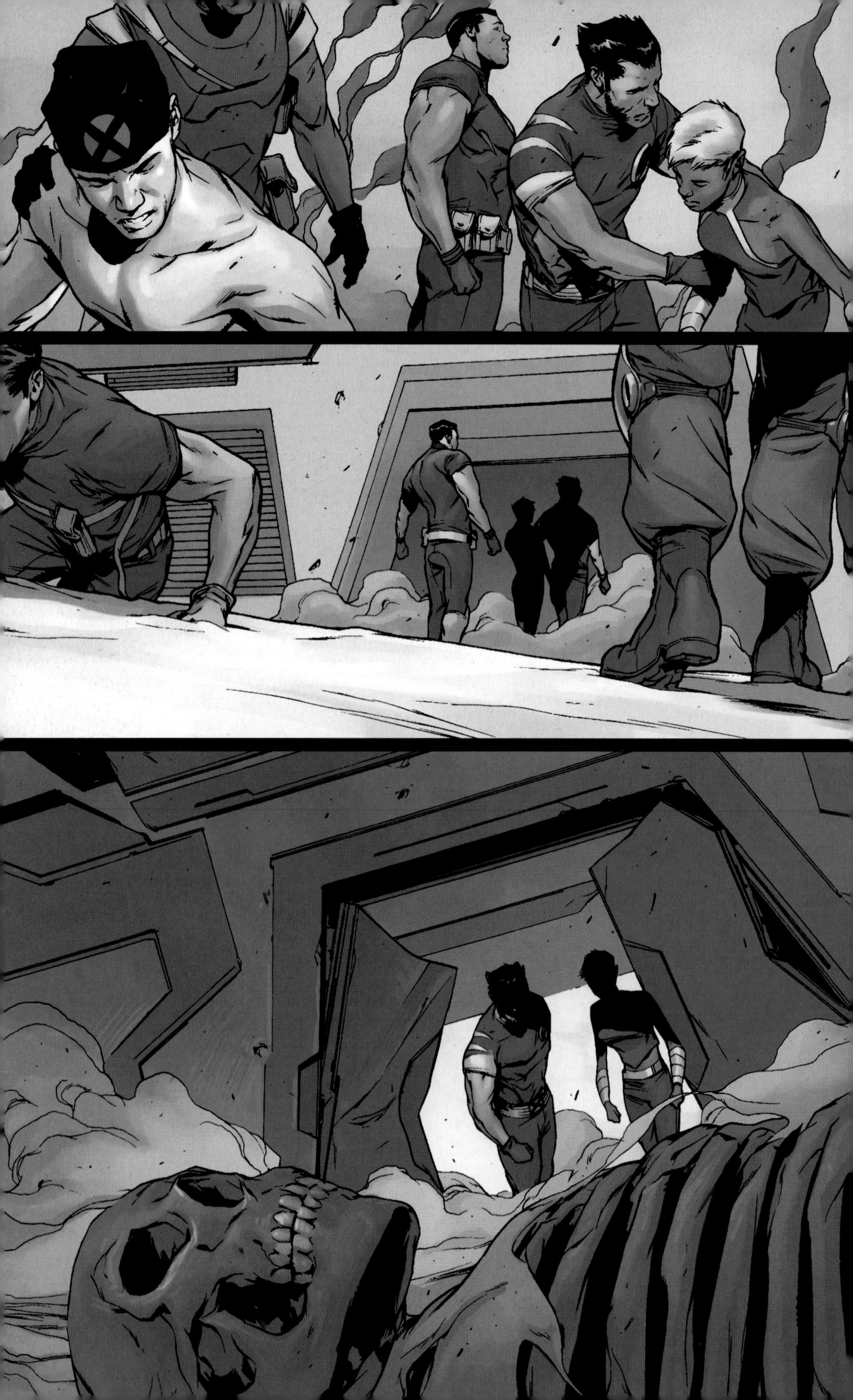

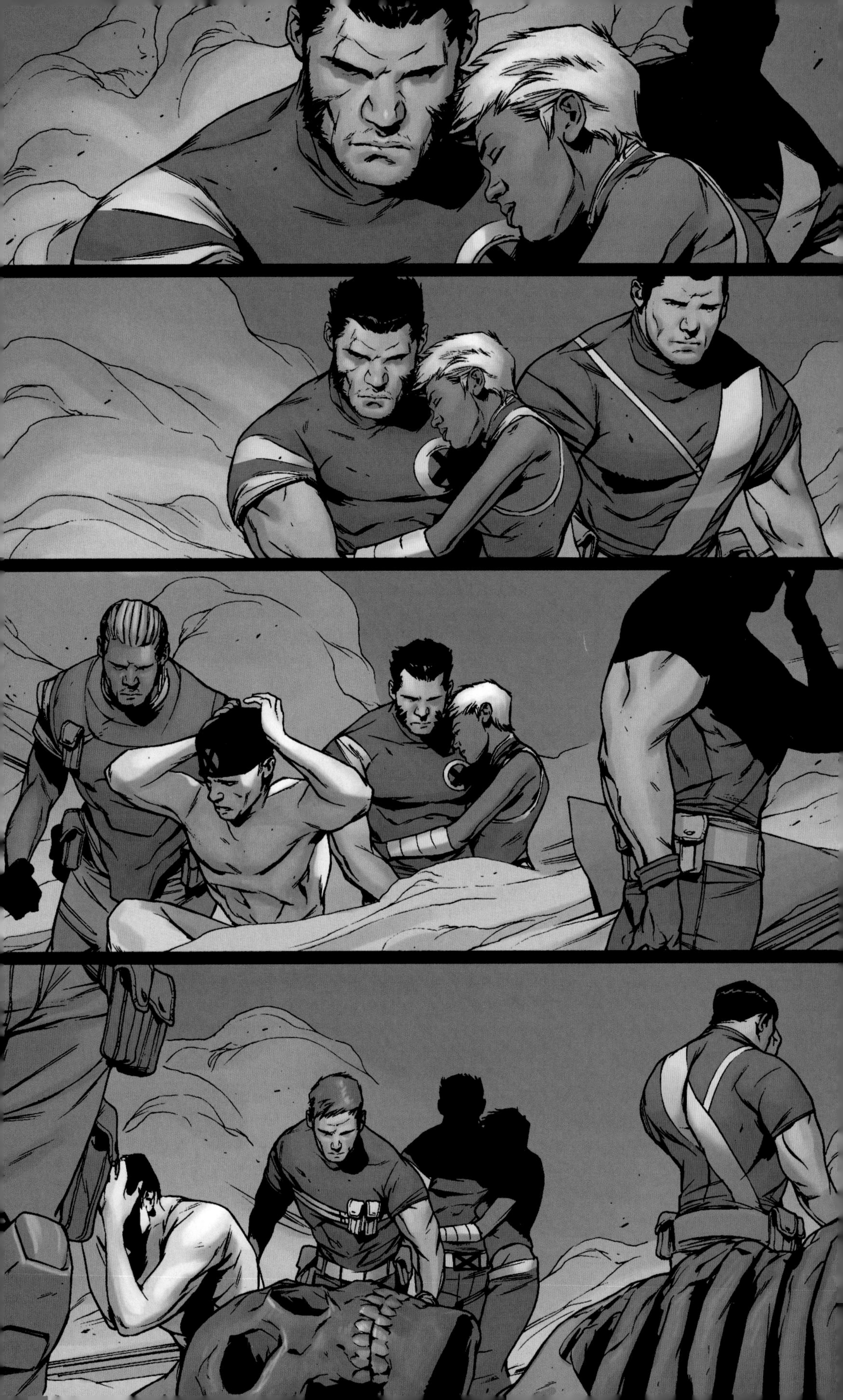

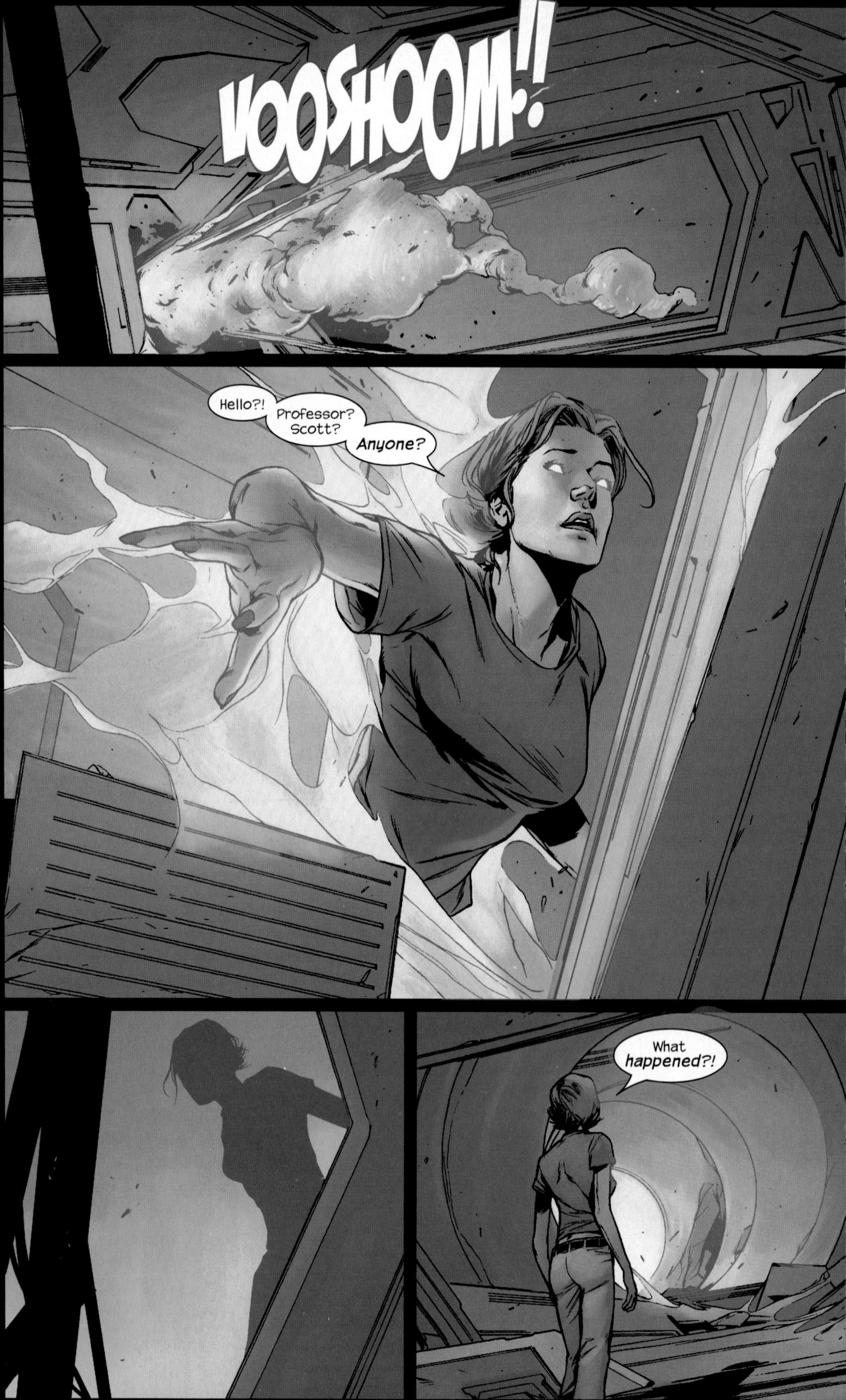
VOOSHOOM!!
Hello?!
Professor? Scott?
Anyone?
What happened?!

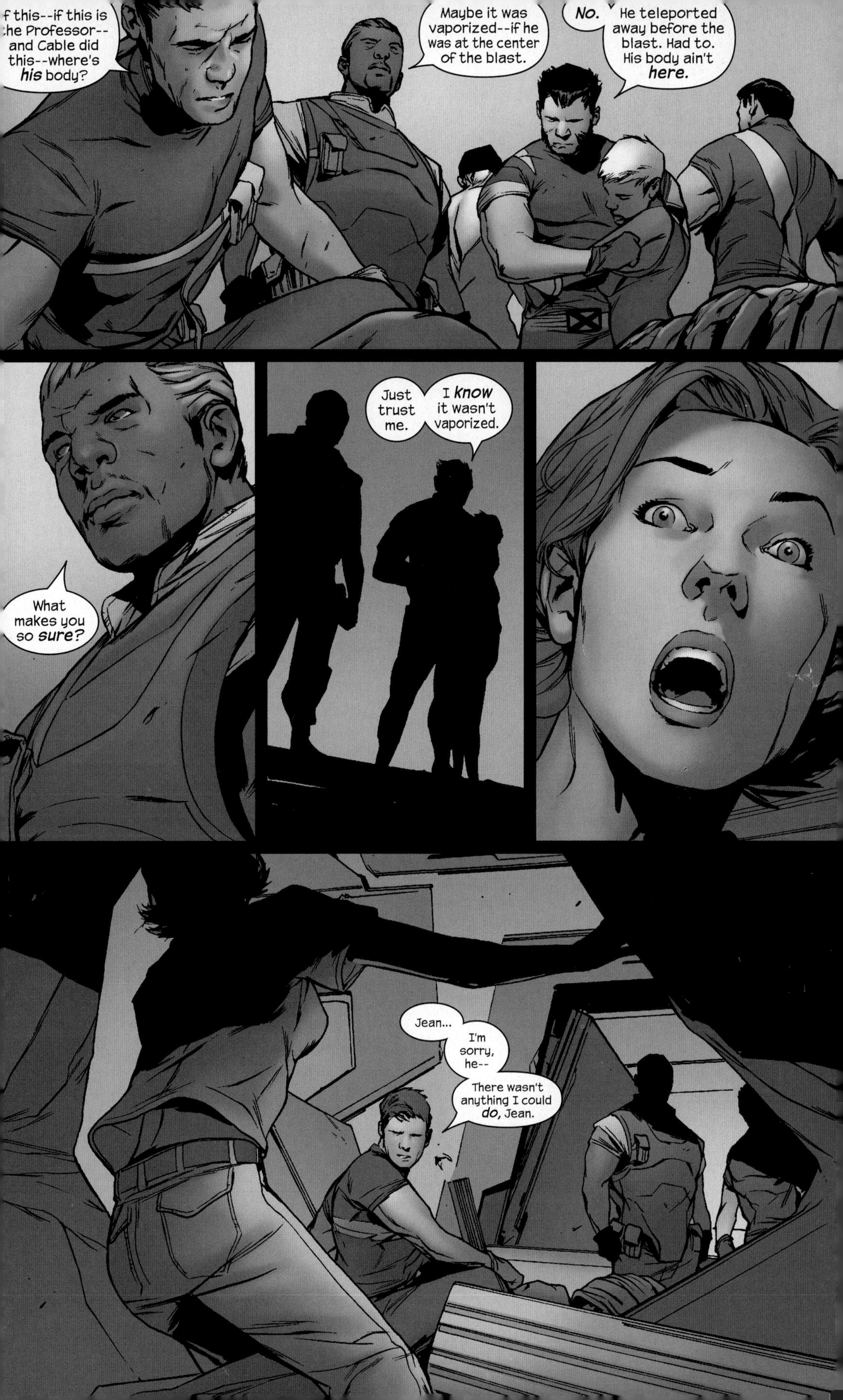

f this--if this is
he Professor--
and Cable did
this--where's
his body?
Maybe it was
vaporized--if he
was at the center
of the blast.
No.
He teleported
away before the
blast. Had to.
His body ain't
here.
What
makes you
so *sure?*
Just
trust
me.
I *know*
it wasn't
vaporized.
Jean...
I'm
sorry,
he--
There wasn't
anything I could
do, Jean.

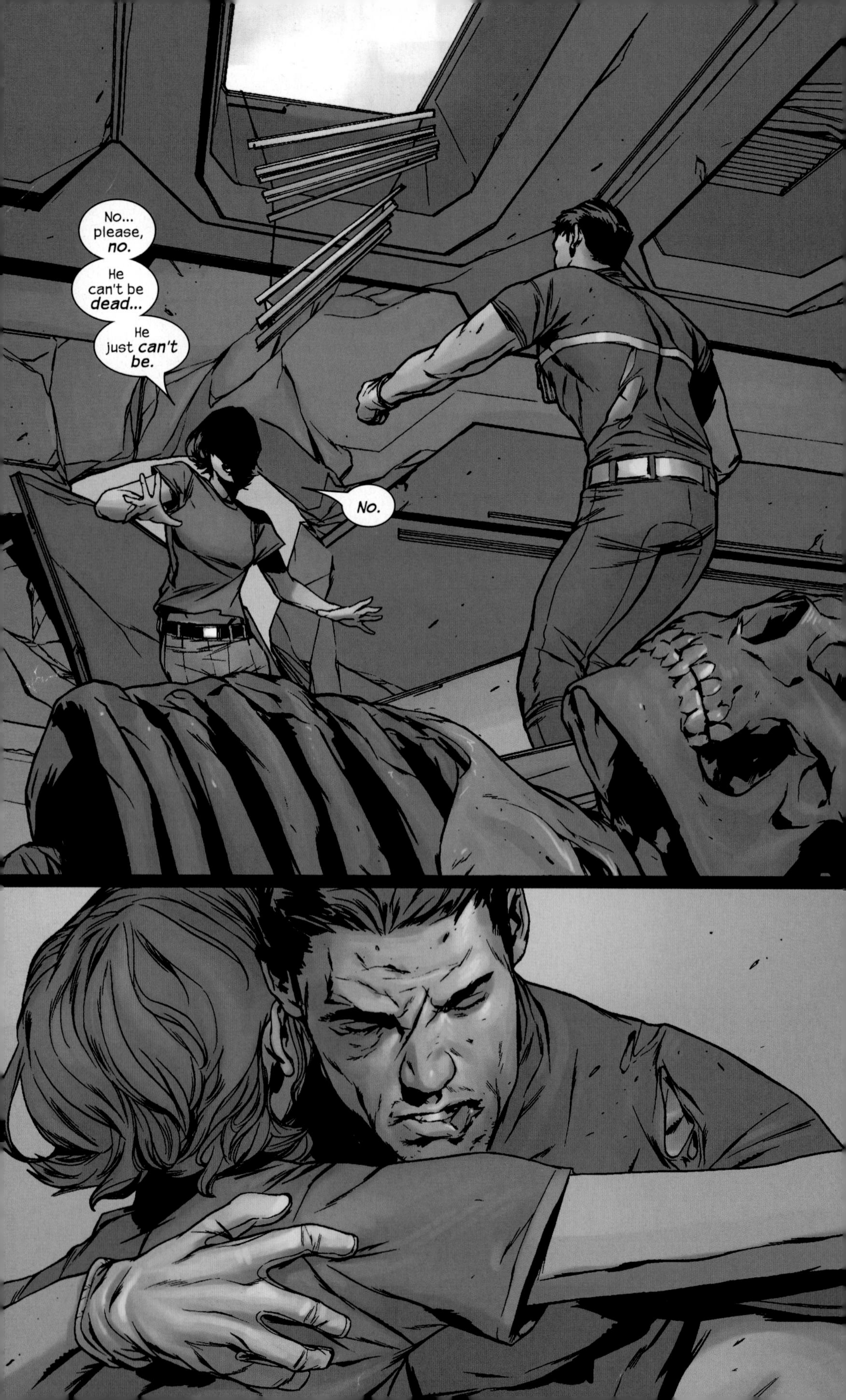
No... please, no.
He can't be dead...
He just can't be.
No.

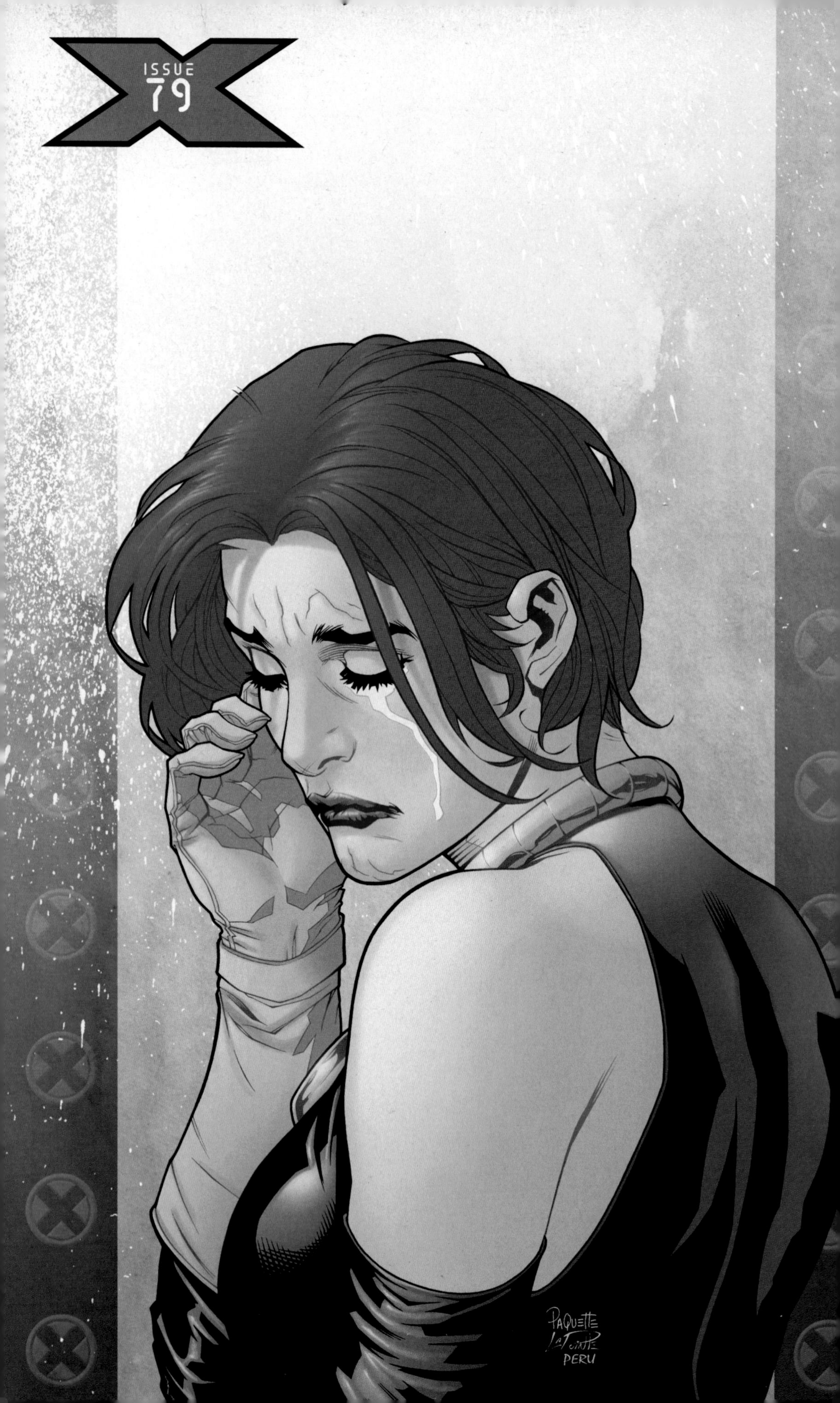
ISSUE
79
PAQUETTE
LaPointe
PERU

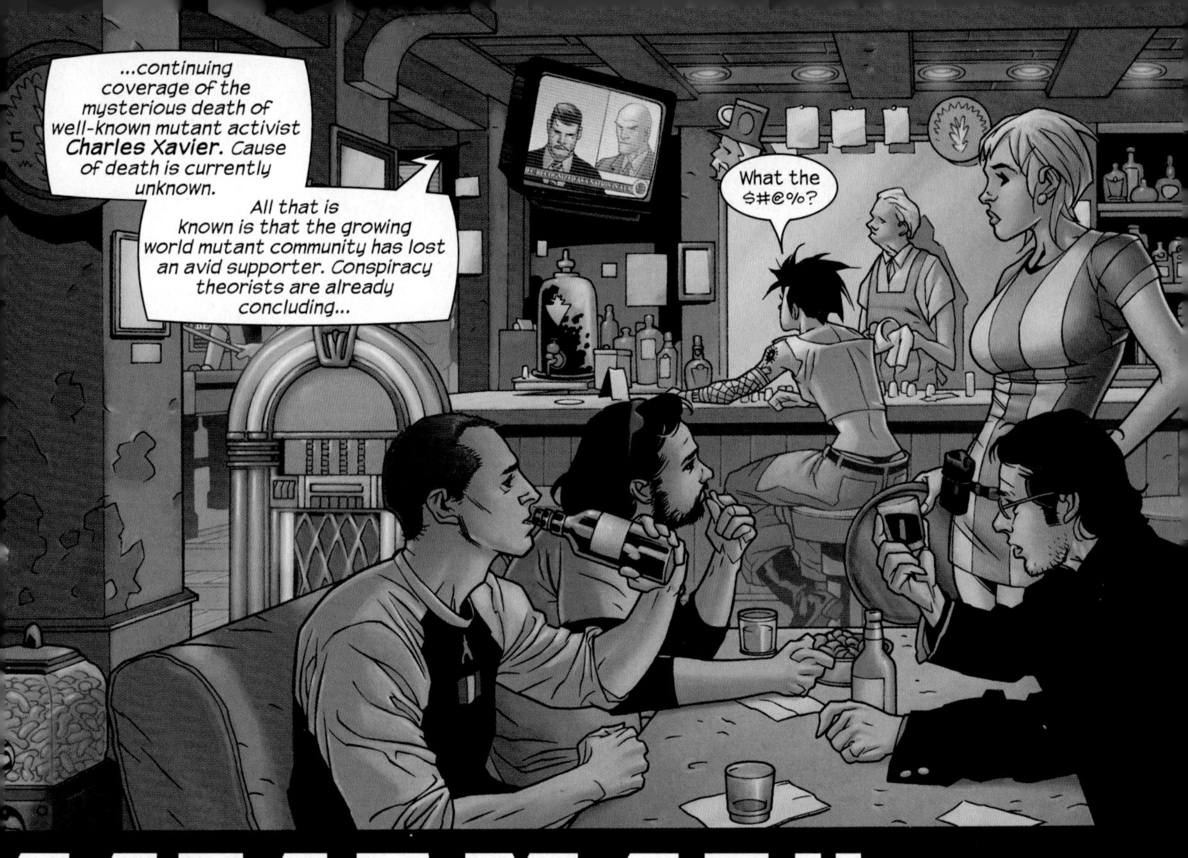
...continuing coverage of the mysterious death of well-known mutant activist Charles Xavier. Cause of death is currently unknown.
All that is known is that the growing world mutant community has lost an avid supporter. Conspiracy theorists are already concluding...
What the $#@%?

AFTERMATH Part 1

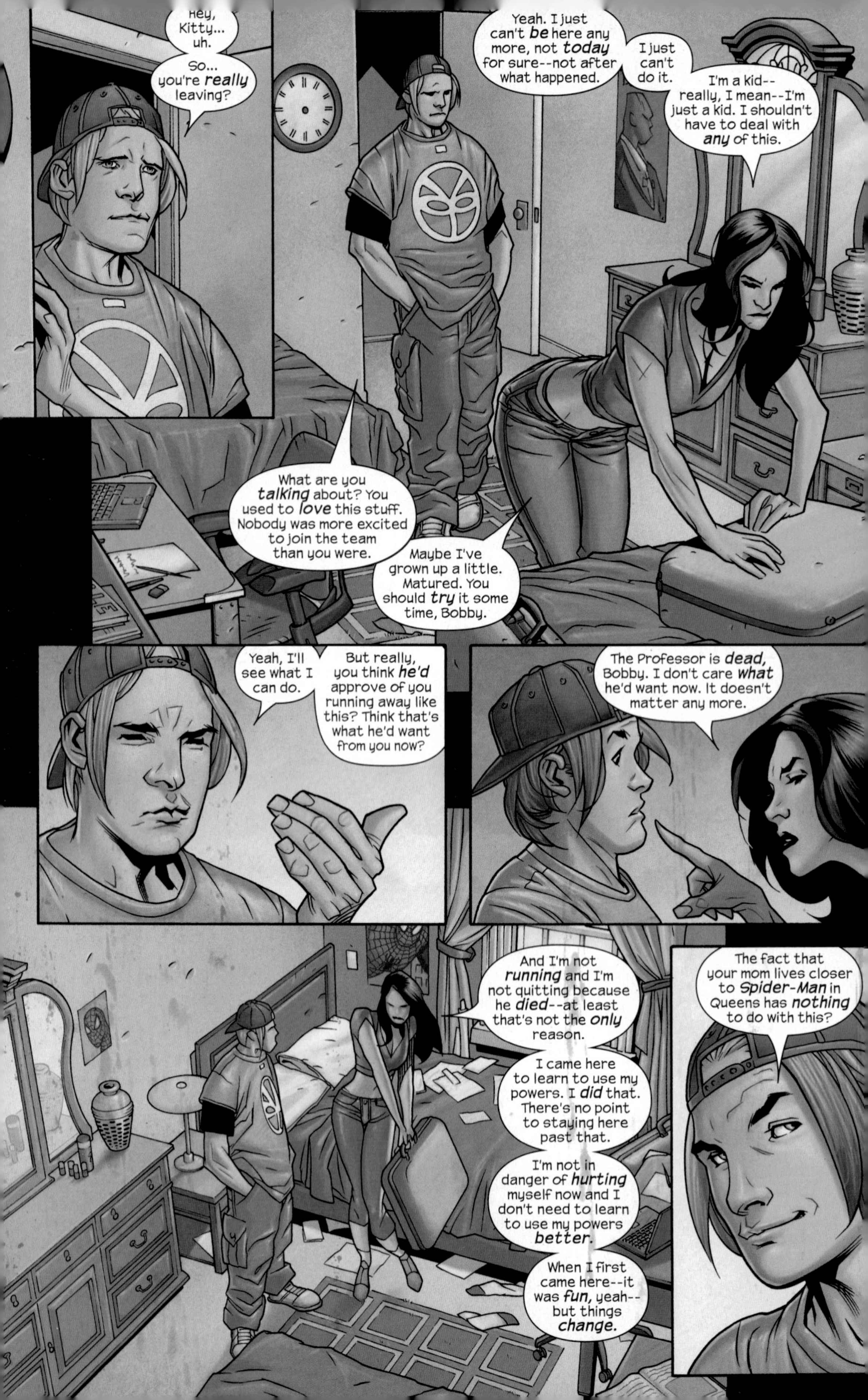
Hey, Kitty... uh.
So... you're really leaving?
Yeah. I just can't be here any more, not today for sure--not after what happened.
I just can't do it.
I'm a kid--really, I mean--I'm just a kid. I shouldn't have to deal with any of this.
What are you talking about? You used to love this stuff. Nobody was more excited to join the team than you were.
Maybe I've grown up a little. Matured. You should try it some time, Bobby.
Yeah, I'll see what I can do.
But really, you think he'd approve of you running away like this? Think that's what he'd want from you now?
The Professor is dead, Bobby. I don't care what he'd want now. It doesn't matter any more.
And I'm not running and I'm not quitting because he died--at least that's not the only reason.
I came here to learn to use my powers. I did that. There's no point to staying here past that.
I'm not in danger of hurting myself now and I don't need to learn to use my powers better.
When I first came here--it was fun, yeah--but things change.
The fact that your mom lives closer to Spider-Man in Queens has nothing to do with this?

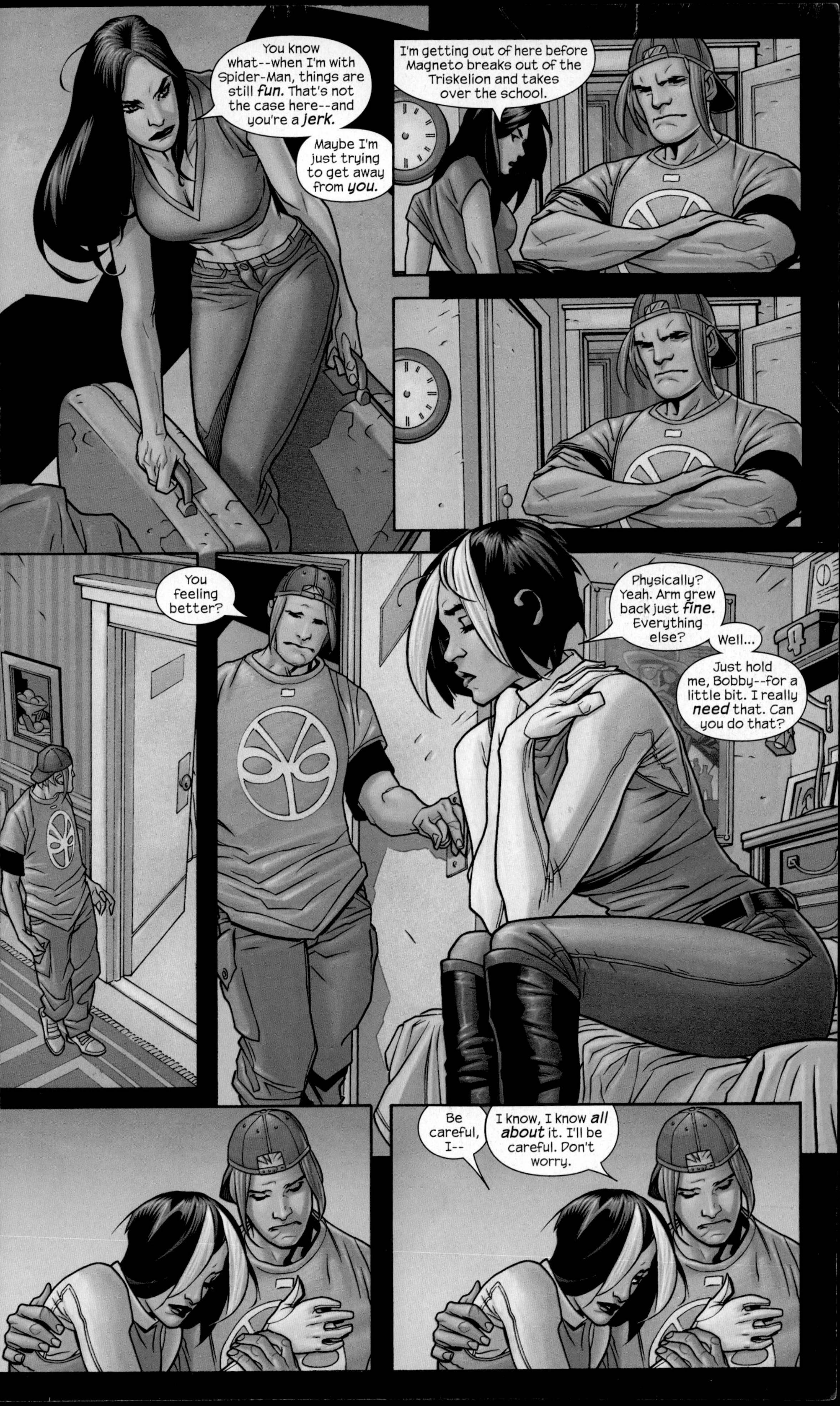

You know what--when I'm with Spider-Man, things are still *fun.* That's not the case here--and you're a ***jerk.***
Maybe I'm just trying to get away from ***you.***
I'm getting out of here before Magneto breaks out of the Triskelion and takes over the school.
You feeling better?
Physically? Yeah. Arm grew back just ***fine.*** Everything else?
Well...
Just hold me, Bobby--for a little bit. I really ***need*** that. Can you do that?
Be careful, I--
I know, I know ***all about*** it. I'll be careful. Don't worry.

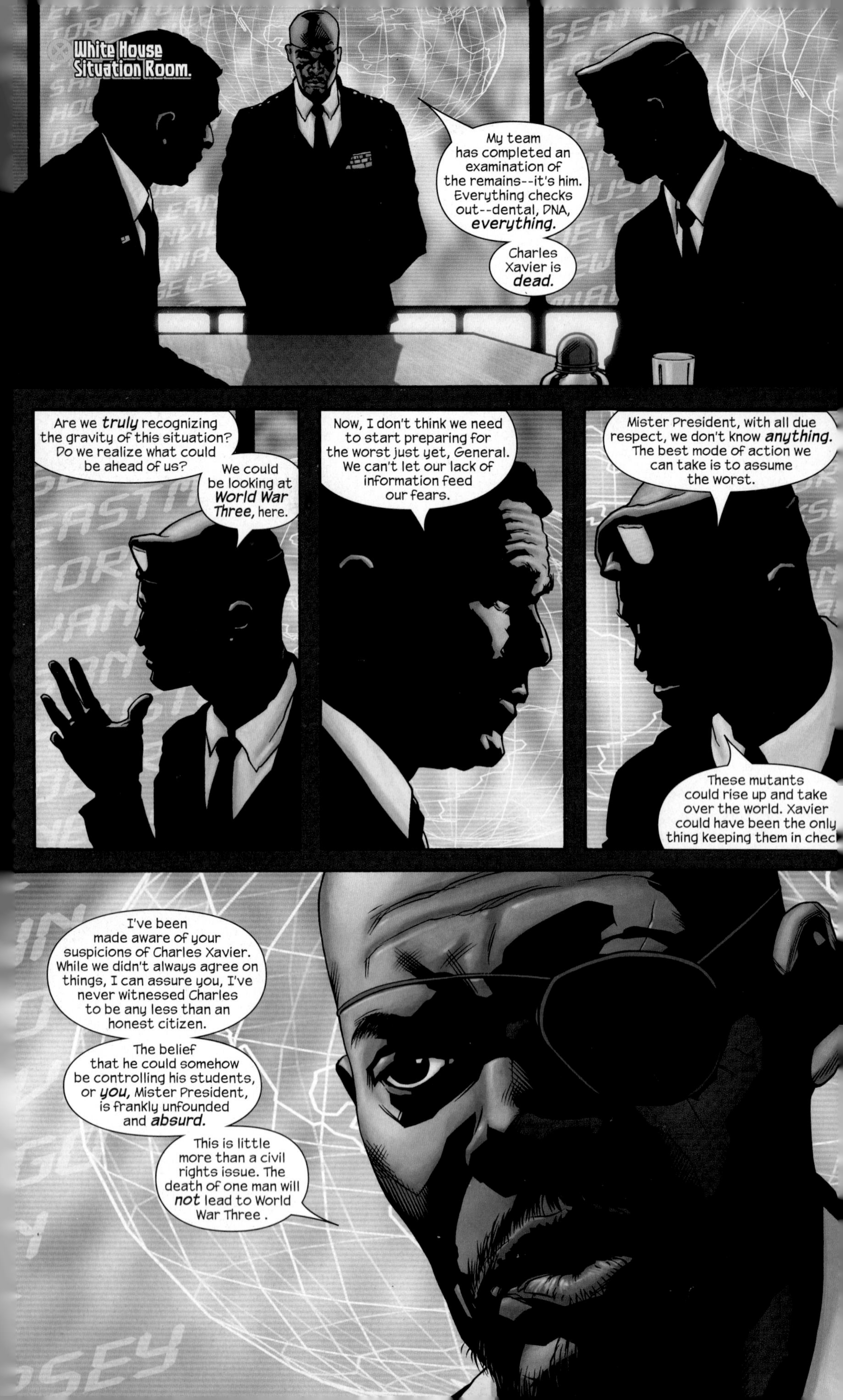
White House Situation Room.
My team has completed an examination of the remains--it's him. Everything checks out--dental, DNA, *everything.*
Charles Xavier is *dead.*
Are we *truly* recognizing the gravity of this situation? Do we realize what could be ahead of us?
We could be looking at *World War Three,* here.
Now, I don't think we need to start preparing for the worst just yet, General. We can't let our lack of information feed our fears.
Mister President, with all due respect, we don't know *anything.* The best mode of action we can take is to assume the worst.
These mutants could rise up and take over the world. Xavier could have been the only thing keeping them in chec
I've been made aware of your suspicions of Charles Xavier. While we didn't always agree on things, I can assure you, I've never witnessed Charles to be any less than an honest citizen.
The belief that he could somehow be controlling his students, or *you,* Mister President, is frankly unfounded and *absurd.*
This is little more than a civil rights issue. The death of one man will *not* lead to World War Three .

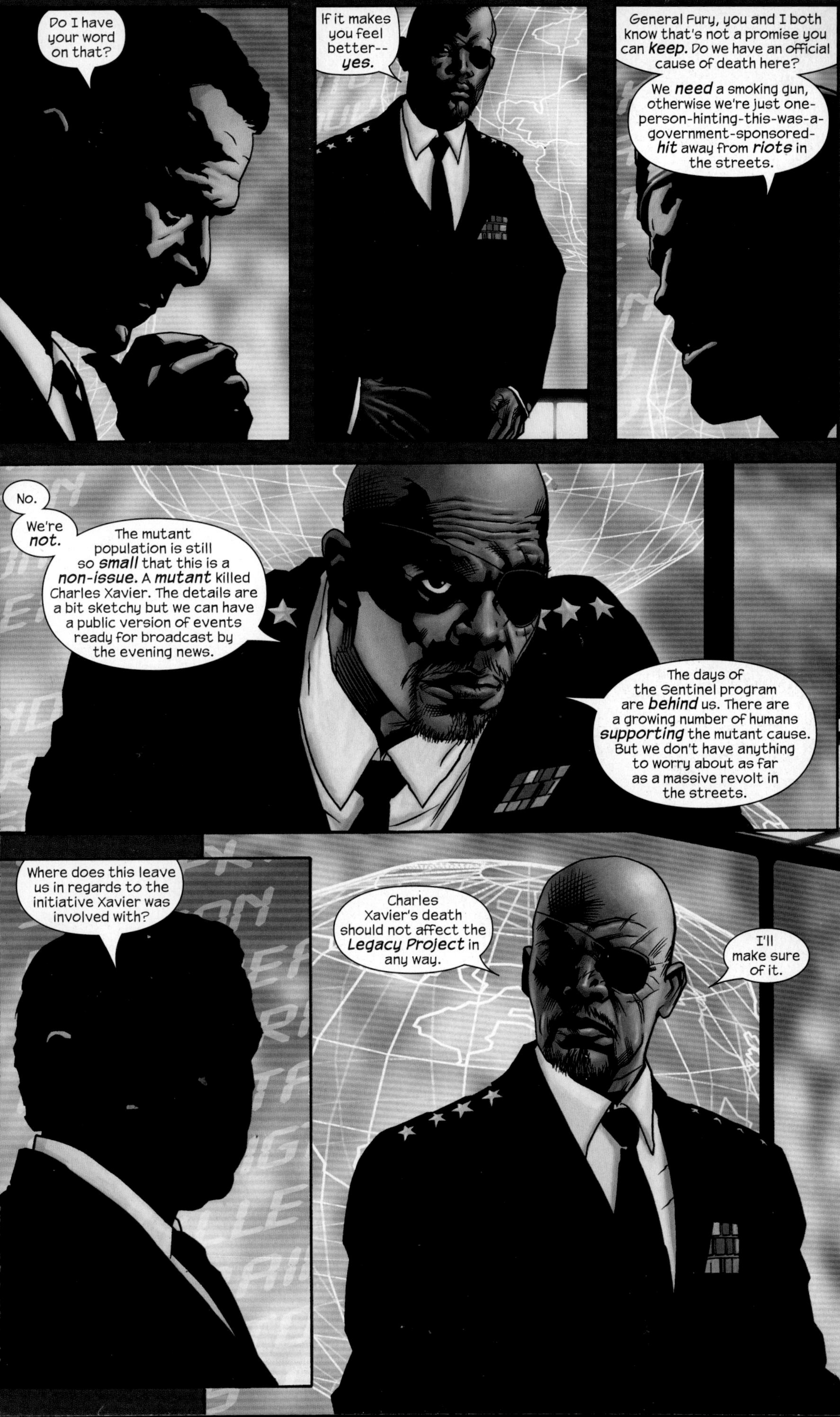
Do I have your word on that?
If it makes you feel better-- yes.
General Fury, you and I both know that's not a promise you can keep. Do we have an official cause of death here?
We need a smoking gun, otherwise we're just one-person-hinting-this-was-a-government-sponsored-hit away from riots in the streets.
No.
We're not.
The mutant population is still so small that this is a non-issue. A mutant killed Charles Xavier. The details are a bit sketchy but we can have a public version of events ready for broadcast by the evening news.
The days of the Sentinel program are behind us. There are a growing number of humans supporting the mutant cause. But we don't have anything to worry about as far as a massive revolt in the streets.
Where does this leave us in regards to the initiative Xavier was involved with?
Charles Xavier's death should not affect the Legacy Project in any way.
I'll make sure of it.

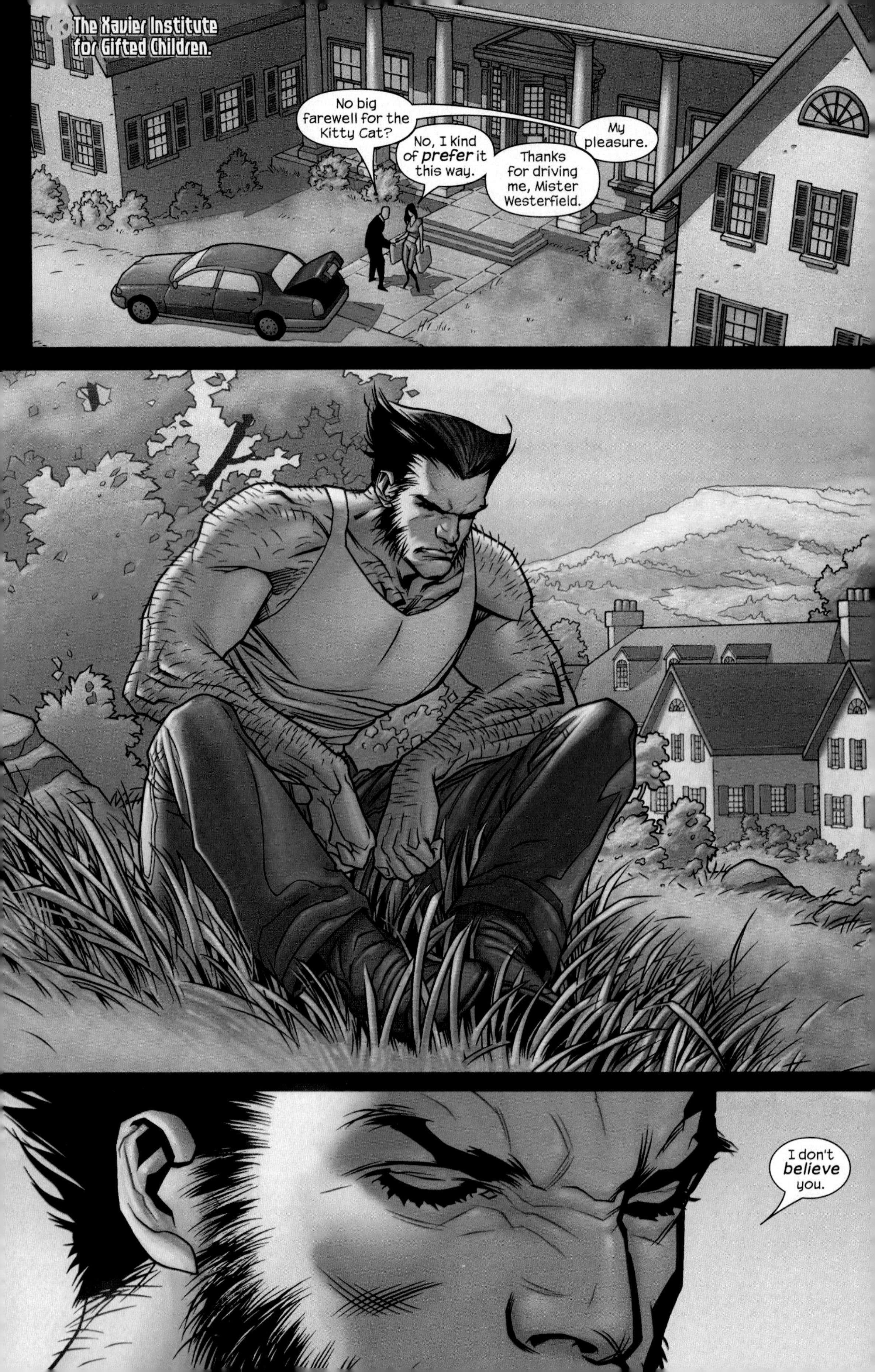
The Xavier Institute for Gifted Children.
No big farewell for the Kitty Cat?
No, I kind of *prefer* it this way.
Thanks for driving me, Mister Westerfield.
My pleasure.
I don't *believe* you.

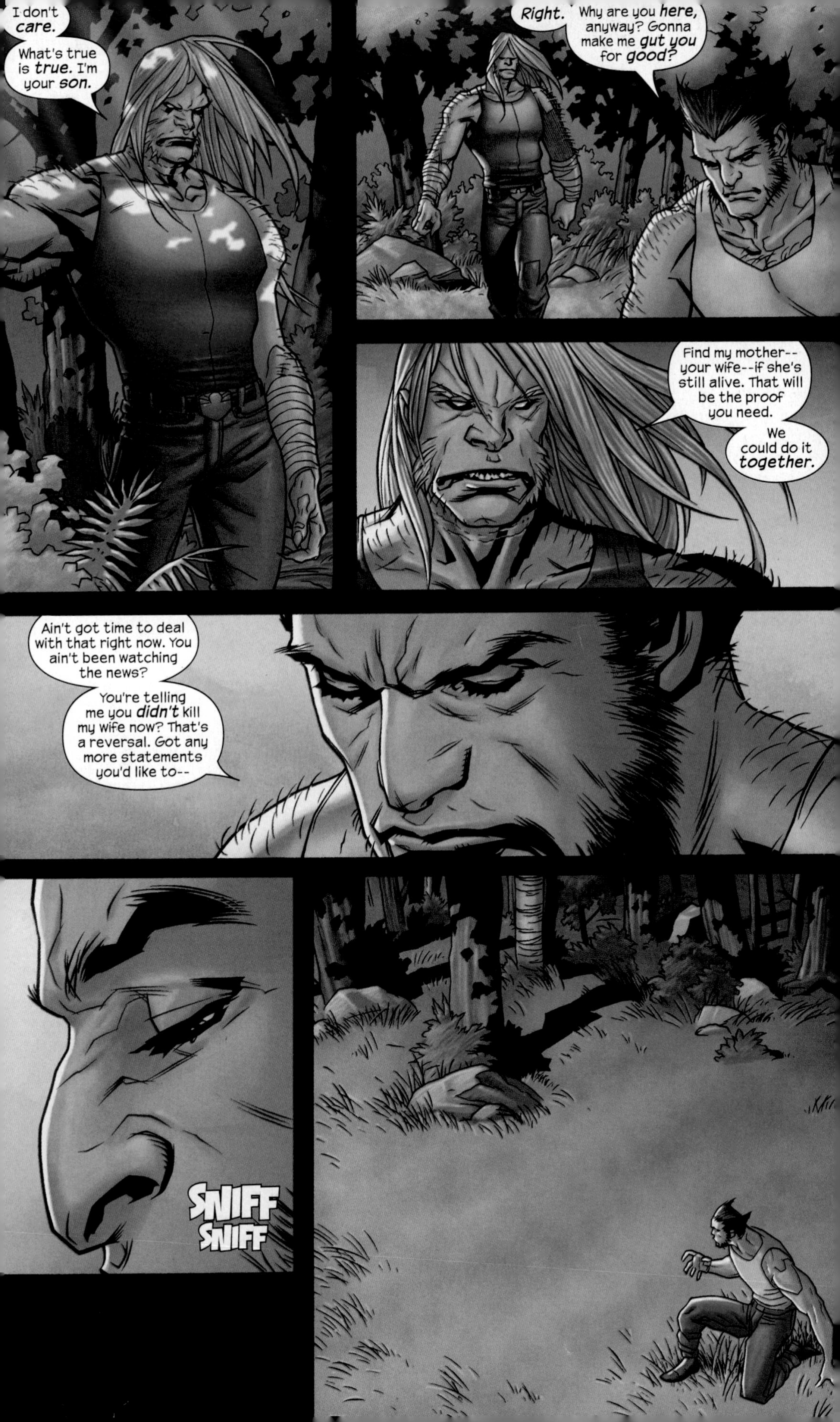

I don't care.
What's true is true. I'm your son.
Right.
Why are you here, anyway? Gonna make me gut you for good?
Find my mother--your wife--if she's still alive. That will be the proof you need.
We could do it together.
Ain't got time to deal with that right now. You ain't been watching the news?
You're telling me you didn't kill my wife now? That's a reversal. Got any more statements you'd like to--
SNIFF SNIFF

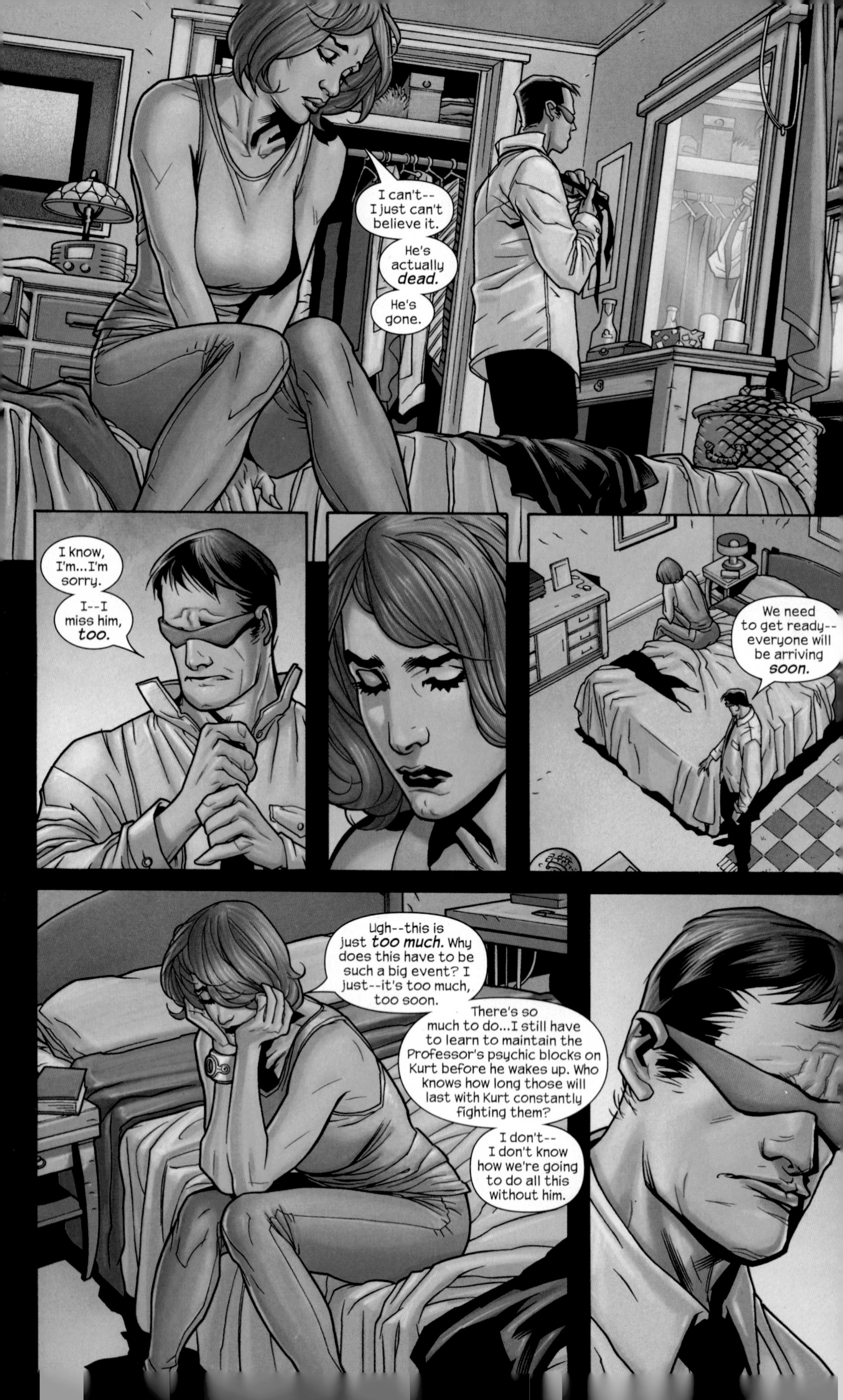

I can't--
I just can't believe it.
He's actually *dead.*
He's gone.
I know, I'm...I'm sorry.
I--I miss him, *too.*
We need to get ready-- everyone will be arriving *soon.*
Ugh--this is just *too much.* Why does this have to be such a big event? I just--it's too much, too soon.
There's so much to do...I still have to learn to maintain the Professor's psychic blocks on Kurt before he wakes up. Who knows how long those will last with Kurt constantly fighting them?
I don't-- I don't know how we're going to do all this without him.

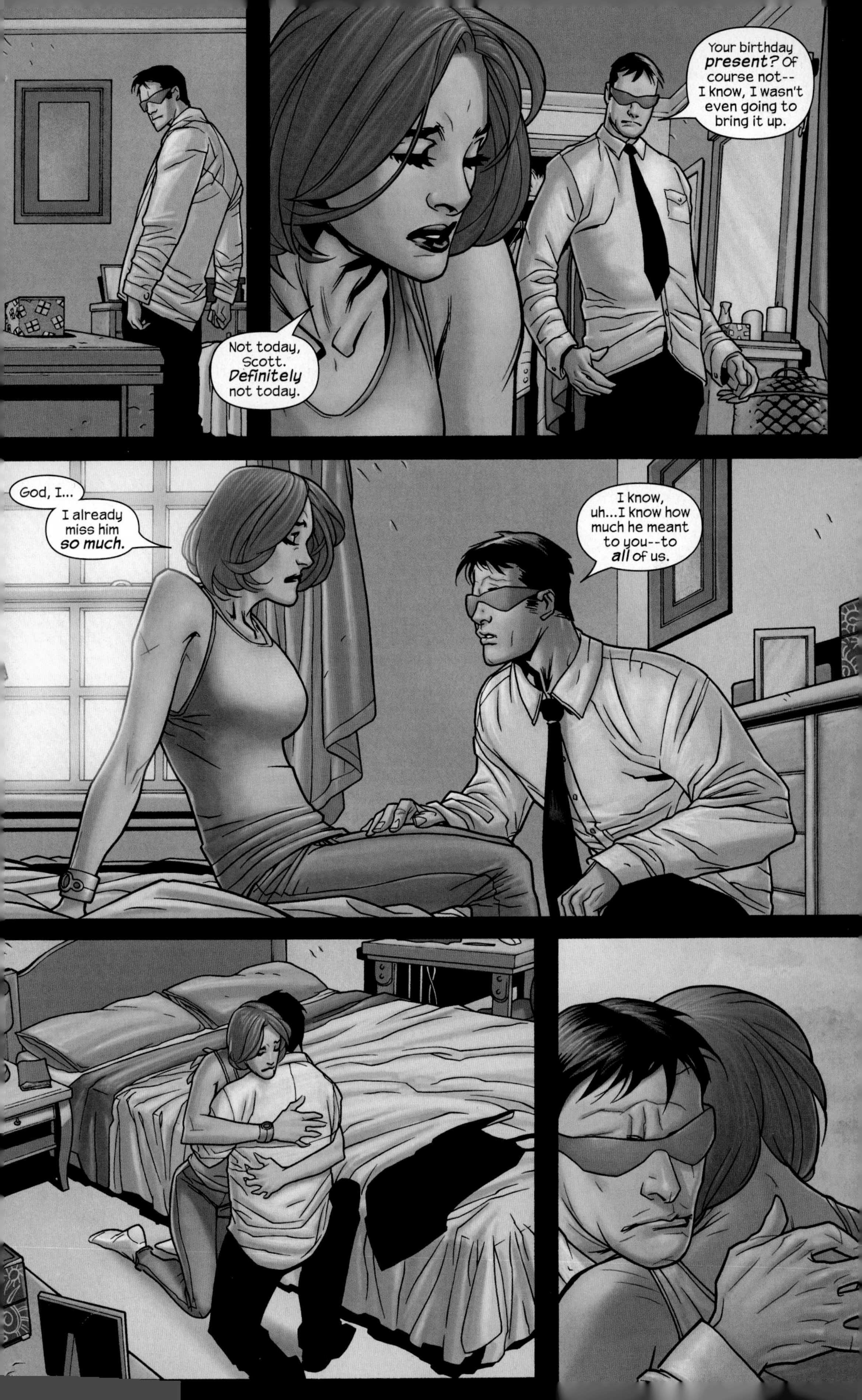
Your birthday present? Of course not-- I know, I wasn't even going to bring it up.
Not today, Scott. Definitely not today.
God, I...
I already miss him so much.
I know, uh...I know how much he meant to you--to all of us.

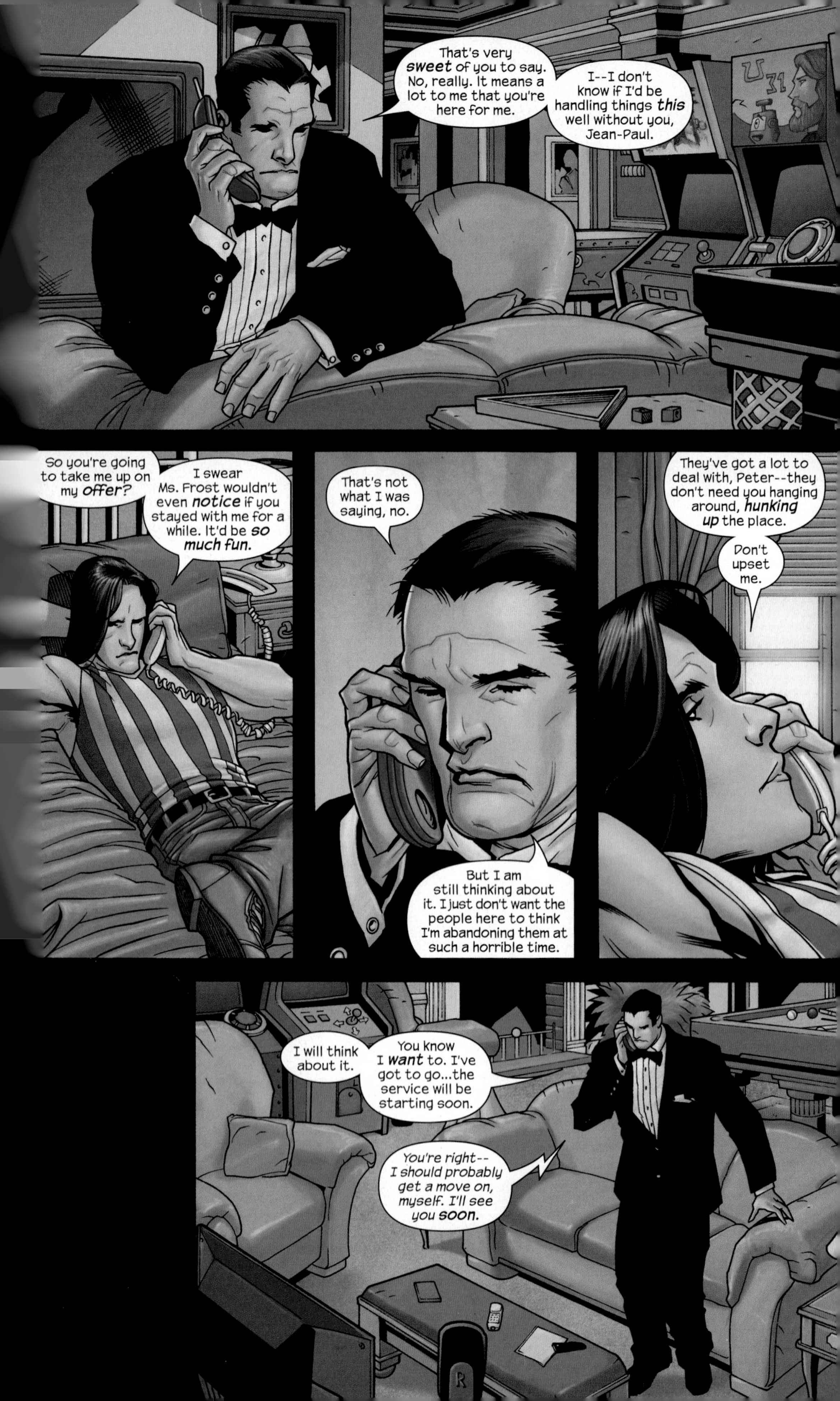
That's very sweet of you to say. No, really. It means a lot to me that you're here for me.
I--I don't know if I'd be handling things this well without you, Jean-Paul.
So you're going to take me up on my offer?
I swear Ms. Frost wouldn't even notice if you stayed with me for a while. It'd be so much fun.
That's not what I was saying, no.
But I am still thinking about it. I just don't want the people here to think I'm abandoning them at such a horrible time.
They've got a lot to deal with, Peter--they don't need you hanging around, hunking up the place.
Don't upset me.
I will think about it.
You know I want to. I've got to go...the service will be starting soon.
You're right-- I should probably get a move on, myself. I'll see you soon.

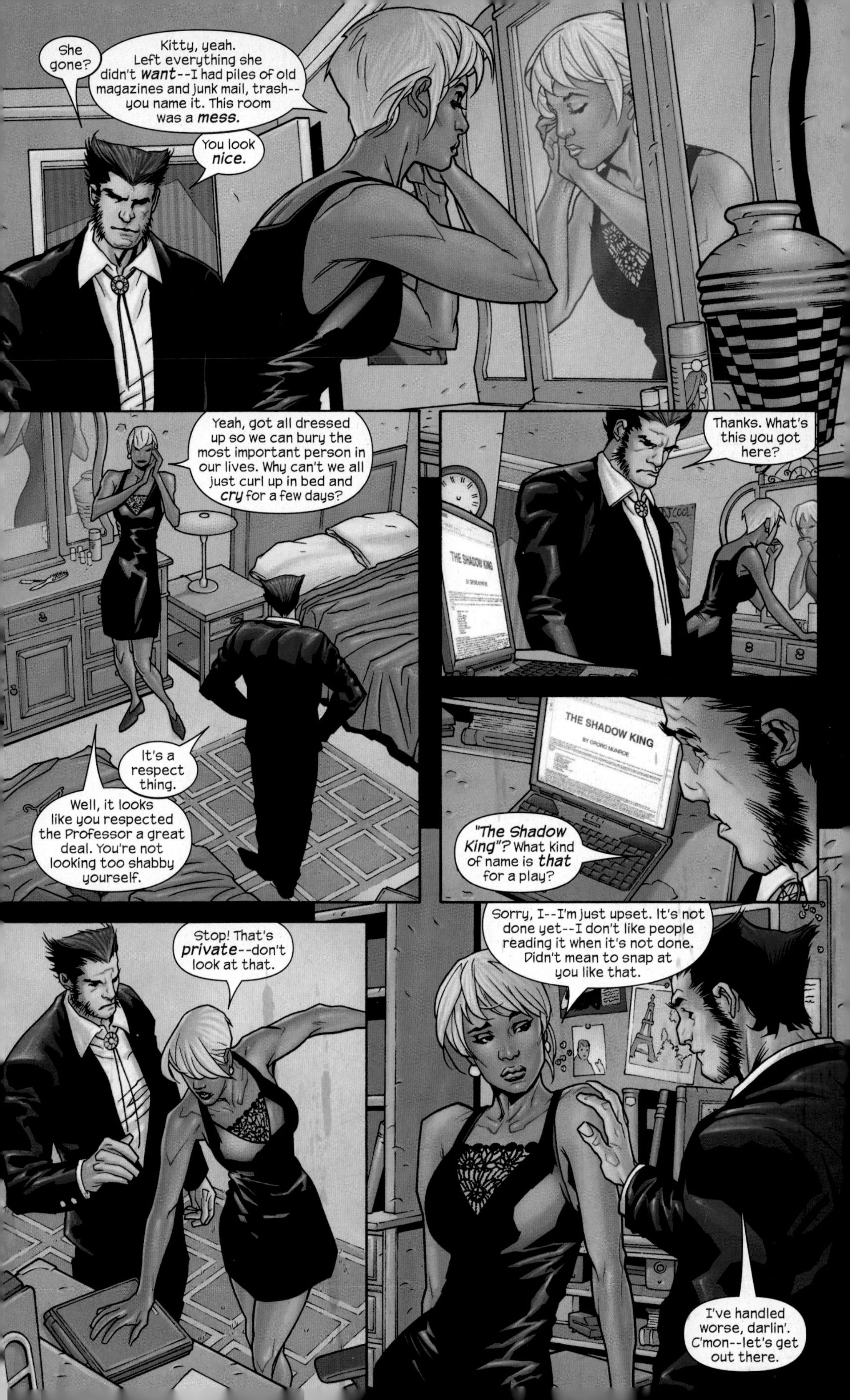
She gone?
Kitty, yeah. Left everything she didn't want--I had piles of old magazines and junk mail, trash--you name it. This room was a mess.
You look nice.
Yeah, got all dressed up so we can bury the most important person in our lives. Why can't we all just curl up in bed and cry for a few days?
It's a respect thing.
Well, it looks like you respected the Professor a great deal. You're not looking too shabby yourself.
Thanks. What's this you got here?
THE SHADOW KING
BY ORORO MUNROE
"The Shadow King"? What kind of name is that for a play?
Stop! That's private--don't look at that.
Sorry, I--I'm just upset. It's not done yet--I don't like people reading it when it's not done. Didn't mean to snap at you like that.
I've handled worse, darlin'. C'mon--let's get out there.

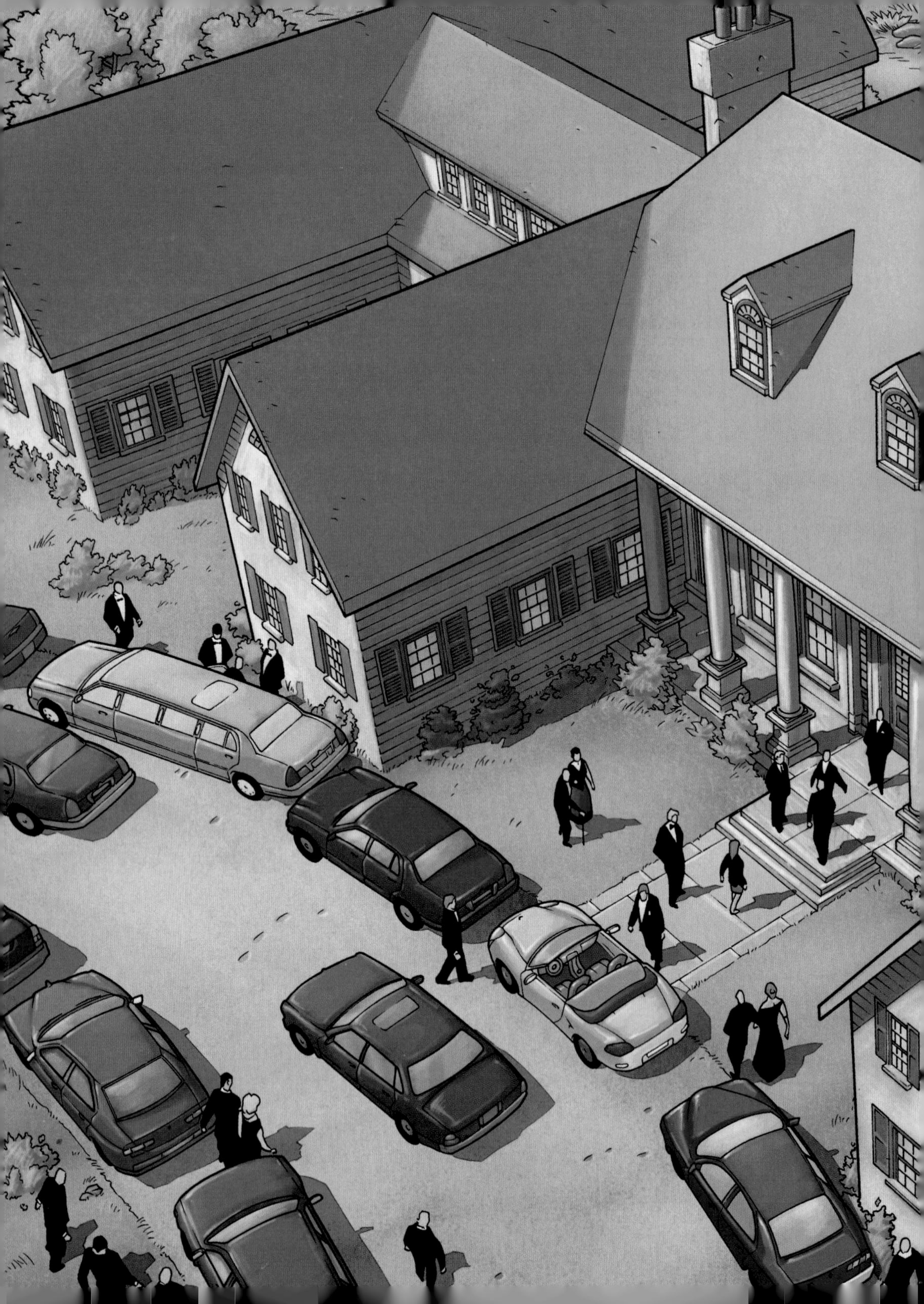

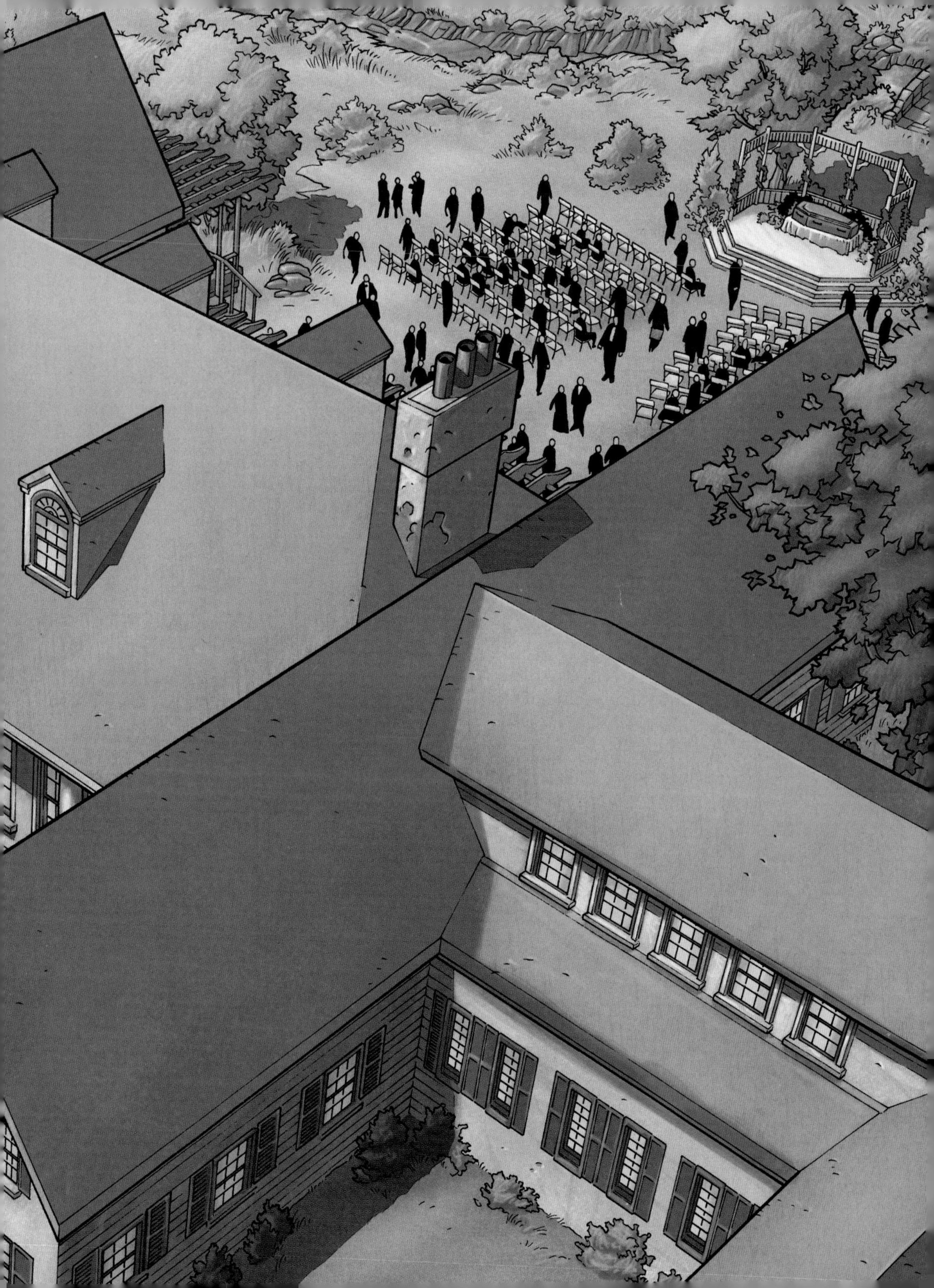

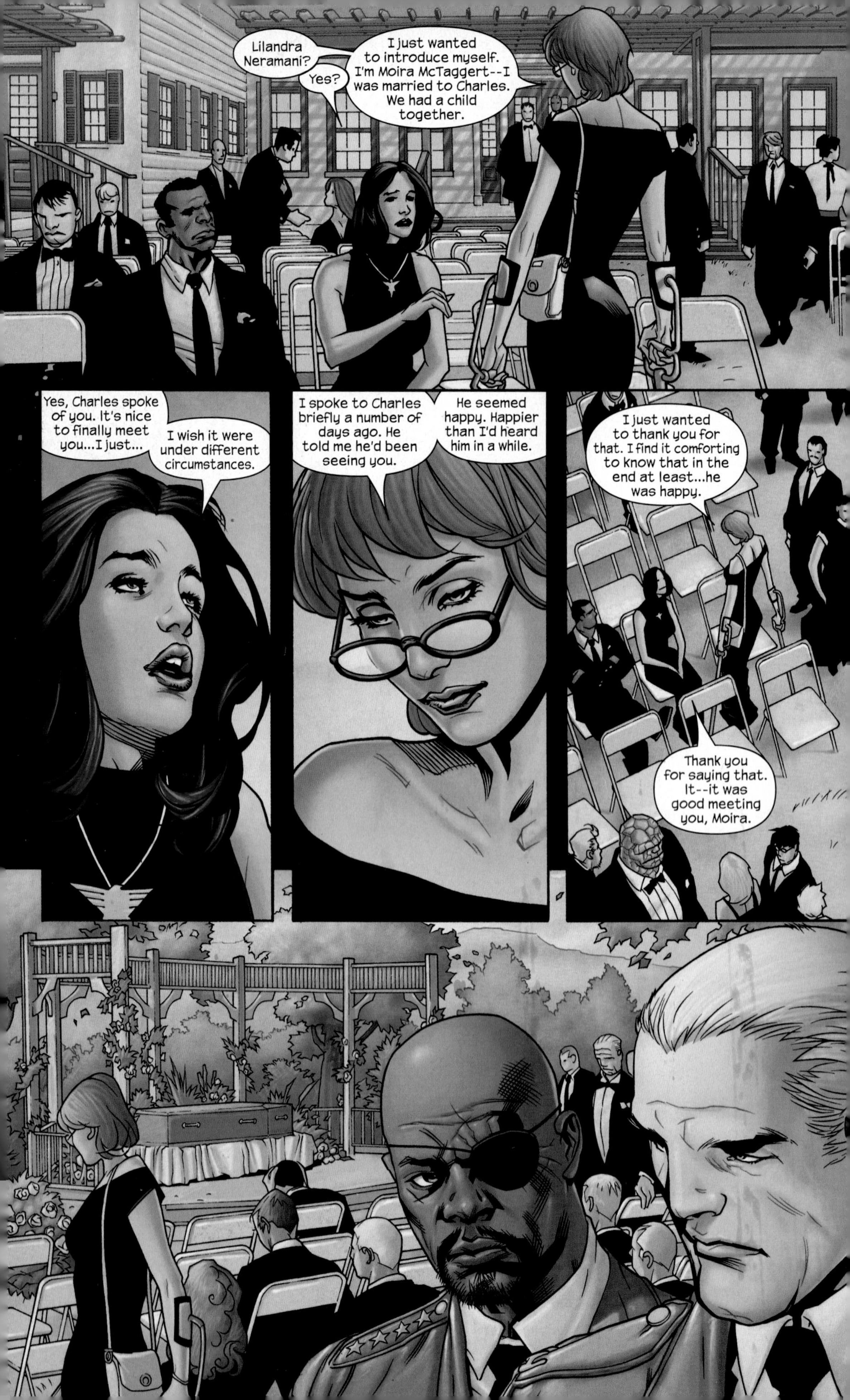

Lilandra Neramani?
Yes?
I just wanted to introduce myself. I'm Moira McTaggert--I was married to Charles. We had a child together.
Yes, Charles spoke of you. It's nice to finally meet you...I just...
I wish it were under different circumstances.
I spoke to Charles briefly a number of days ago. He told me he'd been seeing you.
He seemed happy. Happier than I'd heard him in a while.
I just wanted to thank you for that. I find it comforting to know that in the end at least...he was happy.
Thank you for saying that. It--it was good meeting you, Moira.

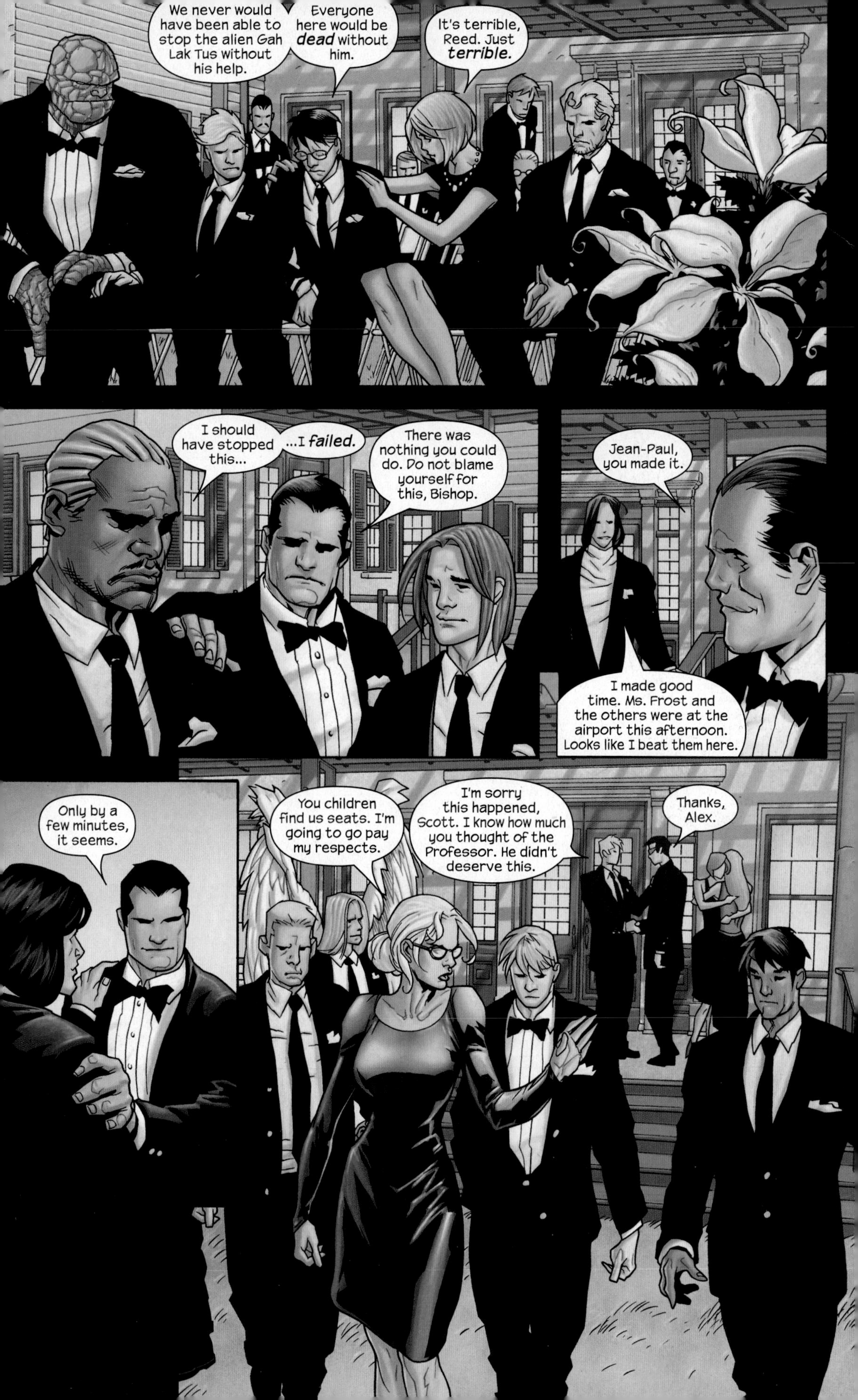
We never would have been able to stop the alien Gah Lak Tus without his help.
Everyone here would be *dead* without him.
It's terrible, Reed. Just *terrible.*
I should have stopped this...
...I *failed.*
There was nothing you could do. Do not blame yourself for this, Bishop.
Jean-Paul, you made it.
I made good time. Ms. Frost and the others were at the airport this afternoon. Looks like I beat them here.
Only by a few minutes, it seems.
You children find us seats. I'm going to go pay my respects.
I'm sorry this happened, Scott. I know how much you thought of the Professor. He didn't deserve this.
Thanks, Alex.

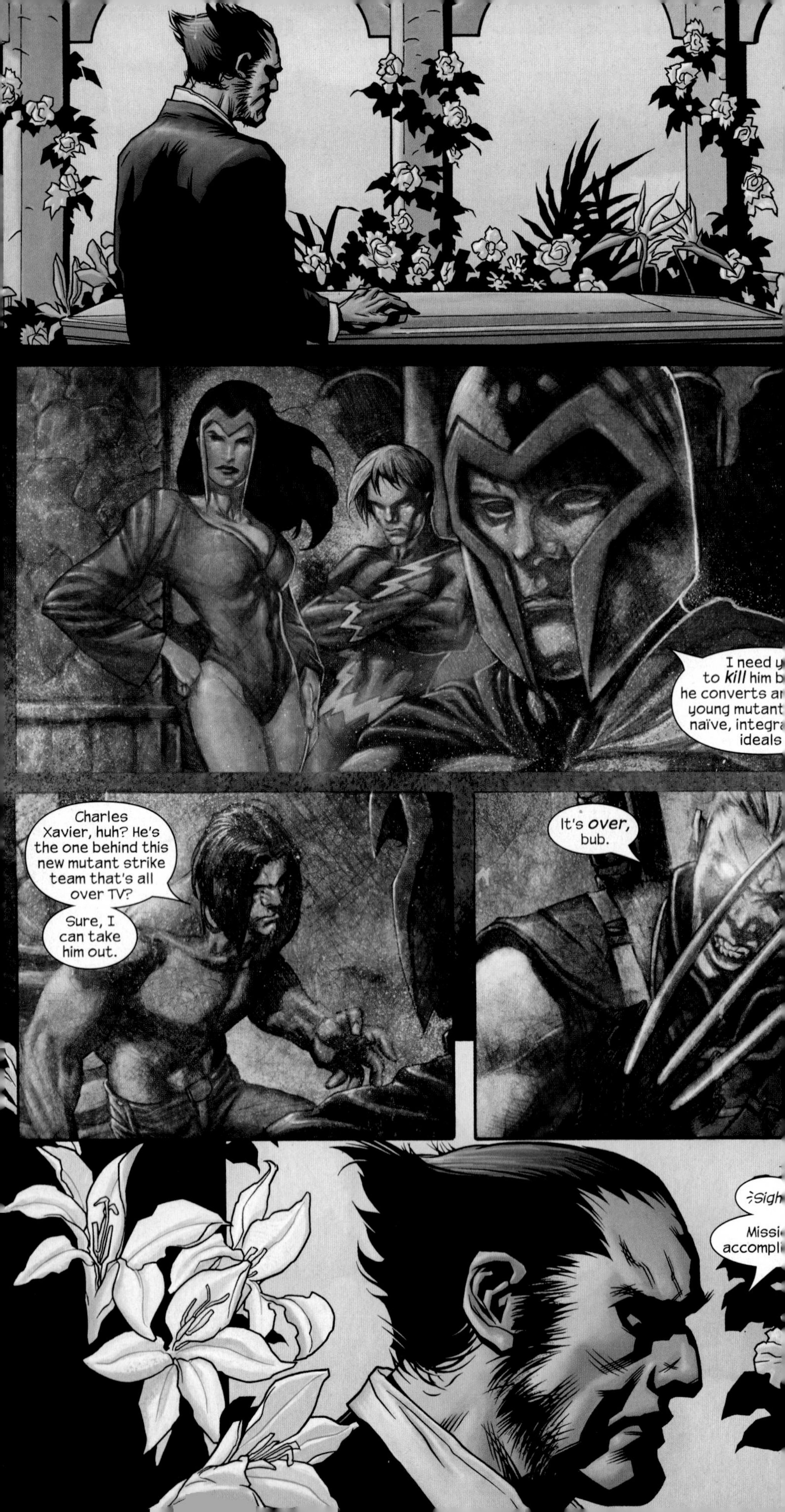
I need y
to kill him b
he converts a
young mutant
naïve, integra
ideals
Charles Xavier, huh? He's the one behind this new mutant strike team that's all over TV?
Sure, I can take him out.
It's over, bub.
Sigh
Missi
accompli

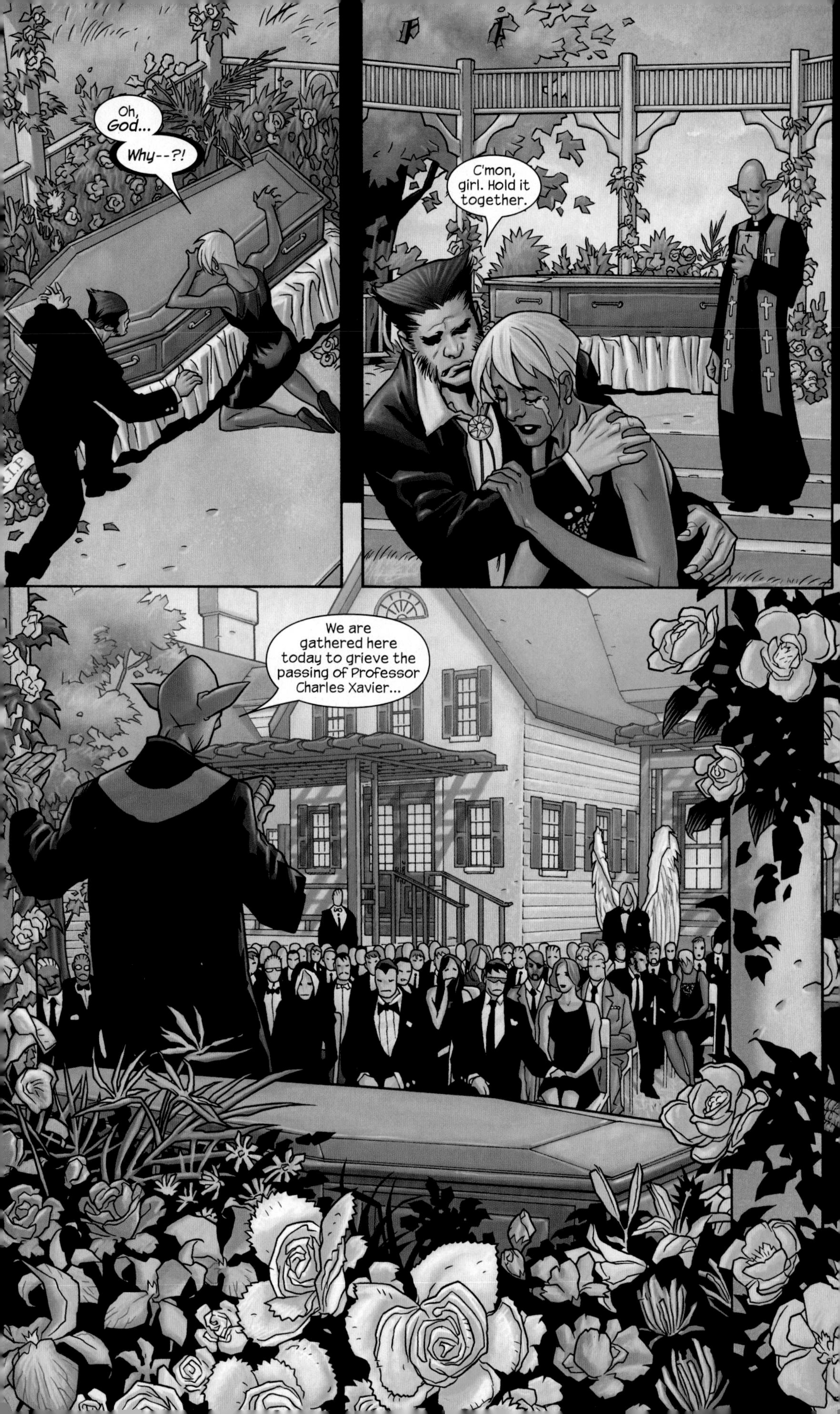

Oh, God...
Why--?!
C'mon, girl. Hold it together.
We are gathered here today to grieve the passing of Professor Charles Xavier...

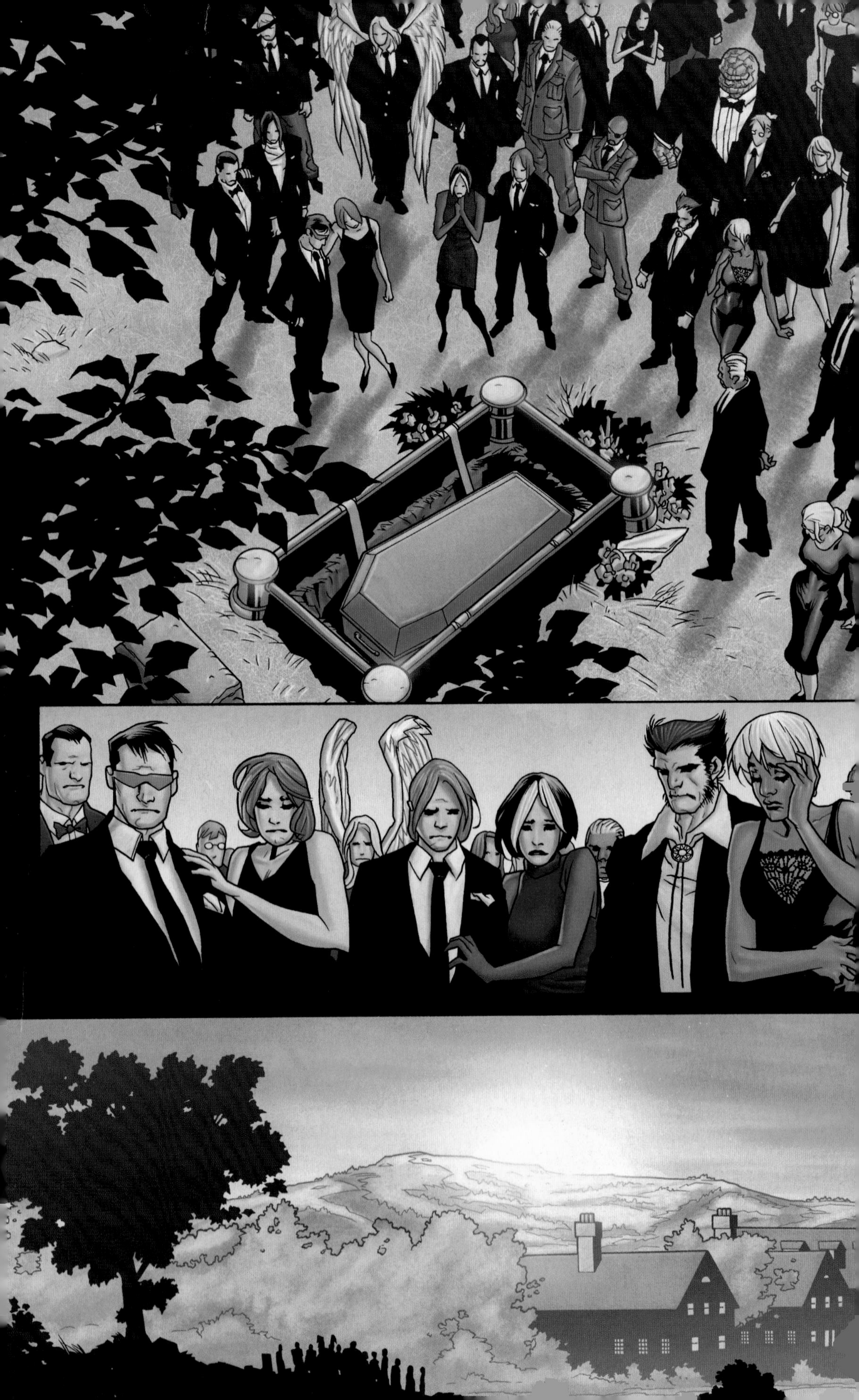

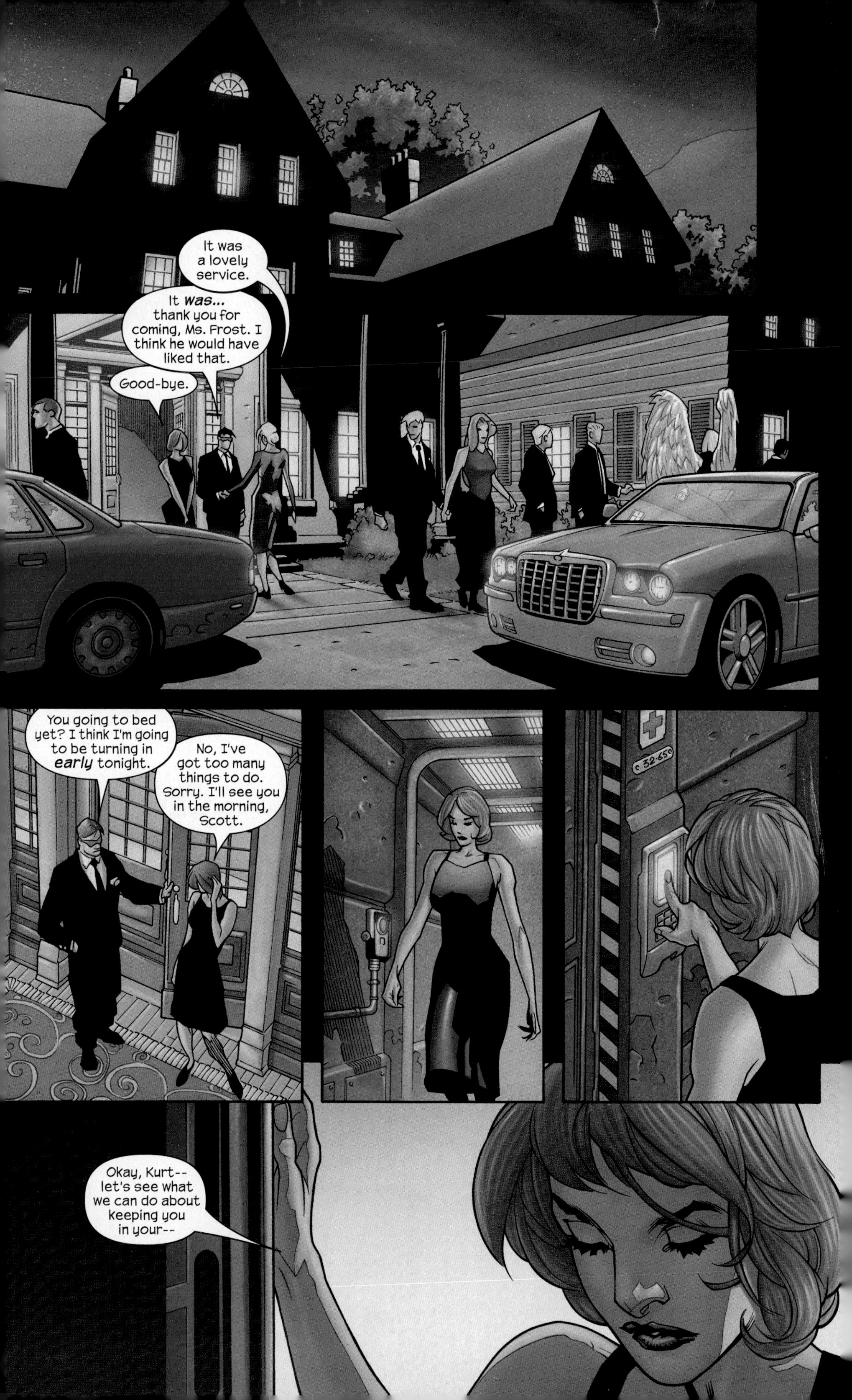
It was a lovely service.
It *was*... thank you for coming, Ms. Frost. I think he would have liked that.
Good-bye.
You going to bed yet? I think I'm going to be turning in *early* tonight.
No, I've got too many things to do. Sorry. I'll see you in the morning, Scott.
32-65
Okay, Kurt-- let's see what we can do about keeping you in your--

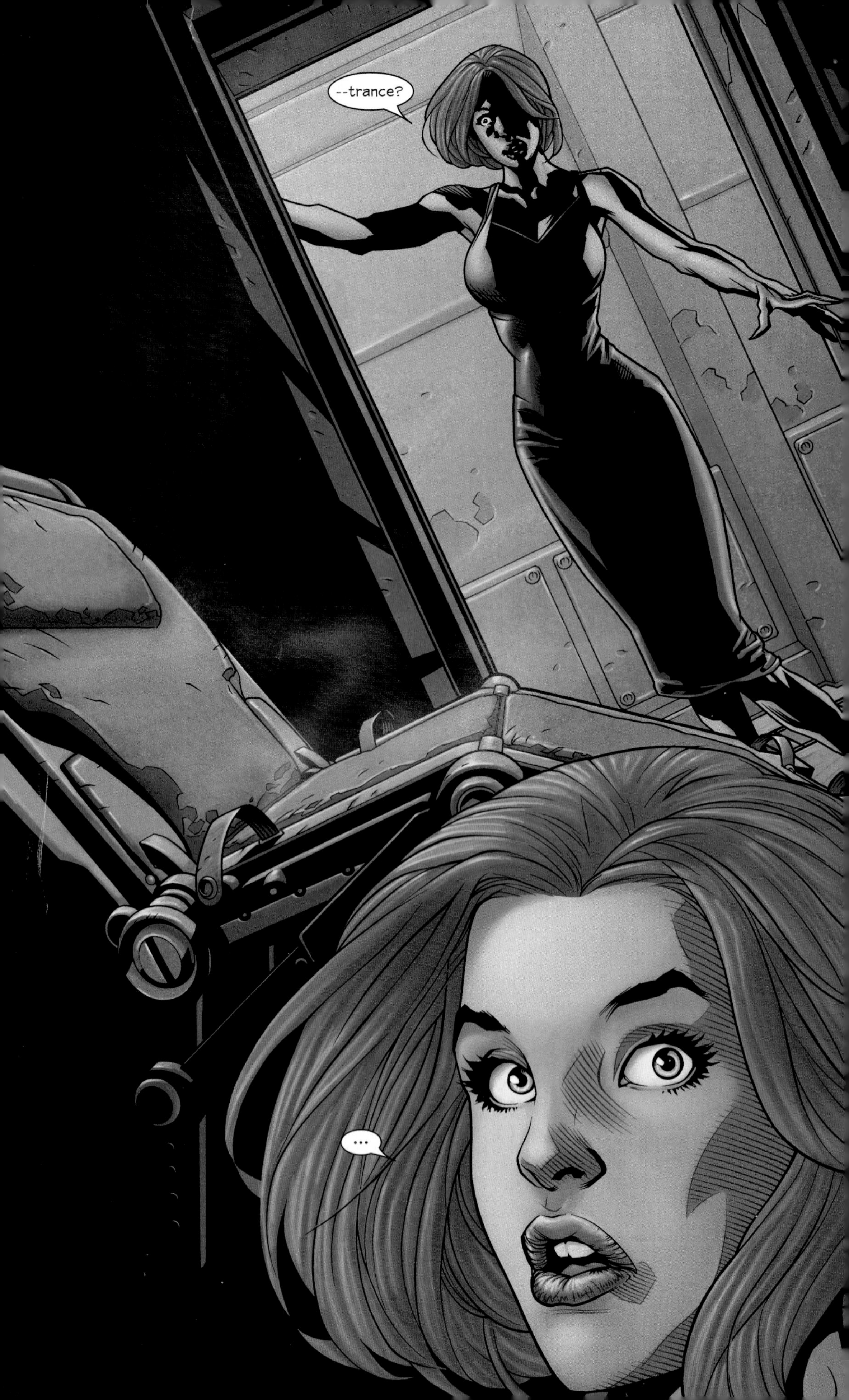
--trance?
...

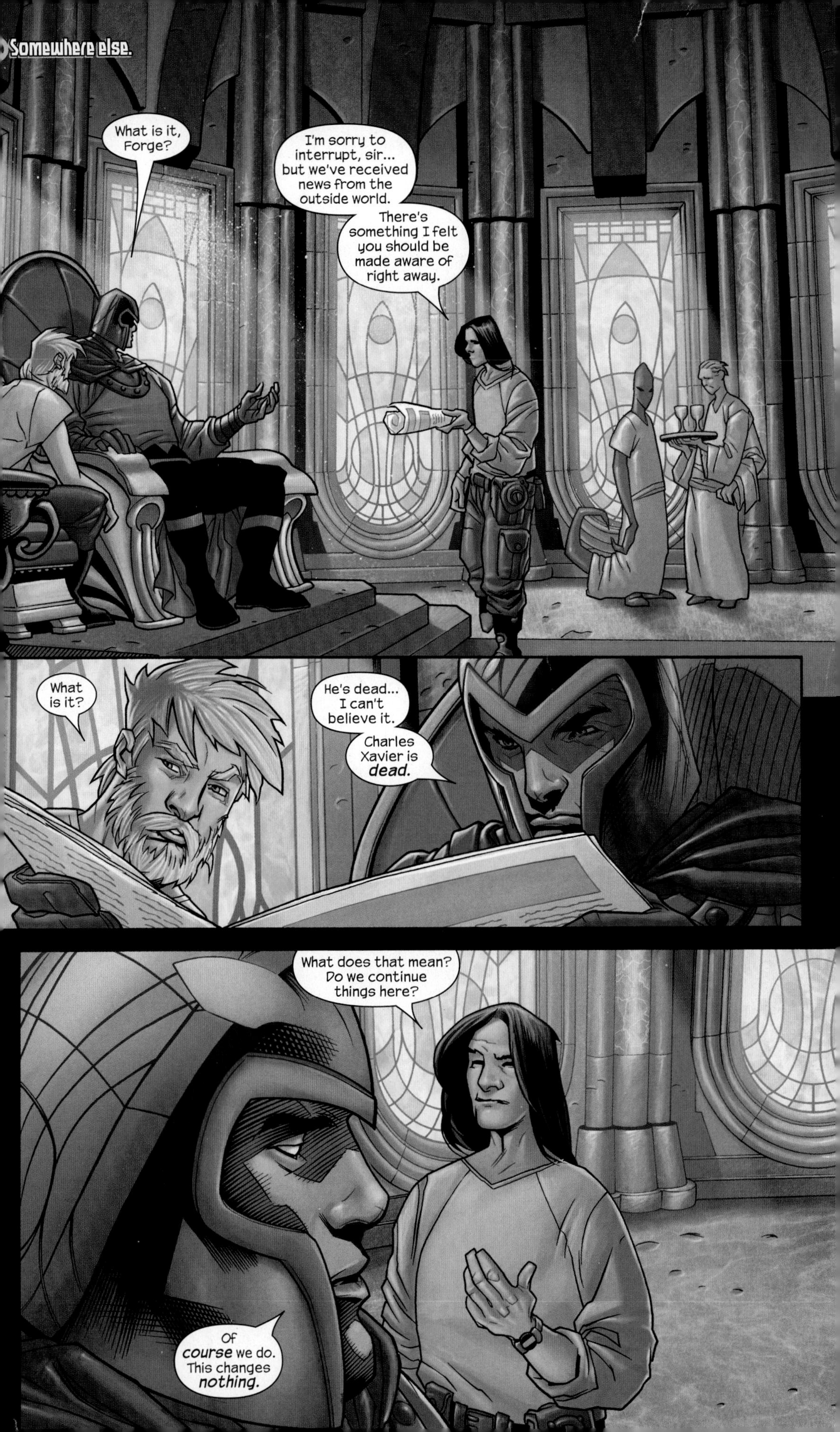
Somewhere else.
What is it, Forge?
I'm sorry to interrupt, sir... but we've received news from the outside world.
There's something I felt you should be made aware of right away.
What is it?
He's dead... I can't believe it.
Charles Xavier is *dead.*
What does that mean? Do we continue things here?
Of *course* we do. This changes *nothing.*

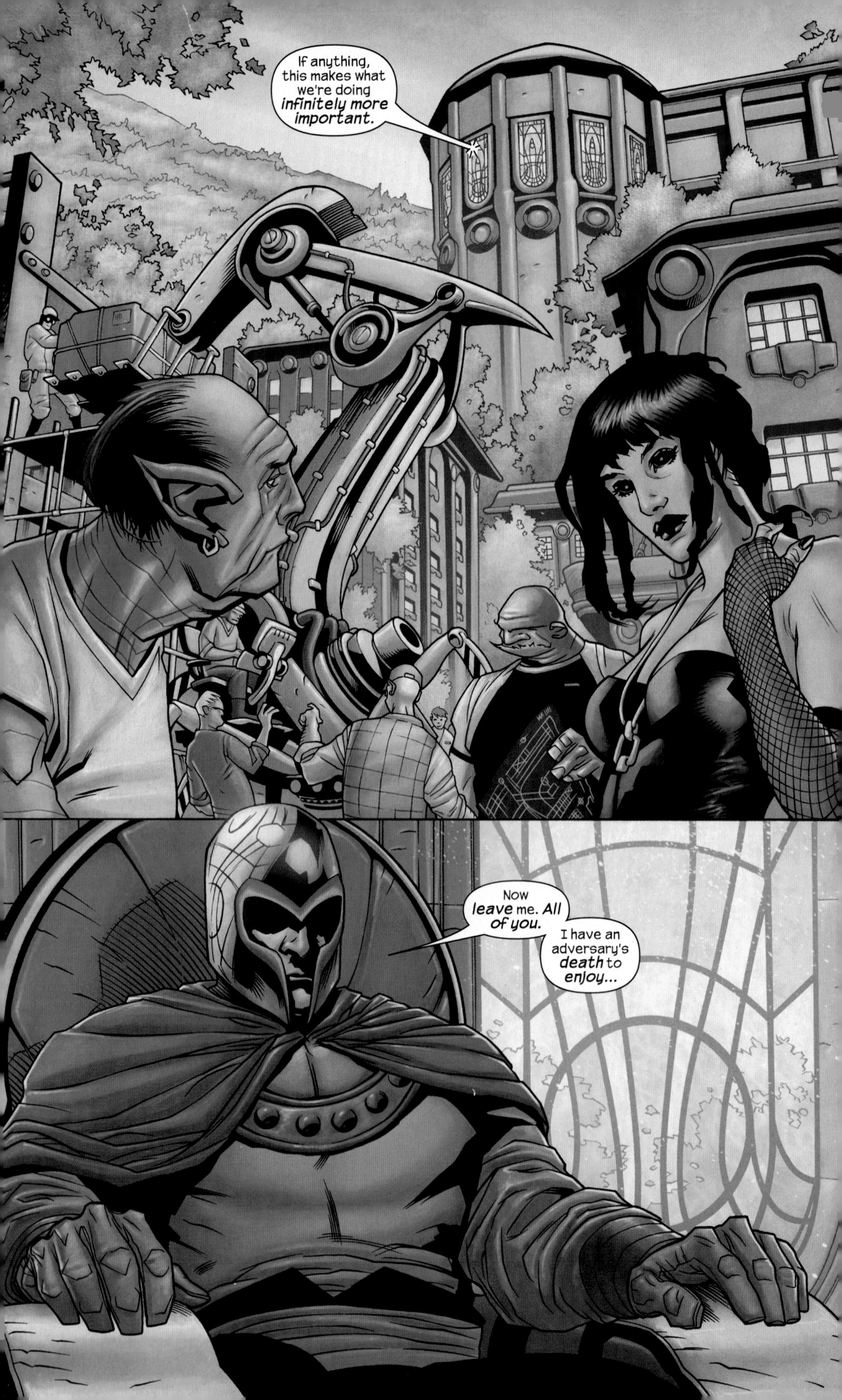

If anything, this makes what we're doing *infinitely more important.*
Now *leave* me. *All of you.*
I have an adversary's *death* to *enjoy*...

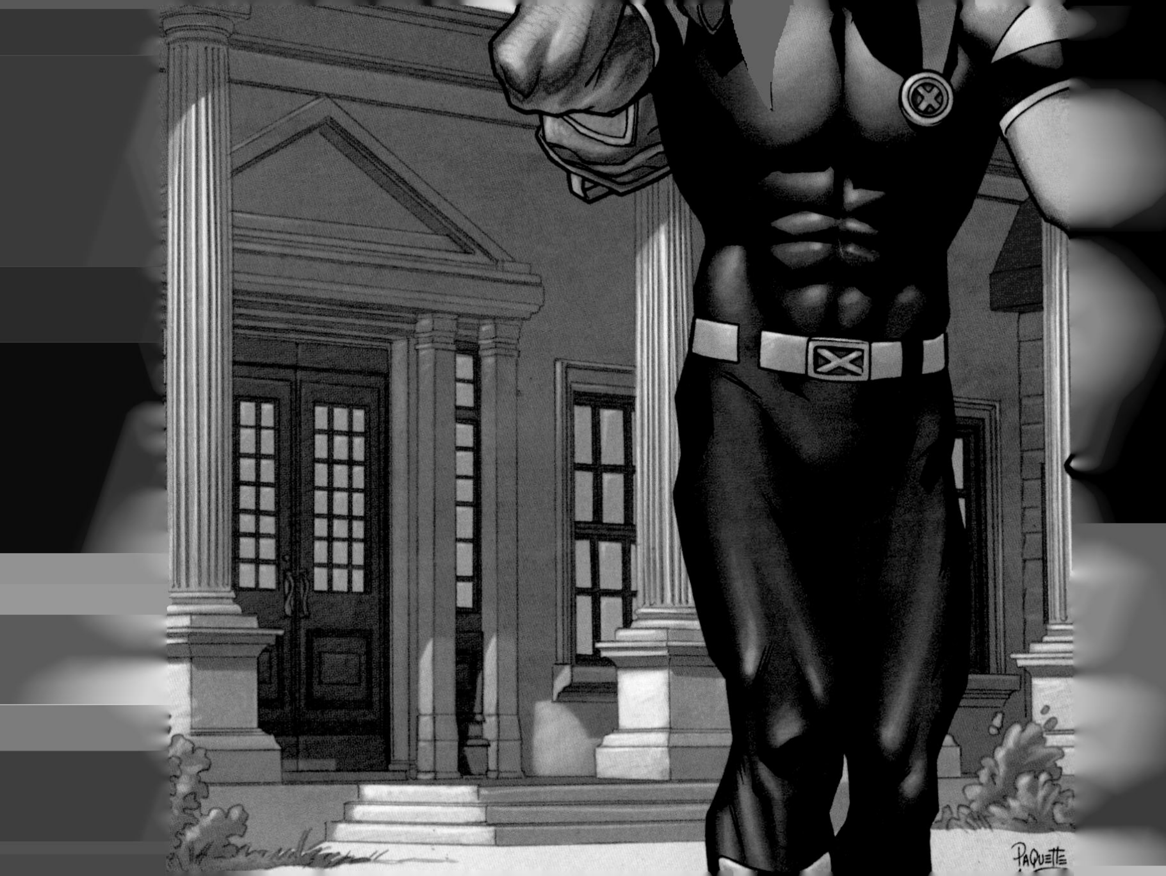
PAQUETTE

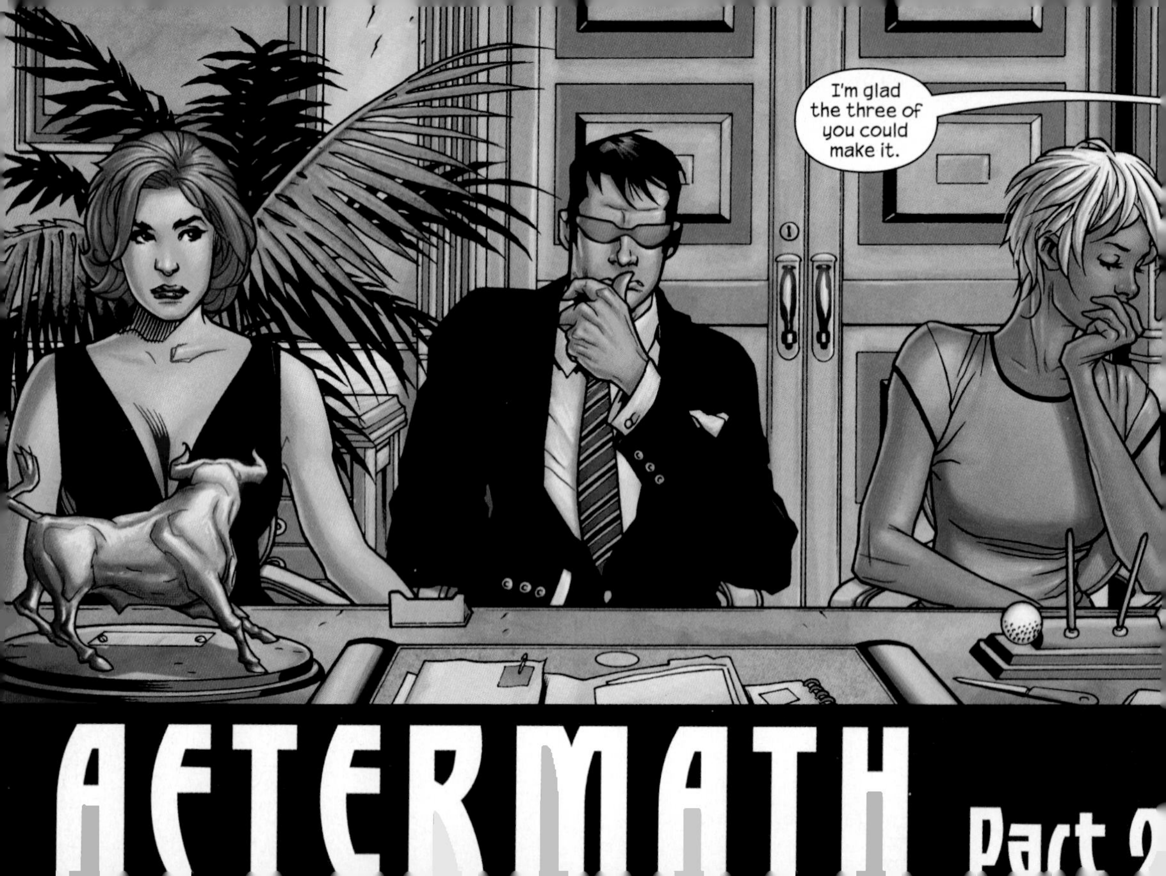

I'm glad the three of you could make it.
AFTERMATH Part 2

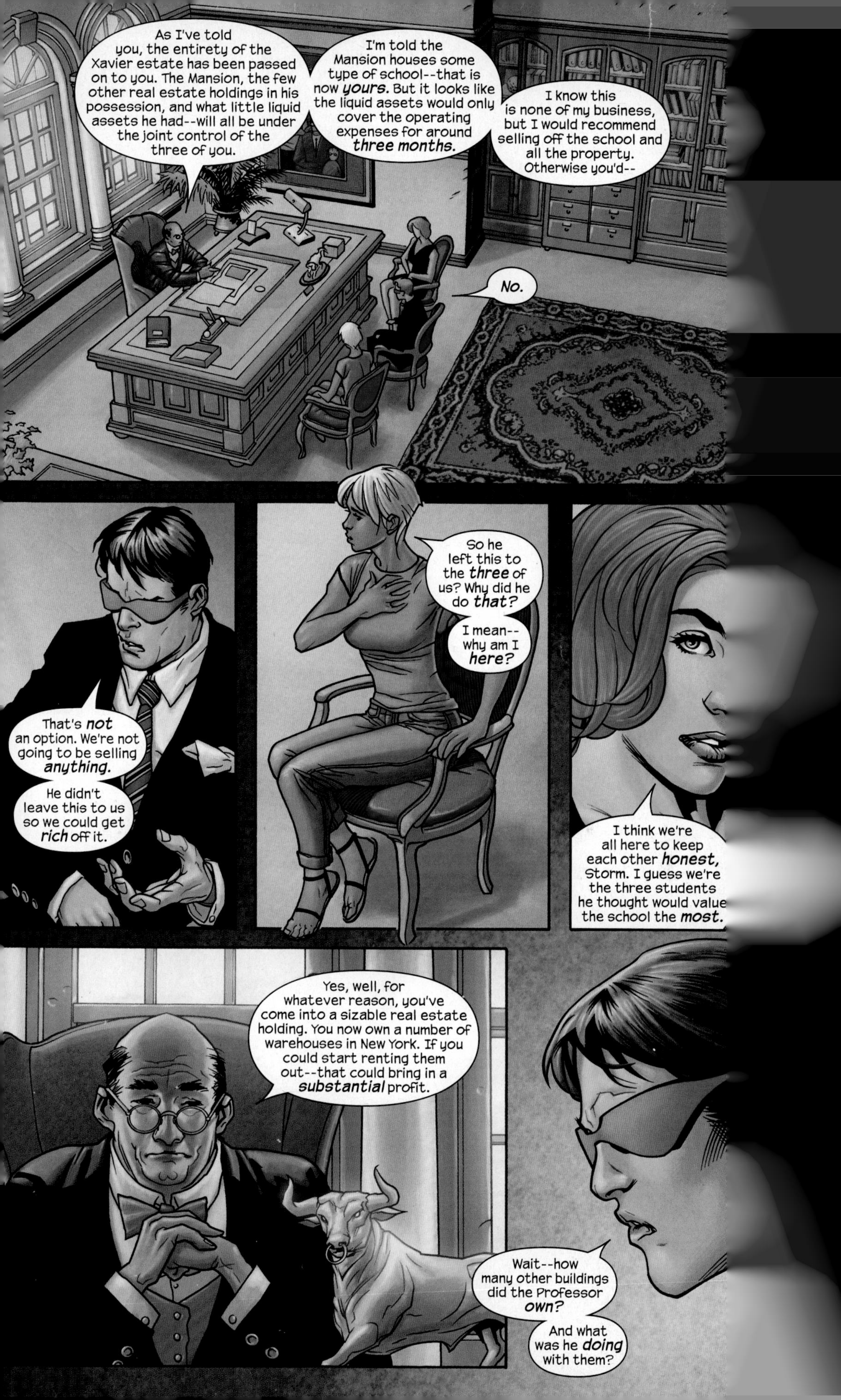
As I've told you, the entirety of the Xavier estate has been passed on to you. The Mansion, the few other real estate holdings in his possession, and what little liquid assets he had--will all be under the joint control of the three of you.
I'm told the Mansion houses some type of school--that is now *yours.* But it looks like the liquid assets would only cover the operating expenses for around *three months.*
I know this is none of my business, but I would recommend selling off the school and all the property. Otherwise you'd--
No.
That's *not* an option. We're not going to be selling *anything.*
He didn't leave this to us so we could get *rich* off it.
So he left this to the *three* of us? Why did he do *that?*
I mean-- why am I *here?*
I think we're all here to keep each other *honest,* Storm. I guess we're the three students he thought would value the school the *most.*
Yes, well, for whatever reason, you've come into a sizable real estate holding. You now own a number of warehouses in New York. If you could start renting them out--that could bring in a *substantial* profit.
Wait--how many other buildings did the Professor *own?*
And what was he *doing* with them?

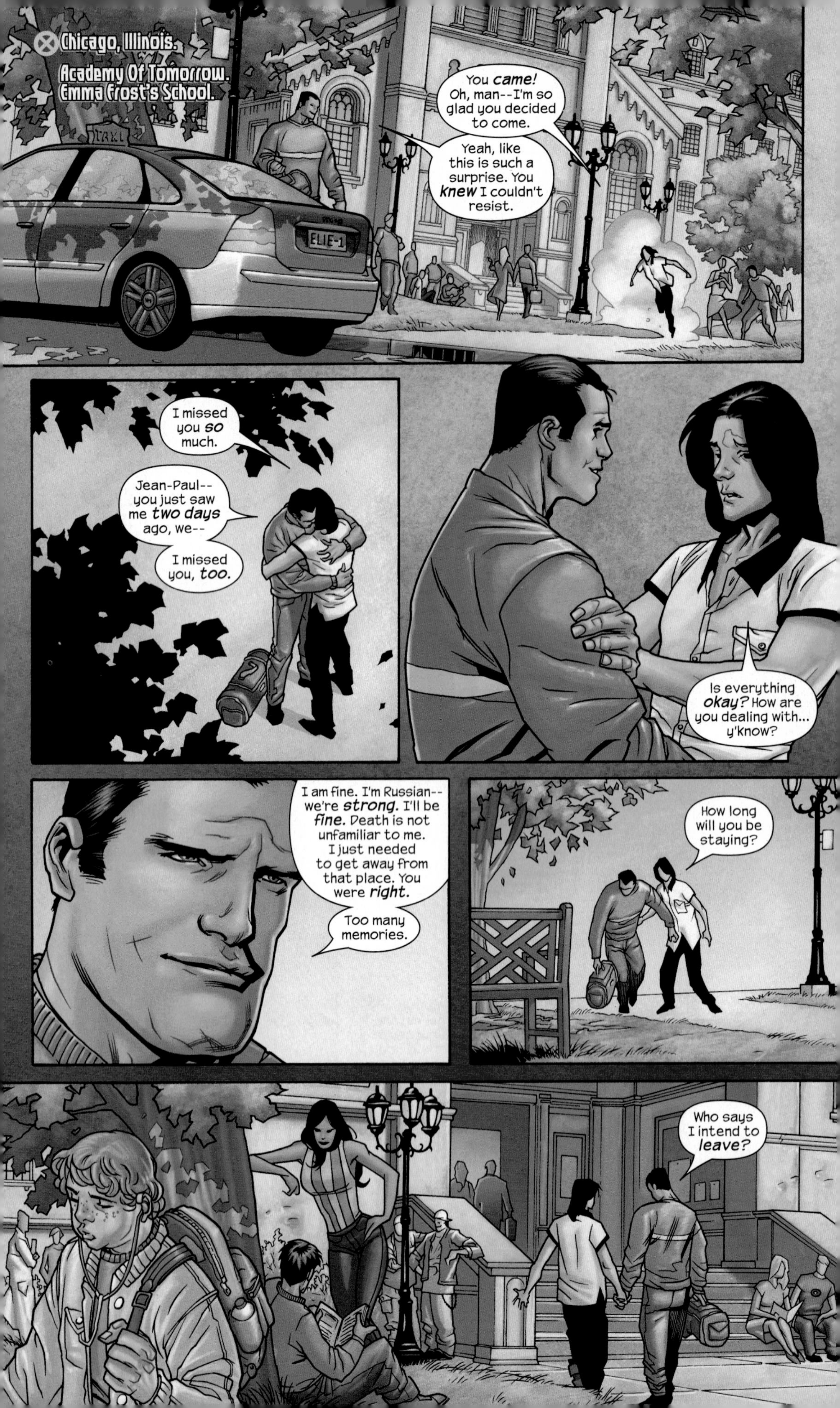
Chicago, Illinois.
Academy Of Tomorrow. Emma Frost's School.
TAXI
ELIE-1
You came! Oh, man--I'm so glad you decided to come.
Yeah, like this is such a surprise. You knew I couldn't resist.
I missed you so much.
Jean-Paul--you just saw me two days ago, we--
I missed you, too.
Is everything okay? How are you dealing with... y'know?
I am fine. I'm Russian--we're strong. I'll be fine. Death is not unfamiliar to me. I just needed to get away from that place. You were right.
Too many memories.
How long will you be staying?
Who says I intend to leave?

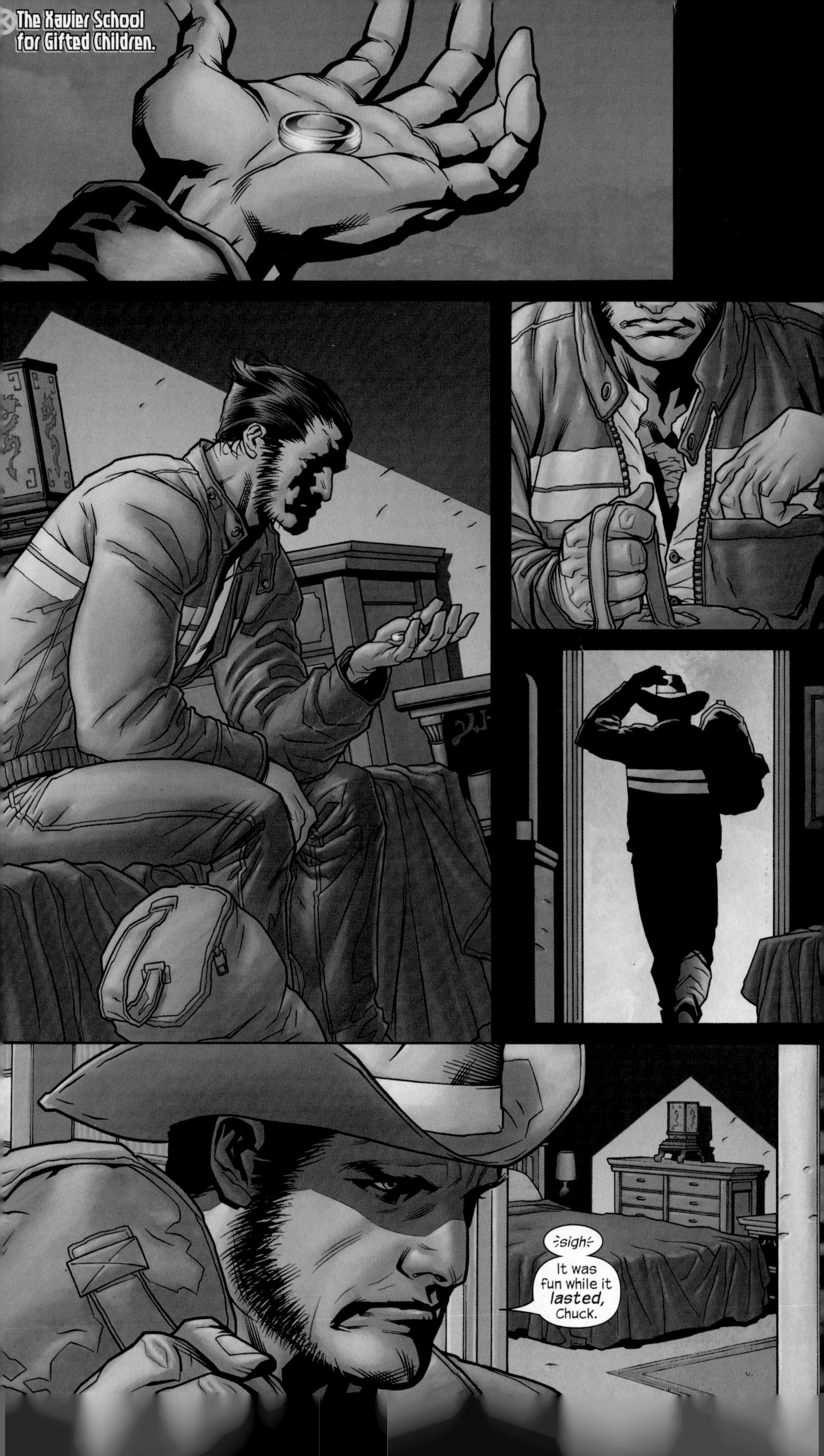

The Xavier School for Gifted Children.
sigh
It was fun while it lasted, Chuck.

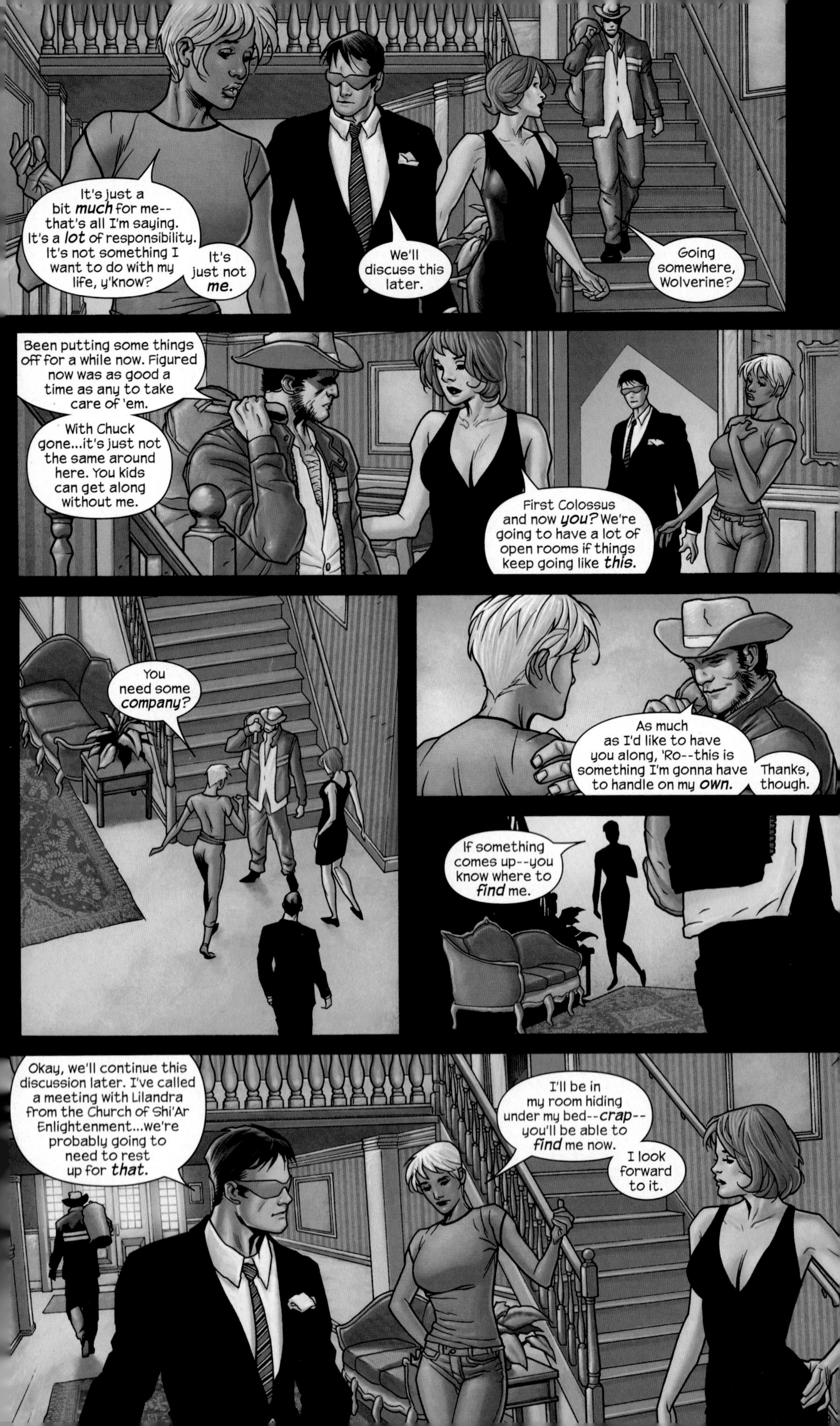
It's just a bit much for me--that's all I'm saying. It's a lot of responsibility. It's not something I want to do with my life, y'know?
It's just not me.
We'll discuss this later.
Going somewhere, Wolverine?
Been putting some things off for a while now. Figured now was as good a time as any to take care of 'em.
With Chuck gone...it's just not the same around here. You kids can get along without me.
First Colossus and now you? We're going to have a lot of open rooms if things keep going like this.
You need some company?
As much as I'd like to have you along, 'Ro--this is something I'm gonna have to handle on my own.
Thanks, though.
If something comes up--you know where to find me.
Okay, we'll continue this discussion later. I've called a meeting with Lilandra from the Church of Shi'Ar Enlightenment...we're probably going to need to rest up for that.
I'll be in my room hiding under my bed--crap--you'll be able to find me now.
I look forward to it.

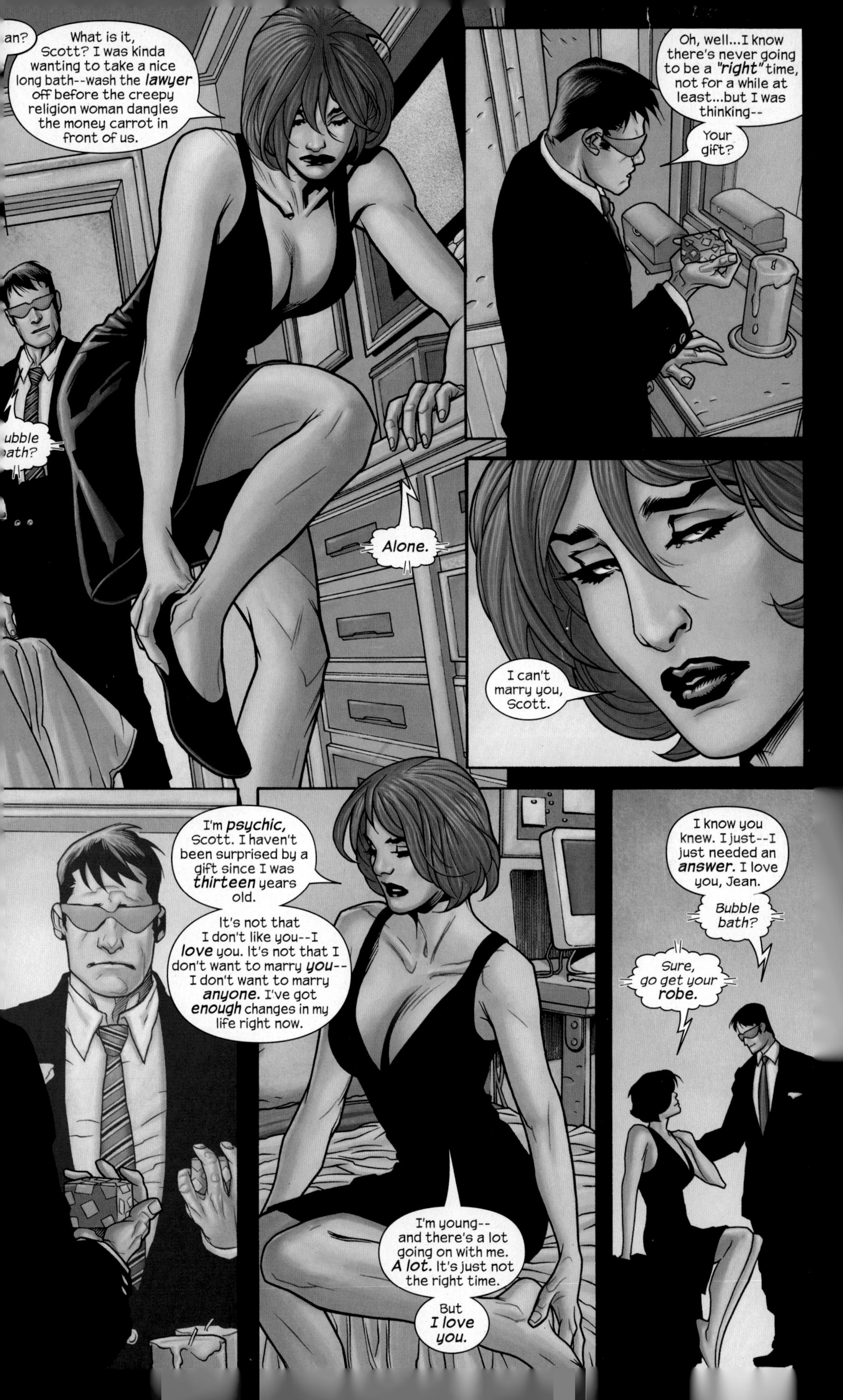
an?
What is it, Scott? I was kinda wanting to take a nice long bath--wash the *lawyer* off before the creepy religion woman dangles the money carrot in front of us.
ubble ath?
Alone.
Oh, well...I know there's never going to be a *"right"* time, not for a while at least...but I was thinking--
Your gift?
I can't marry you, Scott.
I'm *psychic,* Scott. I haven't been surprised by a gift since I was *thirteen* years old.
It's not that I don't like you--I *love* you. It's not that I don't want to marry *you*--I don't want to marry *anyone.* I've got *enough* changes in my life right now.
I'm young--and there's a lot going on with me. *A lot.* It's just not the right time.
But *I love you.*
I know you knew. I just--I just needed an *answer.* I love you, Jean.
Bubble bath?
Sure, go get your *robe.*

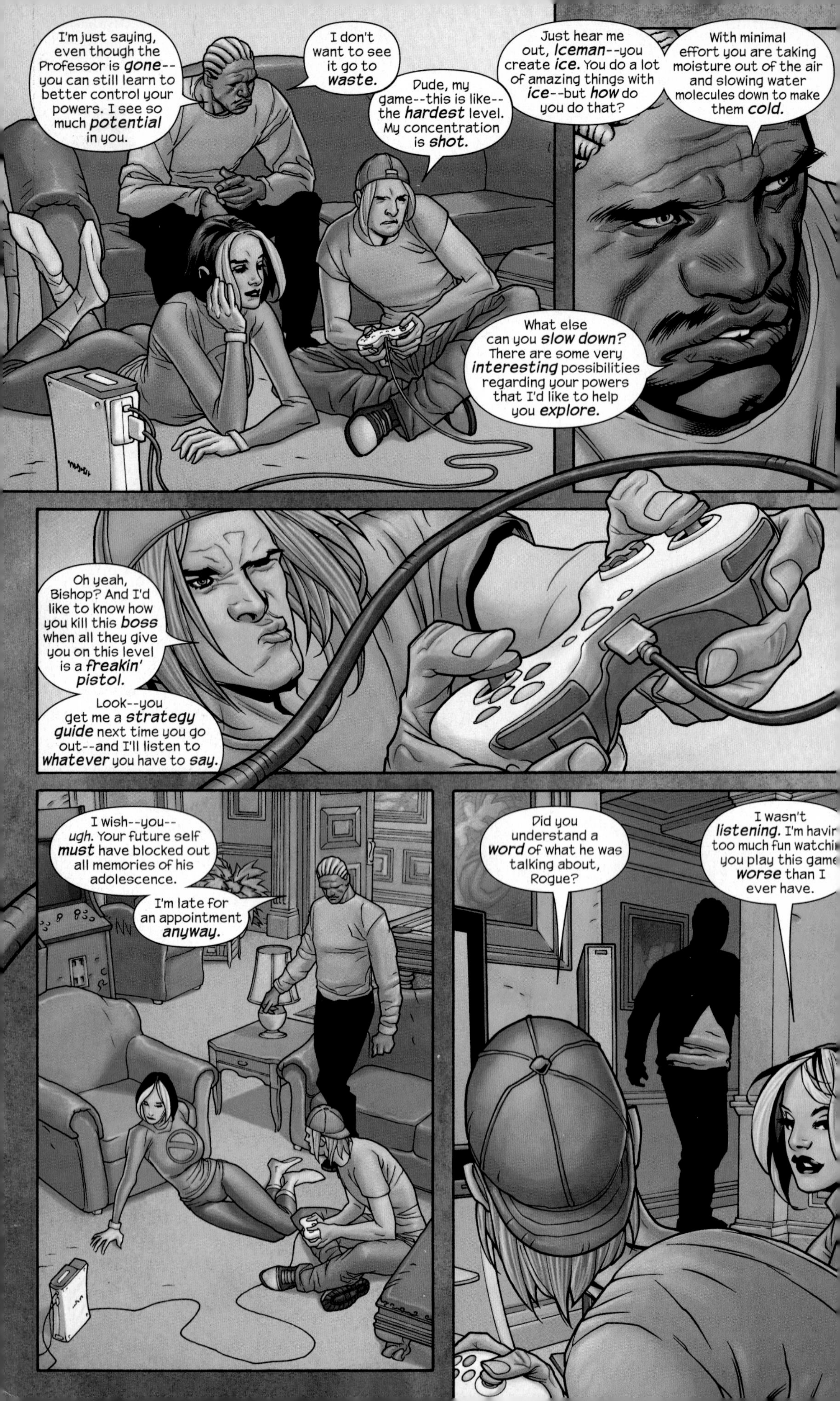
I'm just saying, even though the Professor is gone--you can still learn to better control your powers. I see so much potential in you.
I don't want to see it go to waste.
Dude, my game--this is like--the hardest level. My concentration is shot.
Just hear me out, Iceman--you create ice. You do a lot of amazing things with ice--but how do you do that?
With minimal effort you are taking moisture out of the air and slowing water molecules down to make them cold.
What else can you slow down? There are some very interesting possibilities regarding your powers that I'd like to help you explore.
Oh yeah, Bishop? And I'd like to know how you kill this boss when all they give you on this level is a freakin' pistol.
Look--you get me a strategy guide next time you go out--and I'll listen to whatever you have to say.
I wish--you--ugh. Your future self must have blocked out all memories of his adolescence.
I'm late for an appointment anyway.
Did you understand a word of what he was talking about, Rogue?
I wasn't listening. I'm havi too much fun watchi you play this game worse than I ever have.

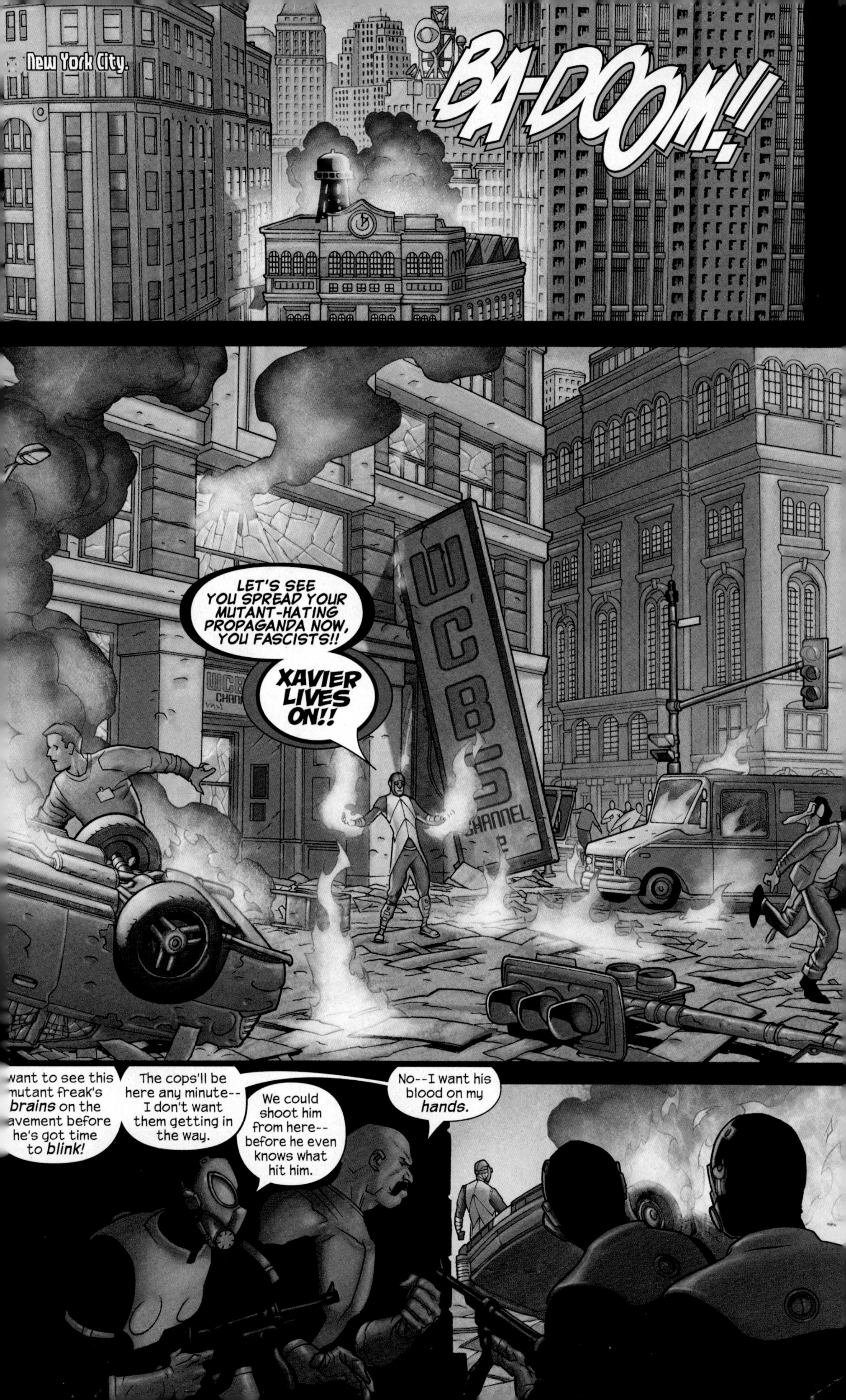
New York City.
BA-DOOM!!
LET'S SEE YOU SPREAD YOUR MUTANT-HATING PROPAGANDA NOW, YOU FASCISTS!!
XAVIER LIVES ON!!
WCBS CHANNEL
want to see this mutant freak's brains on the avement before he's got time to blink!
The cops'll be here any minute-- I don't want them getting in the way.
We could shoot him from here-- before he even knows what hit him.
No--I want his blood on my hands.

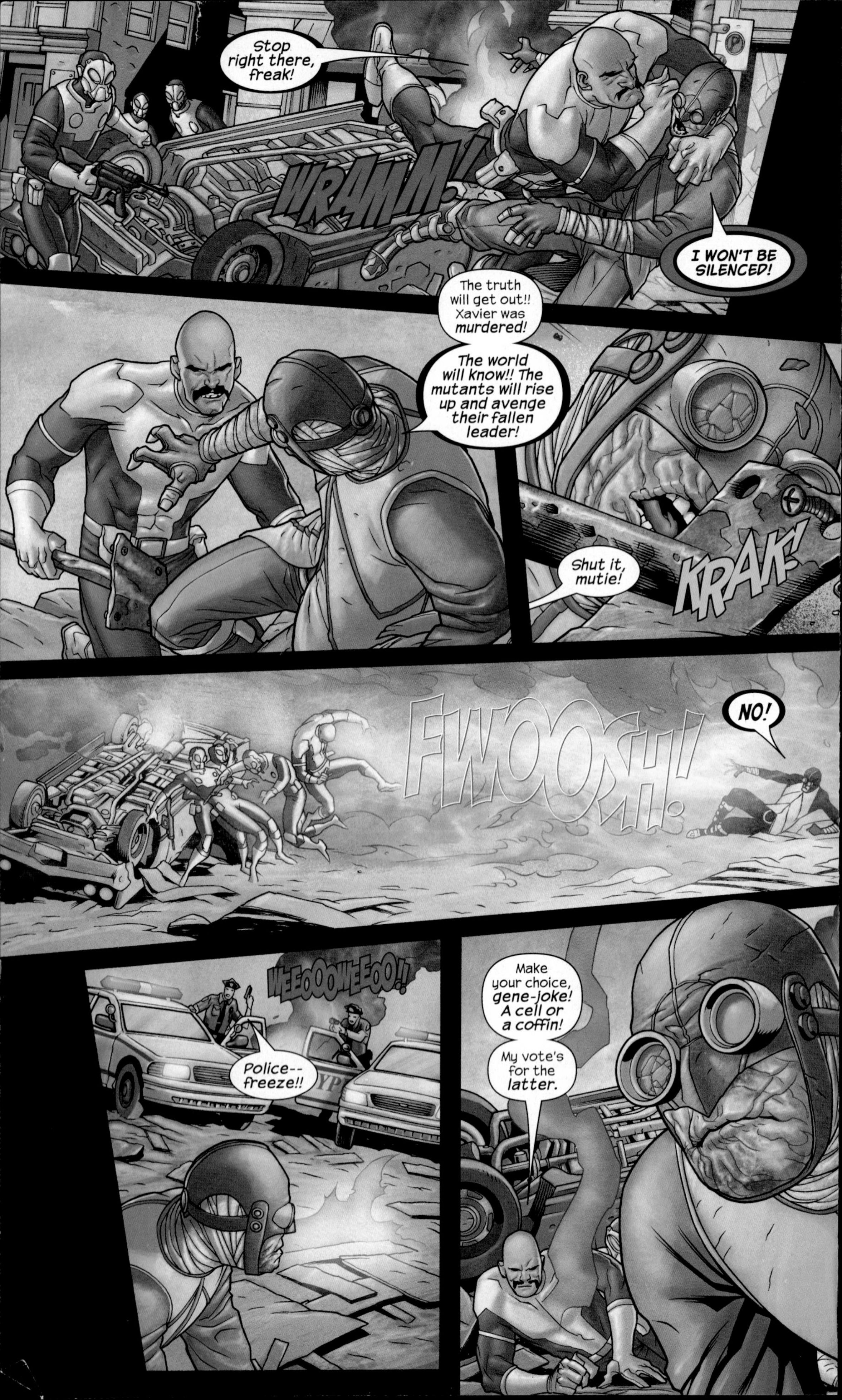

Stop right there, freak!
WRAMM!!
I WON'T BE SILENCED!
The truth will get out!! Xavier was murdered!
The world will know!! The mutants will rise up and avenge their fallen leader!
Shut it, mutie!
KRAK!
FWOOSH!
NO!
WEEOOOWEEOO!!
Police-- freeze!!
Make your choice, gene-joke! A cell or a coffin!
My vote's for the latter.

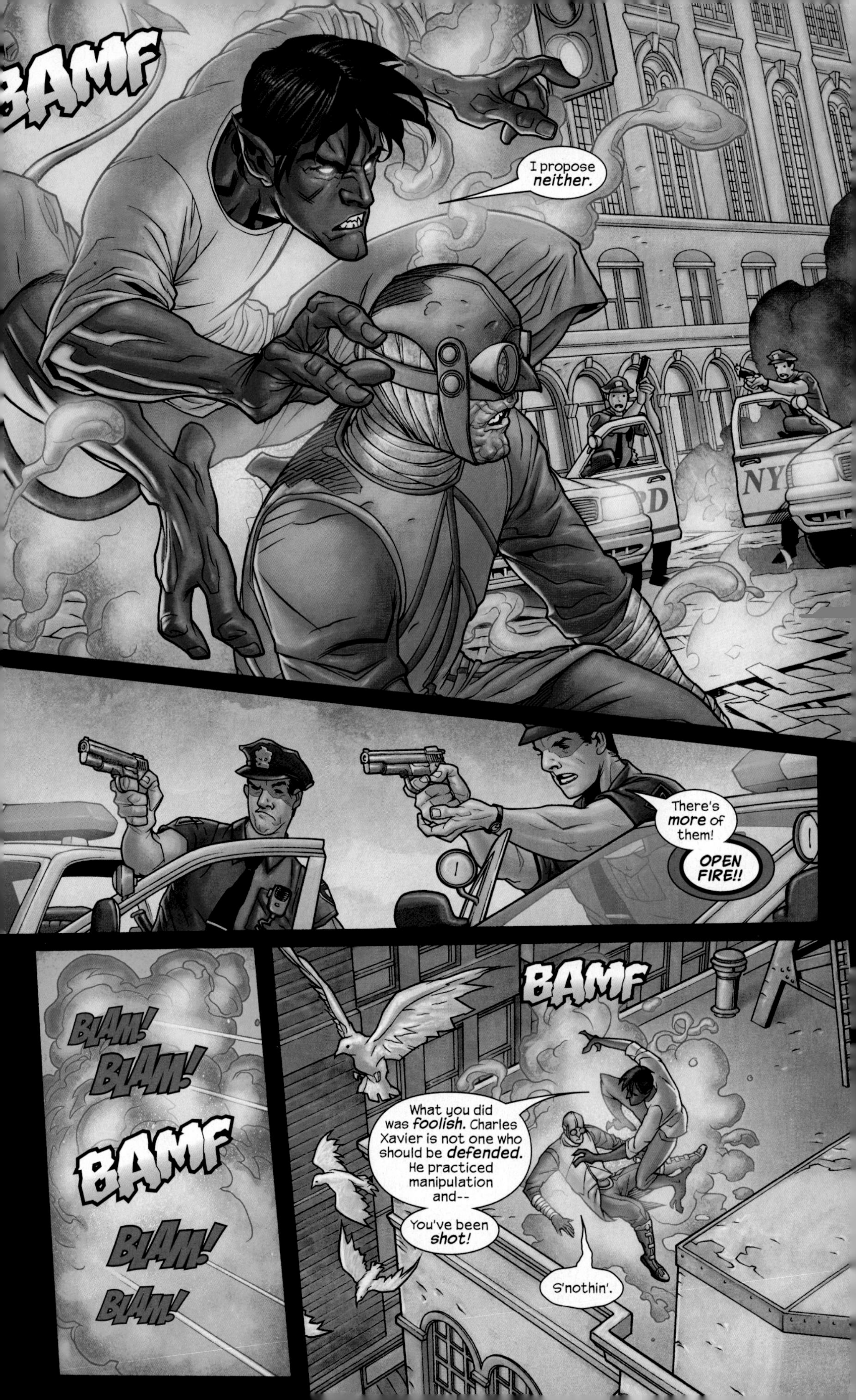
BAMF
I propose neither.
There's more of them!
OPEN FIRE!!
BLAM!
BLAM!
BAMF
BLAM!
BLAM!
BAMF
What you did was foolish. Charles Xavier is not one who should be defended. He practiced manipulation and--
You've been shot!
S'nothin'.

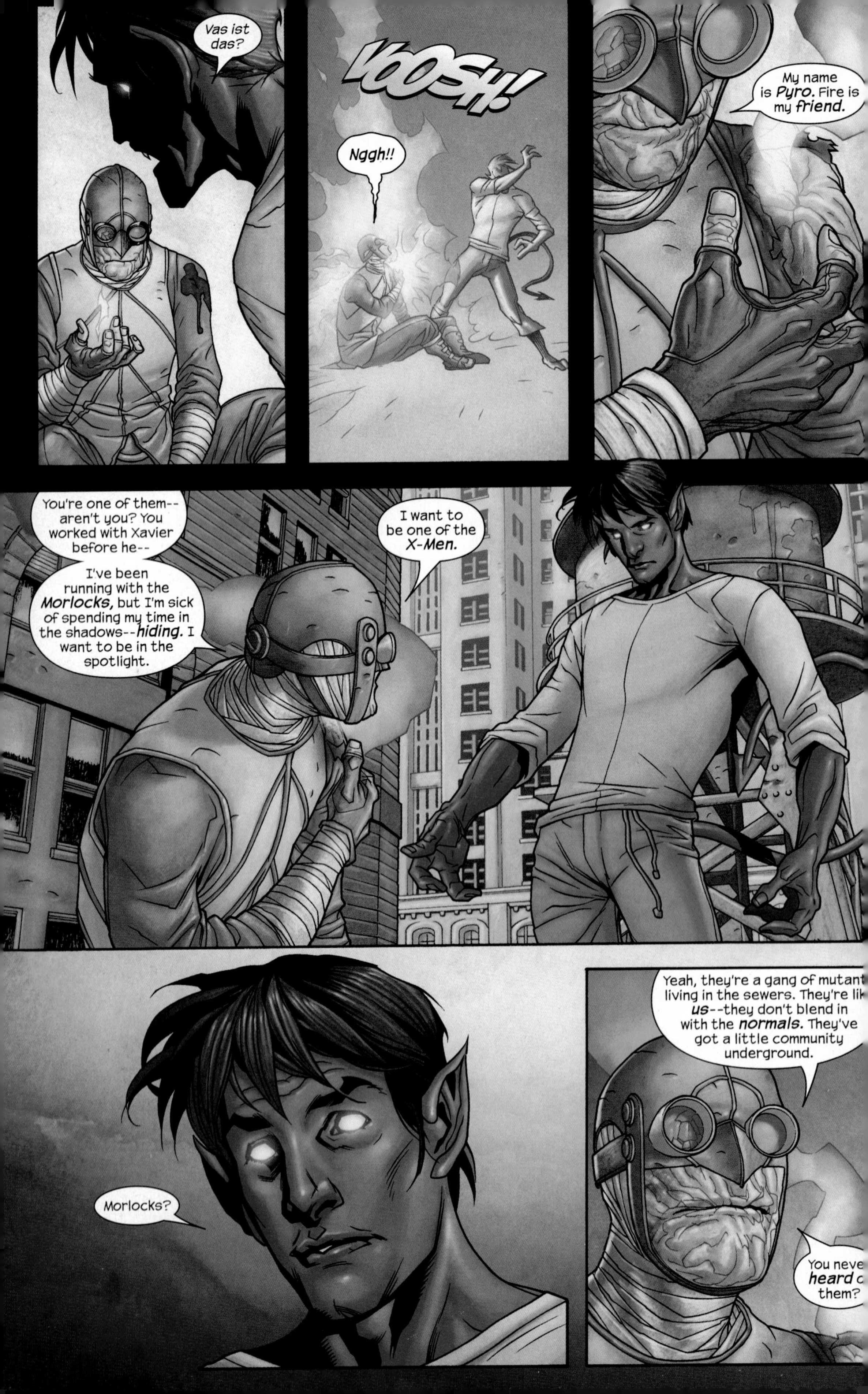
Vas ist das?
VOOSH!
Nggh!!
My name is Pyro. Fire is my friend.
You're one of them--aren't you? You worked with Xavier before he--
I've been running with the Morlocks, but I'm sick of spending my time in the shadows--hiding. I want to be in the spotlight.
I want to be one of the X-Men.
Morlocks?
Yeah, they're a gang of mutant living in the sewers. They're lik us--they don't blend in with the normals. They've got a little community underground.
You neve heard o them?

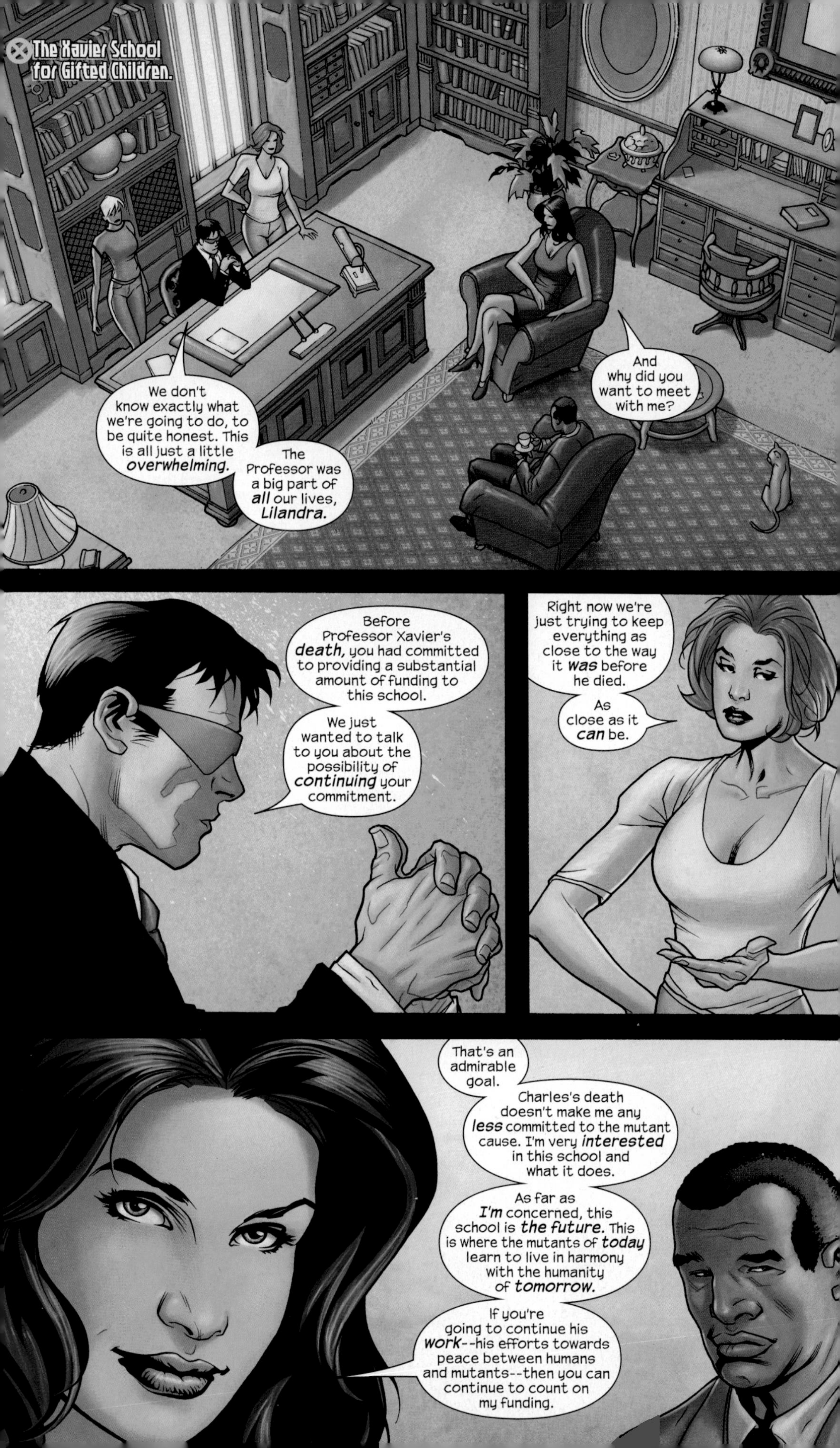
The Xavier School for Gifted Children.
We don't know exactly what we're going to do, to be quite honest. This is all just a little overwhelming.
The Professor was a big part of all our lives, Lilandra.
And why did you want to meet with me?
Before Professor Xavier's death, you had committed to providing a substantial amount of funding to this school.
We just wanted to talk to you about the possibility of continuing your commitment.
Right now we're just trying to keep everything as close to the way it was before he died.
As close as it can be.
That's an admirable goal.
Charles's death doesn't make me any less committed to the mutant cause. I'm very interested in this school and what it does.
As far as I'm concerned, this school is the future. This is where the mutants of today learn to live in harmony with the humanity of tomorrow.
If you're going to continue his work--his efforts towards peace between humans and mutants--then you can continue to count on my funding.

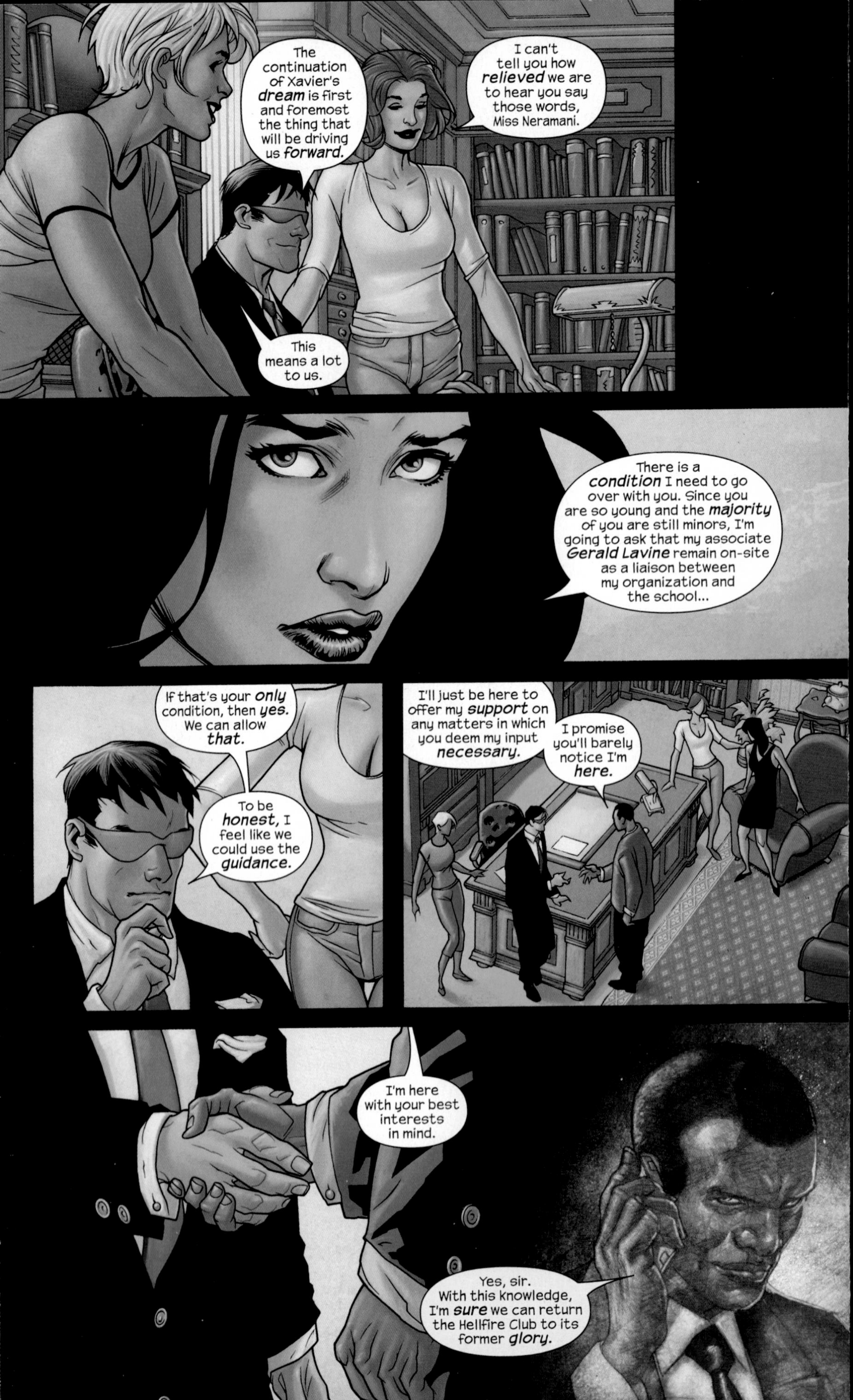
The continuation of Xavier's dream is first and foremost the thing that will be driving us forward.
I can't tell you how relieved we are to hear you say those words, Miss Neramani.
This means a lot to us.
There is a condition I need to go over with you. Since you are so young and the majority of you are still minors, I'm going to ask that my associate Gerald Lavine remain on-site as a liaison between my organization and the school...
If that's your only condition, then yes. We can allow that.
To be honest, I feel like we could use the guidance.
I'll just be here to offer my support on any matters in which you deem my input necessary.
I promise you'll barely notice I'm here.
I'm here with your best interests in mind.
Yes, sir. With this knowledge, I'm sure we can return the Hellfire Club to its former glory.

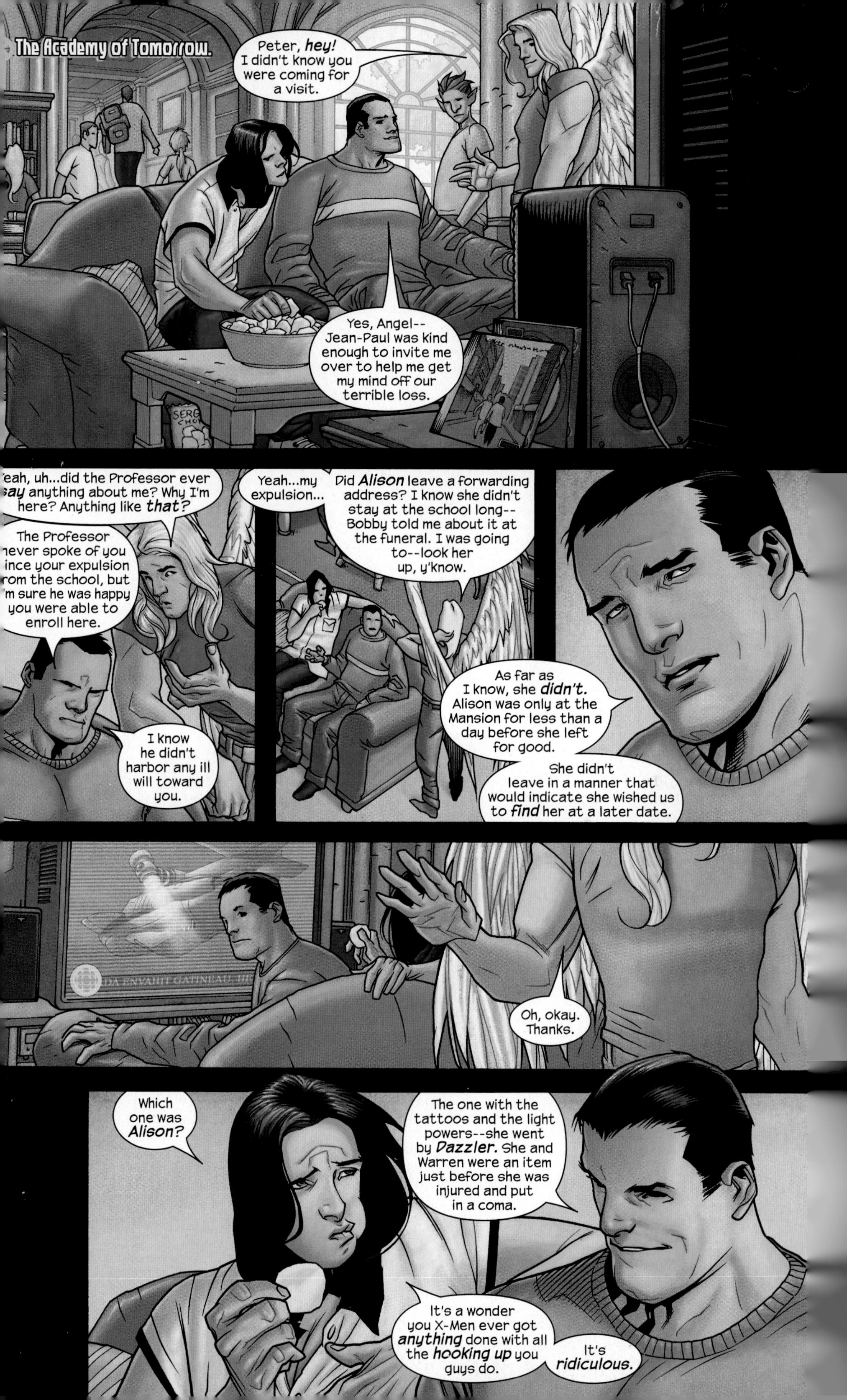
The Academy of Tomorrow.
Peter, hey! I didn't know you were coming for a visit.
Yes, Angel-- Jean-Paul was kind enough to invite me over to help me get my mind off our terrible loss.
eah, uh...did the Professor ever say anything about me? Why I'm here? Anything like that?
The Professor never spoke of you ince your expulsion rom the school, but 'm sure he was happy you were able to enroll here.
I know he didn't harbor any ill will toward you.
Yeah...my expulsion...
Did Alison leave a forwarding address? I know she didn't stay at the school long-- Bobby told me about it at the funeral. I was going to--look her up, y'know.
As far as I know, she didn't. Alison was only at the Mansion for less than a day before she left for good.
She didn't leave in a manner that would indicate she wished us to find her at a later date.
Oh, okay. Thanks.
Which one was Alison?
The one with the tattoos and the light powers--she went by Dazzler. She and Warren were an item just before she was injured and put in a coma.
It's a wonder you X-Men ever got anything done with all the hooking up you guys do.
It's ridiculous.

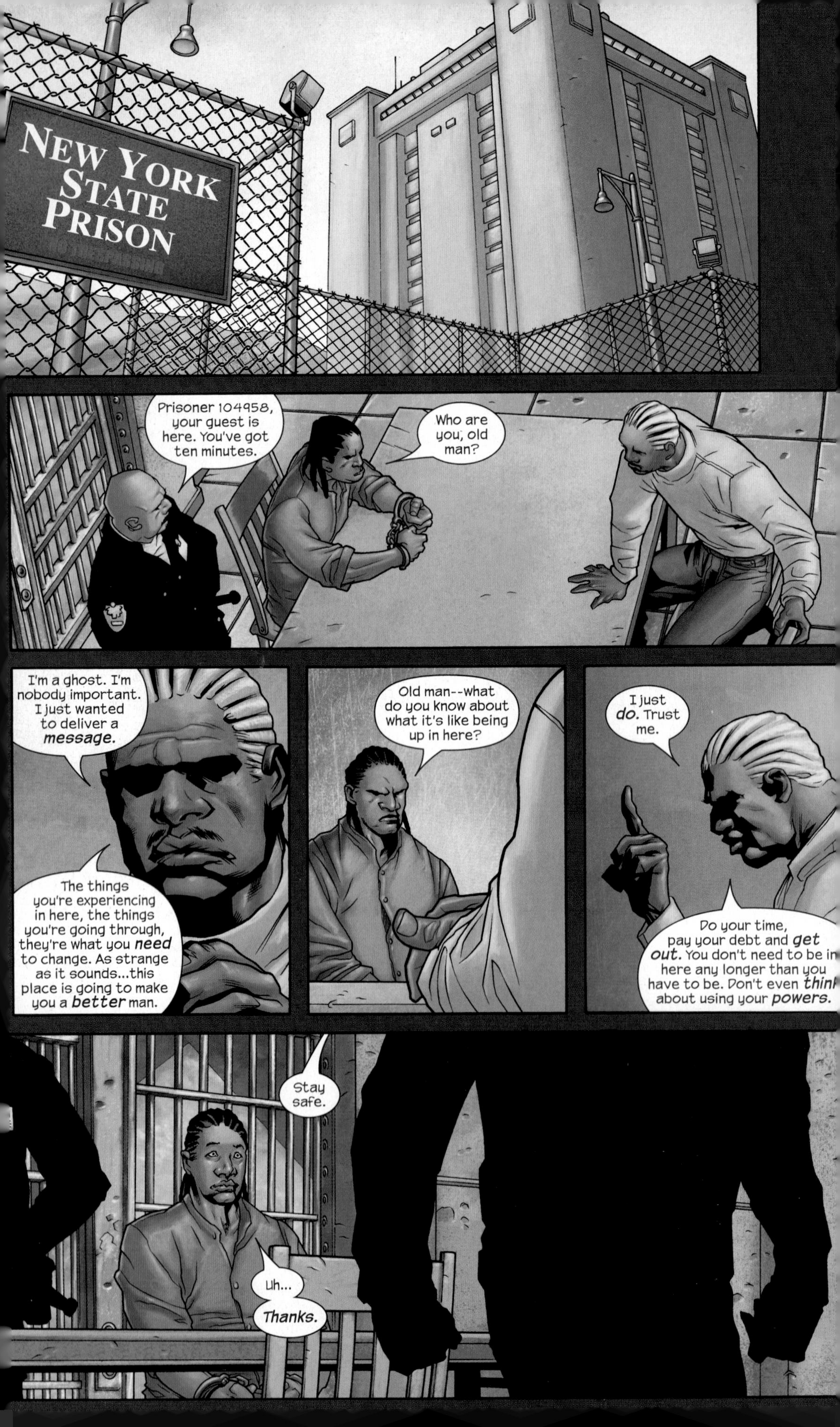
NEW YORK STATE PRISON
Prisoner 104958, your guest is here. You've got ten minutes.
Who are you, old man?
I'm a ghost. I'm nobody important. I just wanted to deliver a *message.*
The things you're experiencing in here, the things you're going through, they're what you *need* to change. As strange as it sounds...this place is going to make you a *better* man.
Old man--what do you know about what it's like being up in here?
I just *do.* Trust me.
Do your time, pay your debt and *get out.* You don't need to be in here any longer than you have to be. Don't even think about using your *powers.*
Stay safe.
Uh...
Thanks.

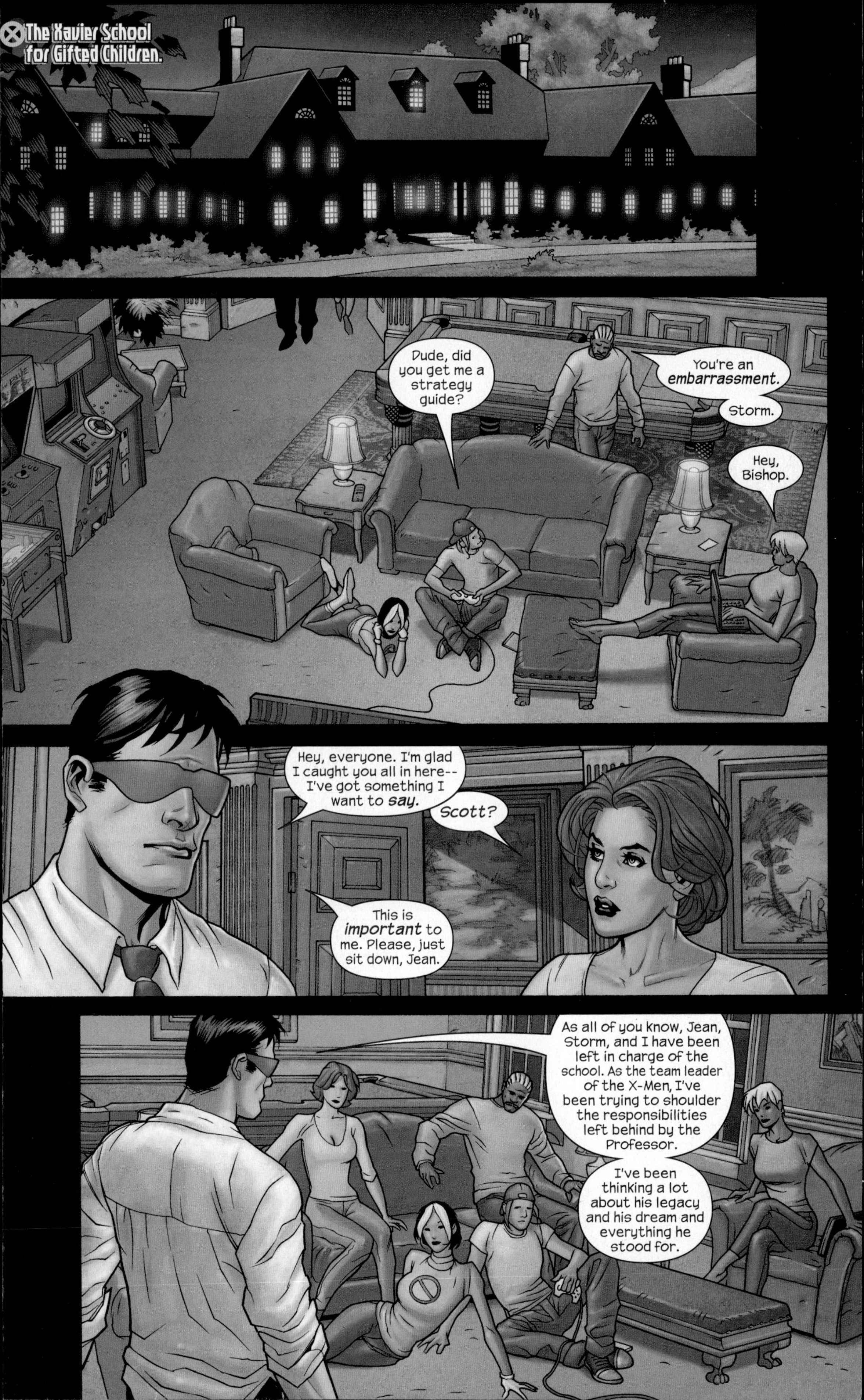

The Xavier School for Gifted Children.
Dude, did you get me a strategy guide?
You're an *embarrassment.*
Storm.
Hey, Bishop.
Hey, everyone. I'm glad I caught you all in here-- I've got something I want to *say.*
Scott?
This is *important* to me. Please, just sit down, Jean.
As all of you know, Jean, Storm, and I have been left in charge of the school. As the team leader of the X-Men, I've been trying to shoulder the responsibilities left behind by the Professor.
I've been thinking a lot about his legacy and his dream and everything he stood for.

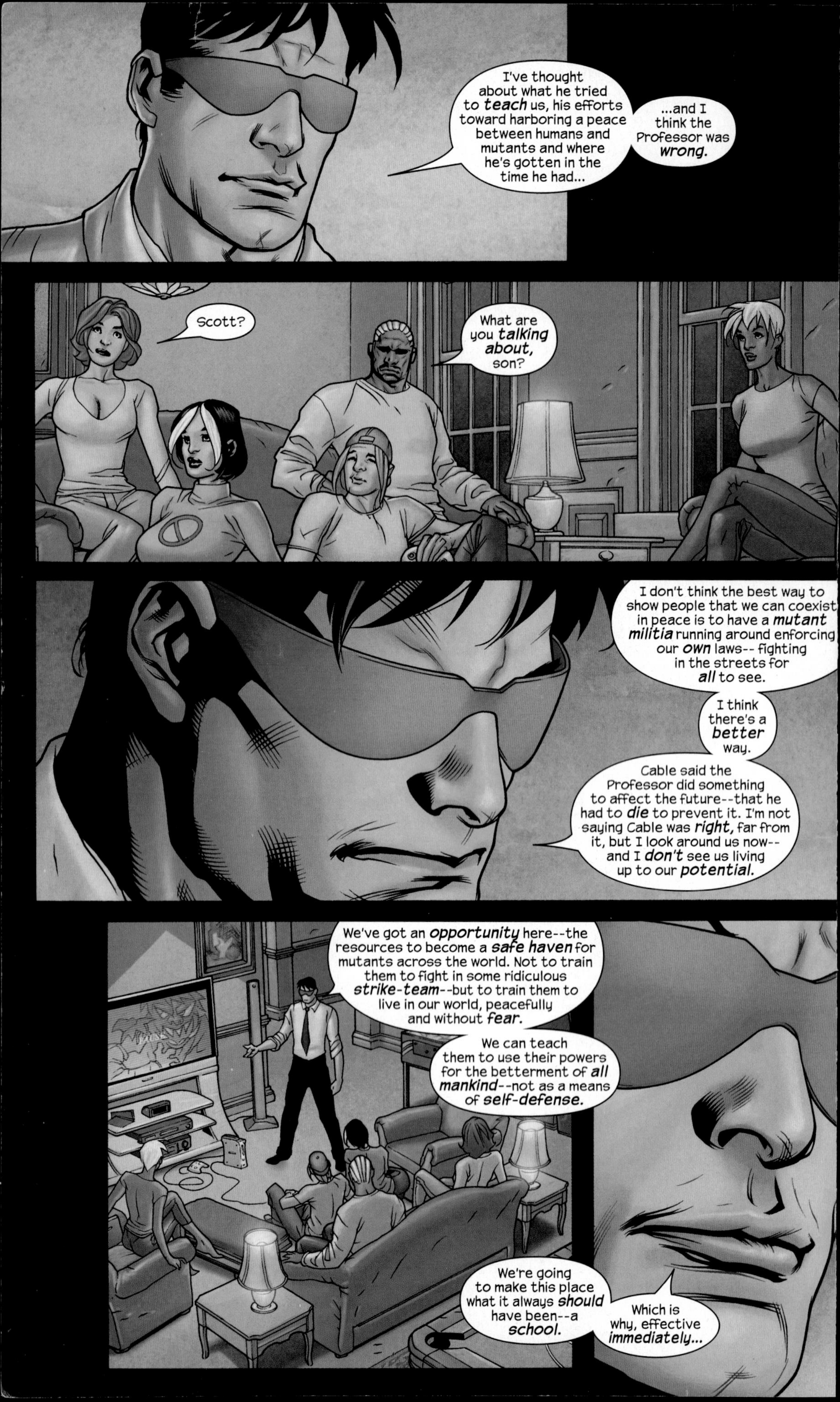
I've thought about what he tried to teach us, his efforts toward harboring a peace between humans and mutants and where he's gotten in the time he had...
...and I think the Professor was wrong.
Scott?
What are you talking about, son?
I don't think the best way to show people that we can coexist in peace is to have a mutant militia running around enforcing our own laws-- fighting in the streets for all to see.
I think there's a better way.
Cable said the Professor did something to affect the future--that he had to die to prevent it. I'm not saying Cable was right, far from it, but I look around us now--and I don't see us living up to our potential.
We've got an opportunity here--the resources to become a safe haven for mutants across the world. Not to train them to fight in some ridiculous strike-team--but to train them to live in our world, peacefully and without fear.
We can teach them to use their powers for the betterment of all mankind--not as a means of self-defense.
We're going to make this place what it always should have been--a school.
Which is why, effective immediately...

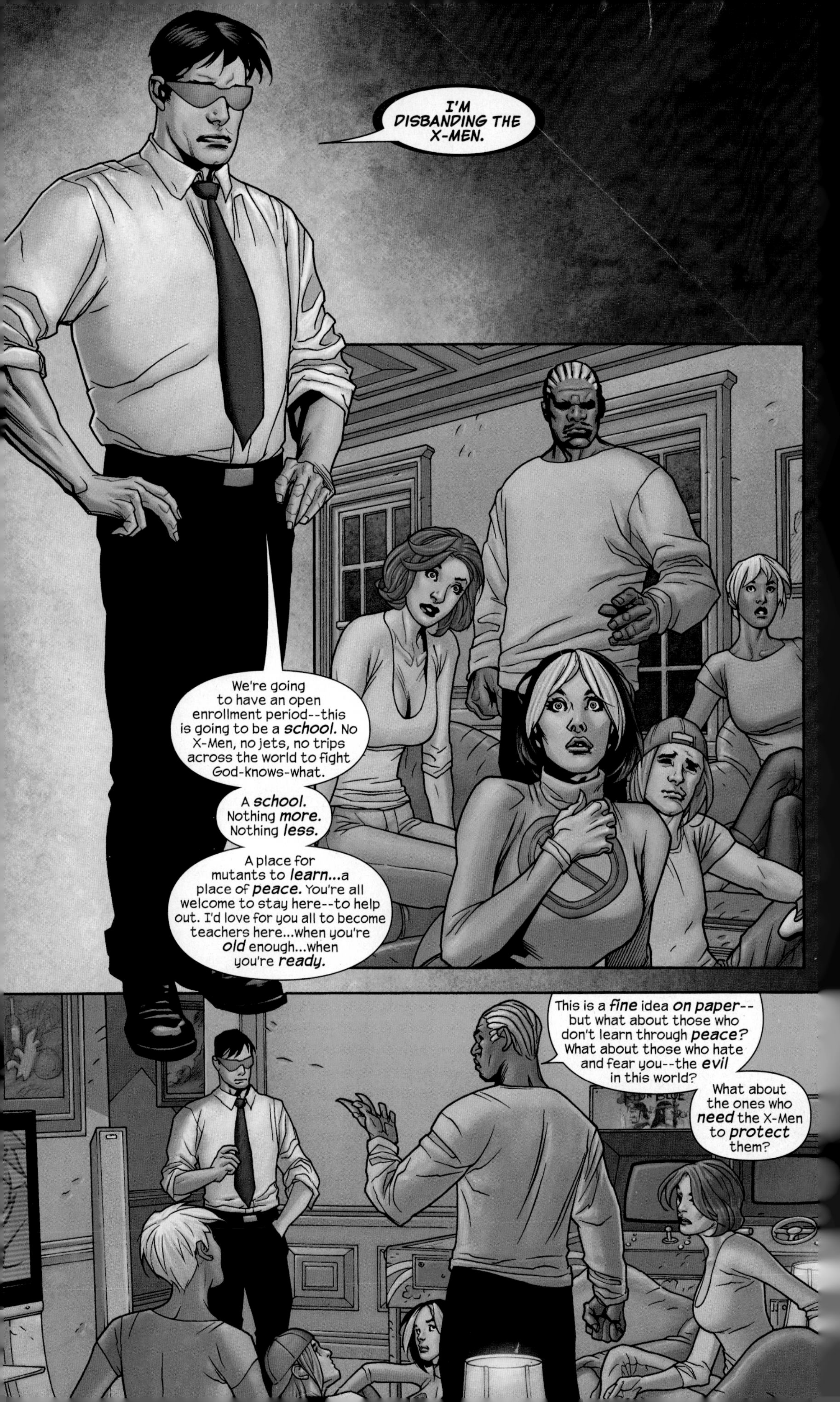
I'M DISBANDING THE X-MEN.
We're going to have an open enrollment period--this is going to be a *school.* No X-Men, no jets, no trips across the world to fight God-knows-what.
A *school.* Nothing *more.* Nothing *less.*
A place for mutants to *learn...*a place of *peace.* You're all welcome to stay here--to help out. I'd love for you all to become teachers here...when you're *old* enough...when you're *ready.*
This is a *fine* idea *on paper*--but what about those who don't learn through *peace?* What about those who hate and fear you--the *evil* in this world?
What about the ones who *need* the X-Men to *protect* them?

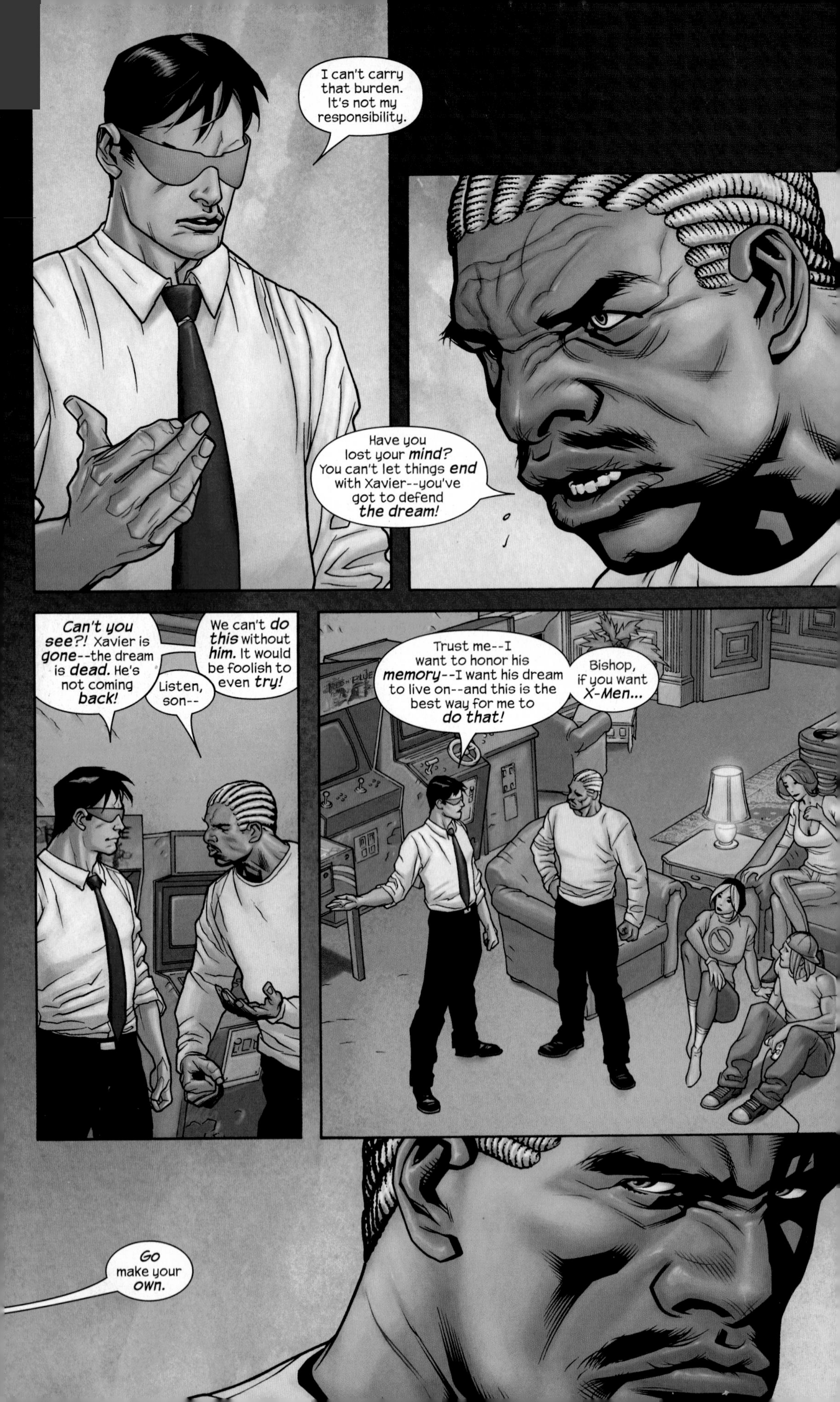

I can't carry that burden. It's not my responsibility.
Have you lost your *mind?* You can't let things *end* with Xavier--you've got to defend ***the dream!***
Can't you see?! Xavier is ***gone***--the dream is ***dead.*** He's not coming ***back!***
Listen, son--
We can't ***do this*** without ***him.*** It would be foolish to even ***try!***
Trust me--I want to honor his ***memory***--I want his dream to live on--and this is the best way for me to ***do that!***
Bishop, if you want ***X-Men...***
Go make your ***own.***

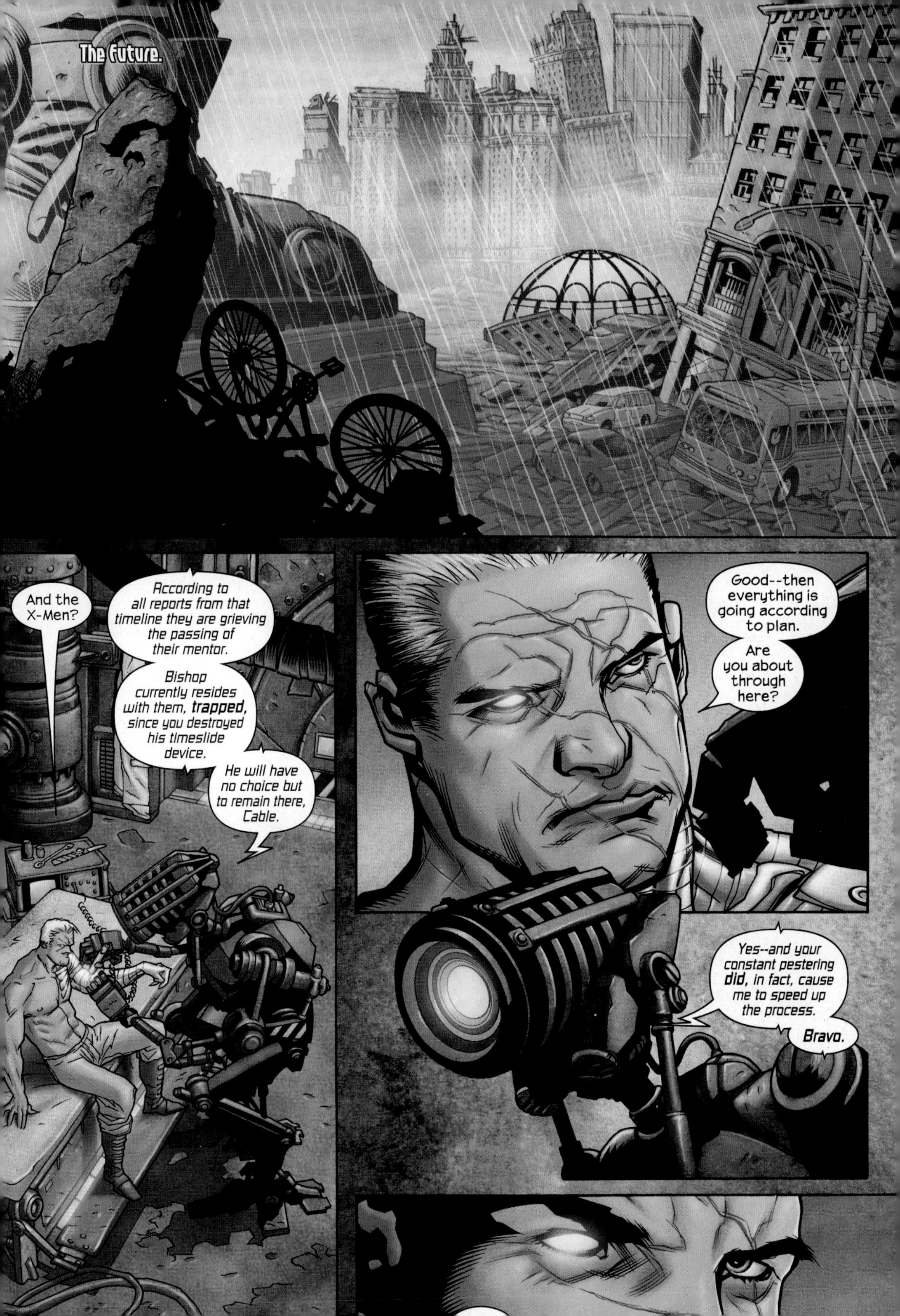
The Future.
And the X-Men?
According to all reports from that timeline they are grieving the passing of their mentor.
Bishop currently resides with them, trapped, since you destroyed his timeslide device.
He will have no choice but to remain there, Cable.
Good--then everything is going according to plan.
Are you about through here?
Yes--and your constant pestering did, in fact, cause me to speed up the process.
Bravo.

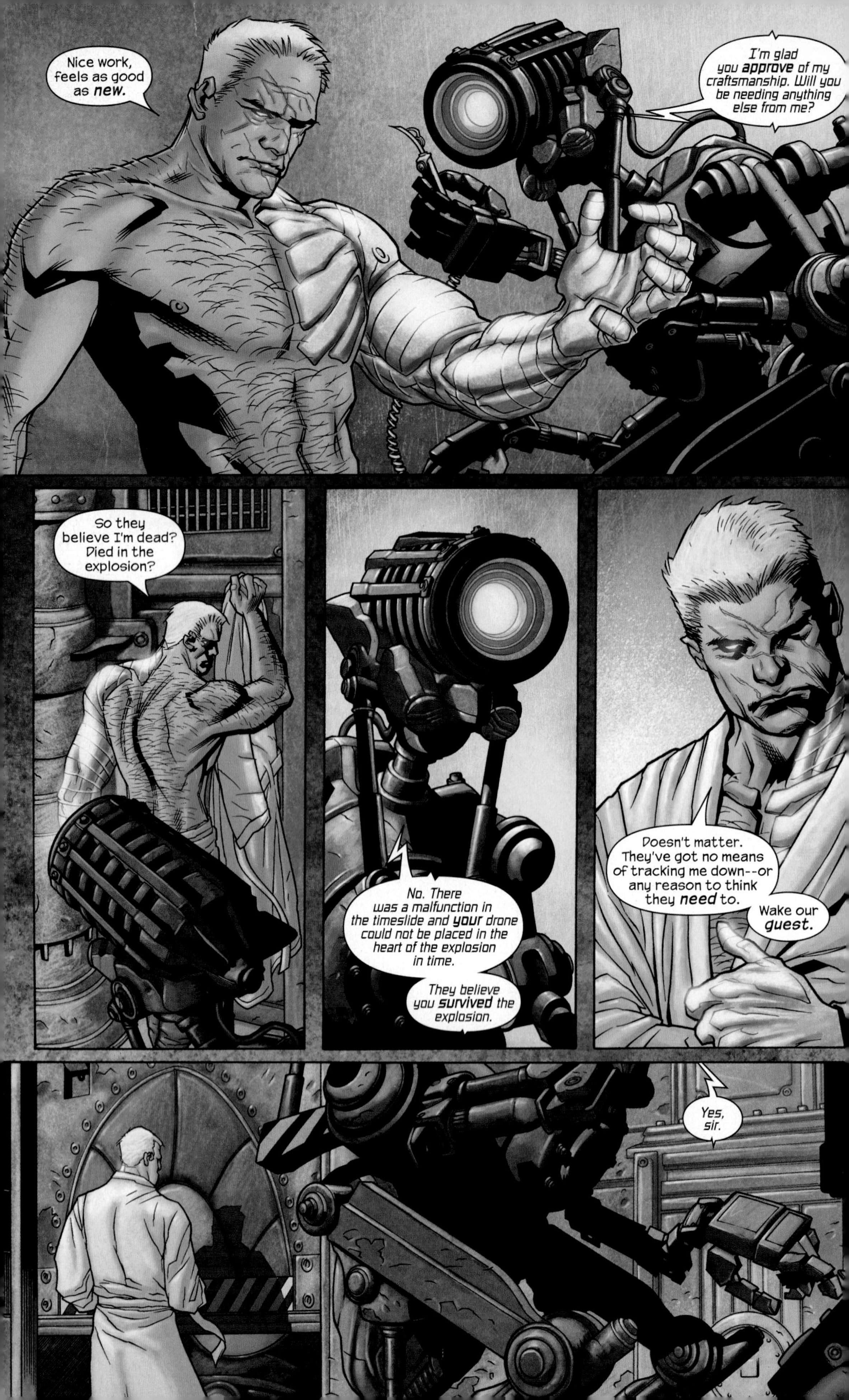
Nice work, feels as good as new.
I'm glad you approve of my craftsmanship. Will you be needing anything else from me?
So they believe I'm dead? Died in the explosion?
No. There was a malfunction in the timeslide and your drone could not be placed in the heart of the explosion in time.
They believe you survived the explosion.
Doesn't matter. They've got no means of tracking me down--or any reason to think they need to.
Wake our guest.
Yes, sir.

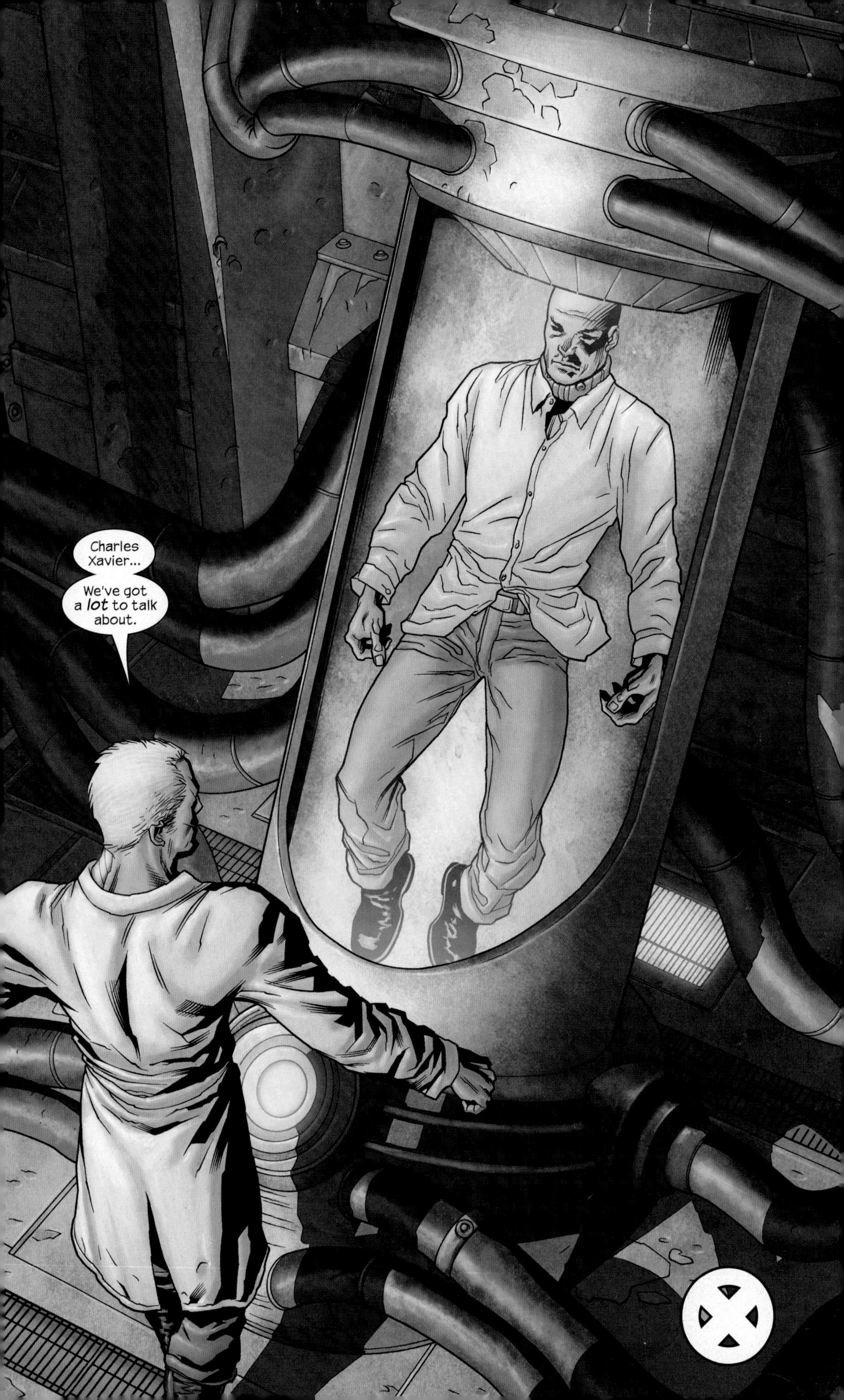
Charles Xavier...
We've got a *lot* to talk about.

PREVIOUSLY:

Charles Xavier's former lover, Emma Frost, has opened a school for gifted students in Chicago. Frost's Academy of Tomorrow is designed to teach students to live with their powers, as opposed to (what she sees as) Xavier's increasingly militaristic Institute for Gifted Children.

Though the Academy students have many ties to the X-Men, including brothers and boyfriends (current and past), the two teams have often met as rivals.

Among Frost's students are not only mutants, but also gifted humans...

Emma Frost
HEADMISTRESS

Alex Summers
HAVOK

Sam Guthrie
CANNONBALL

Roberto Decosta
SUNSPOT

Lorna Dane
POLARIS

Doug Ramsey
...NOTHING

EXTRACURRICULAR

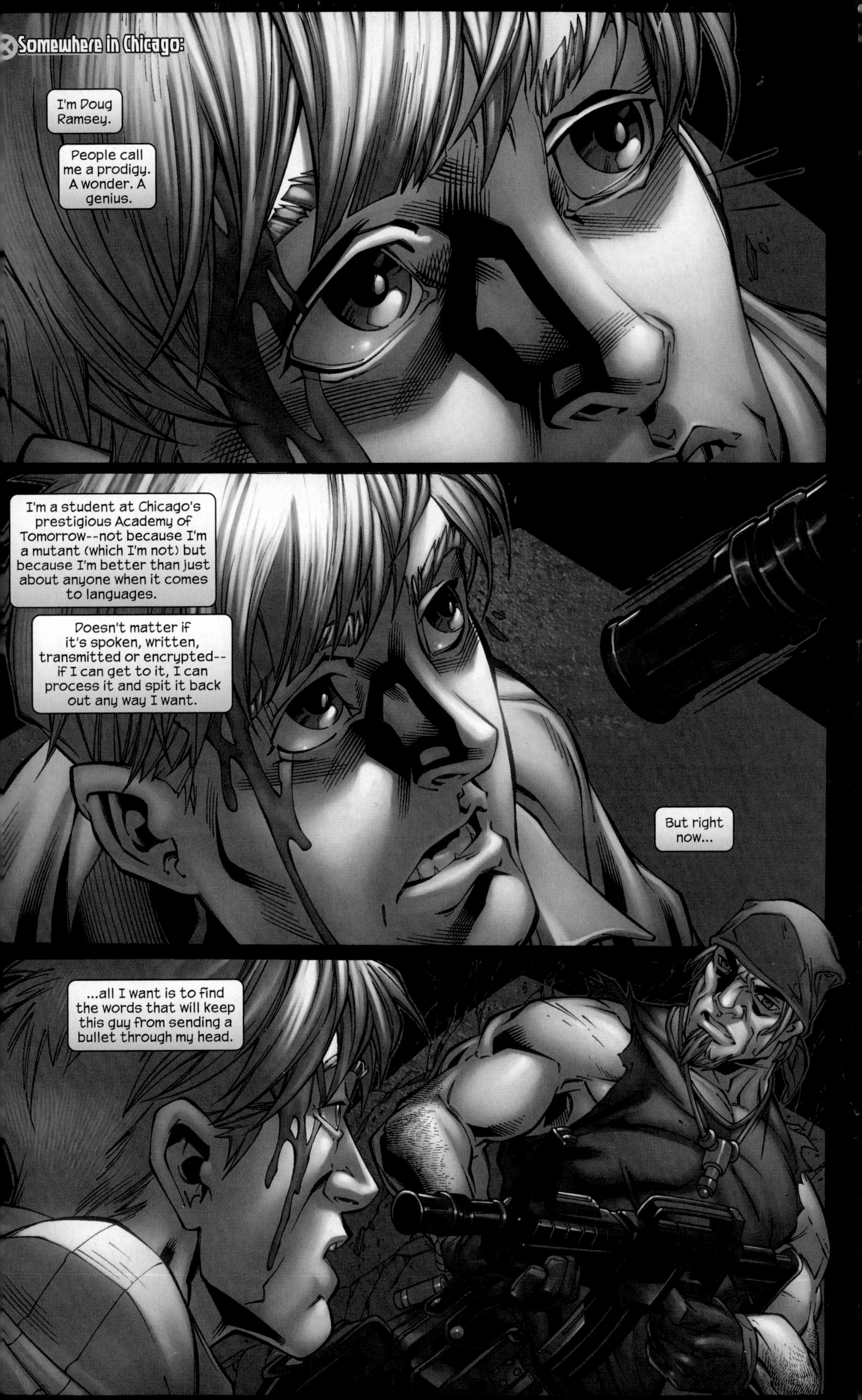
Somewhere in Chicago:
I'm Doug Ramsey.
People call me a prodigy. A wonder. A genius.
I'm a student at Chicago's prestigious Academy of Tomorrow--not because I'm a mutant (which I'm not) but because I'm better than just about anyone when it comes to languages.
Doesn't matter if it's spoken, written, transmitted or encrypted--if I can get to it, I can process it and spit it back out any way I want.
But right now...
...all I want is to find the words that will keep this guy from sending a bullet through my head.

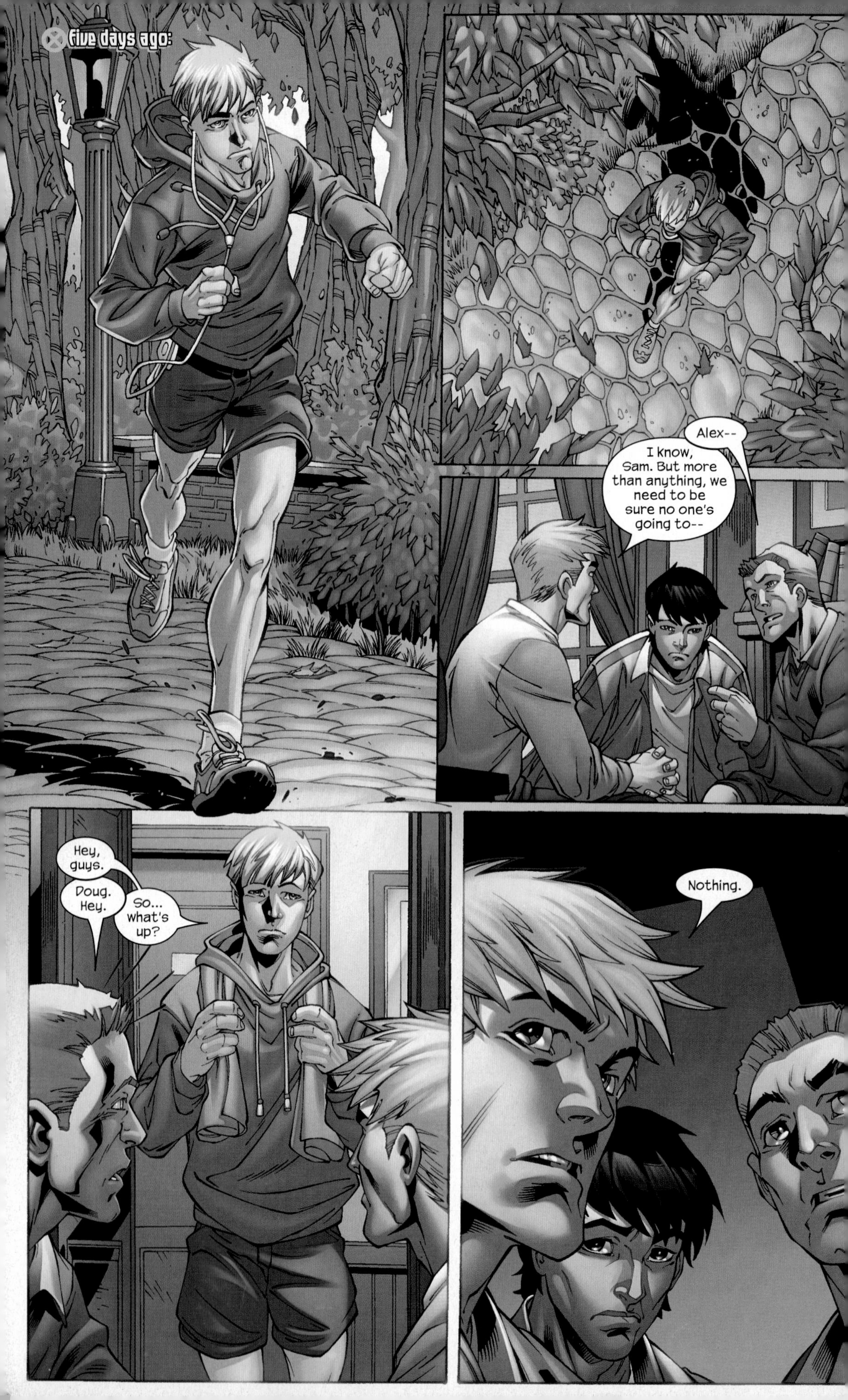
five days ago:
Alex--
I know, Sam. But more than anything, we need to be sure no one's going to--
Hey, guys.
Doug. Hey.
So... what's up?
Nothing.

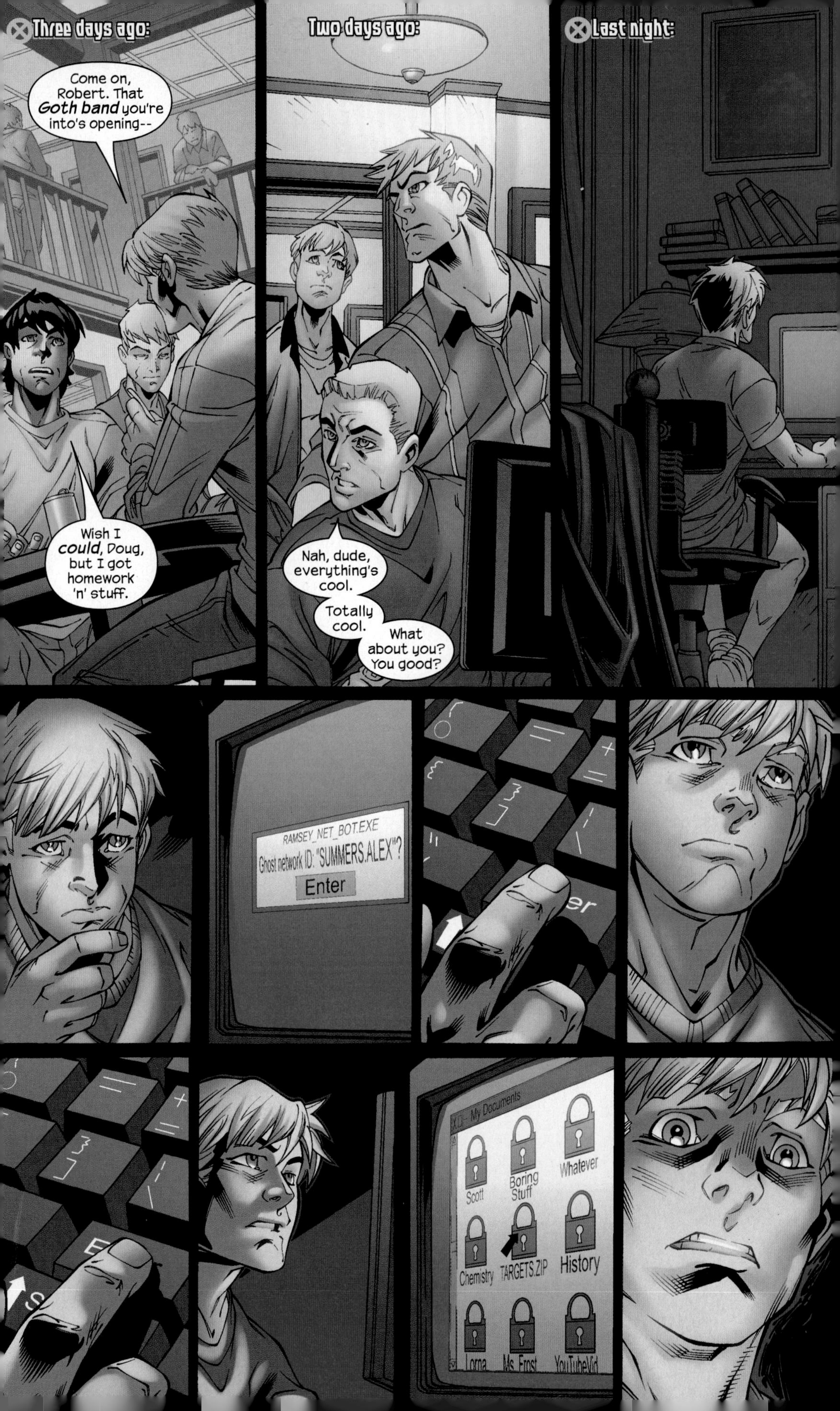

Three days ago:
Come on, Robert. That Goth band you're into's opening--
Wish I could, Doug, but I got homework 'n' stuff.
Two days ago:
Nah, dude, everything's cool.
Totally cool.
What about you? You good?
Last night:
RAMSEY_NET_BOT.EXE
Ghost network ID: "SUMMERS.ALEX"?
Enter
My Documents
Scott
Boring Stuff
Whatever
Chemistry
TARGETS.ZIP
History
Lorna
Ms. Frost
YouTubeVid

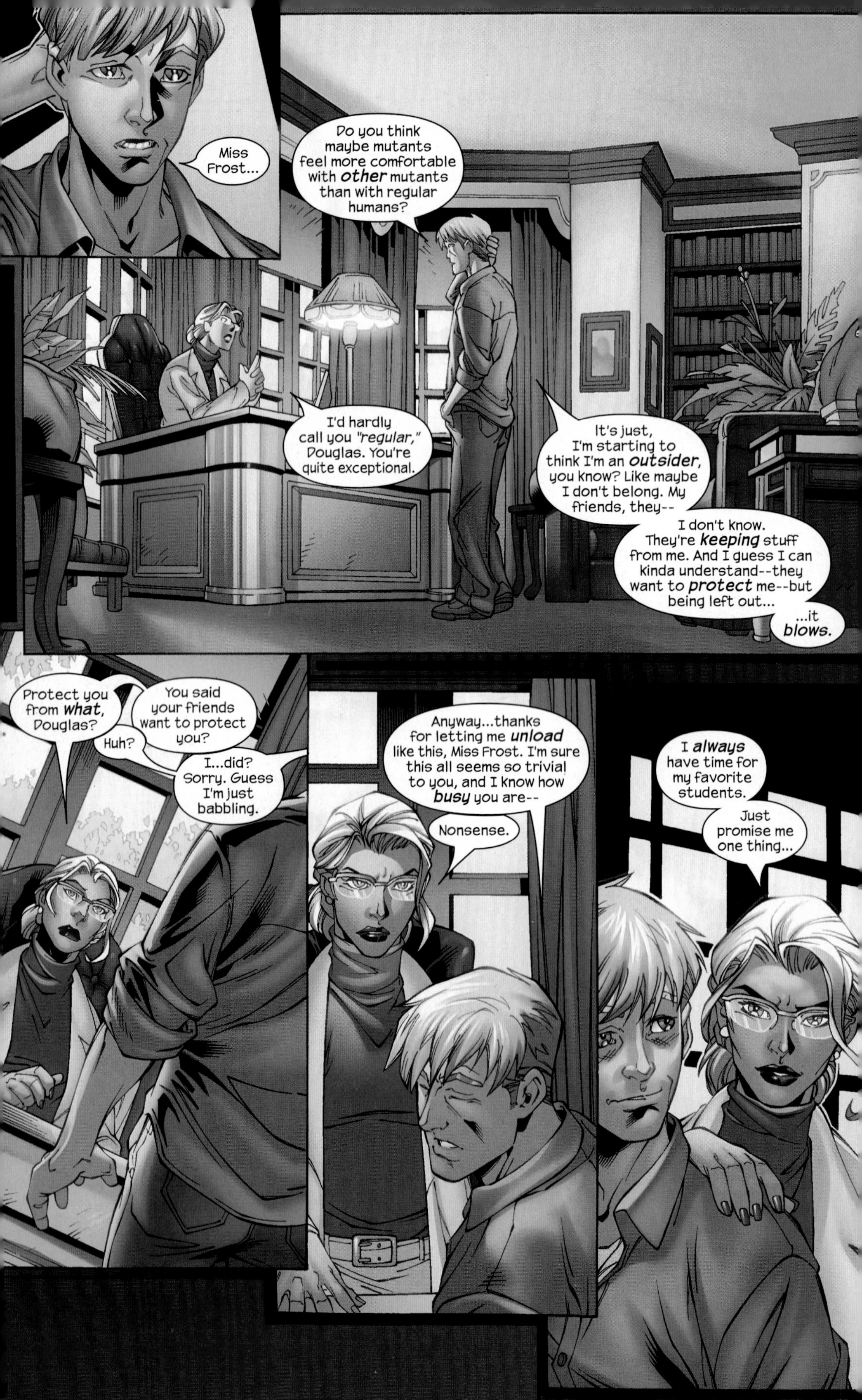

Miss Frost...
Do you think maybe mutants feel more comfortable with other mutants than with regular humans?
I'd hardly call you "regular," Douglas. You're quite exceptional.
It's just, I'm starting to think I'm an outsider, you know? Like maybe I don't belong. My friends, they--
I don't know. They're keeping stuff from me. And I guess I can kinda understand--they want to protect me--but being left out...
...it blows.
Protect you from what, Douglas?
You said your friends want to protect you?
Huh?
I...did? Sorry. Guess I'm just babbling.
Anyway...thanks for letting me unload like this, Miss Frost. I'm sure this all seems so trivial to you, and I know how busy you are--
Nonsense.
I always have time for my favorite students.
Just promise me one thing...

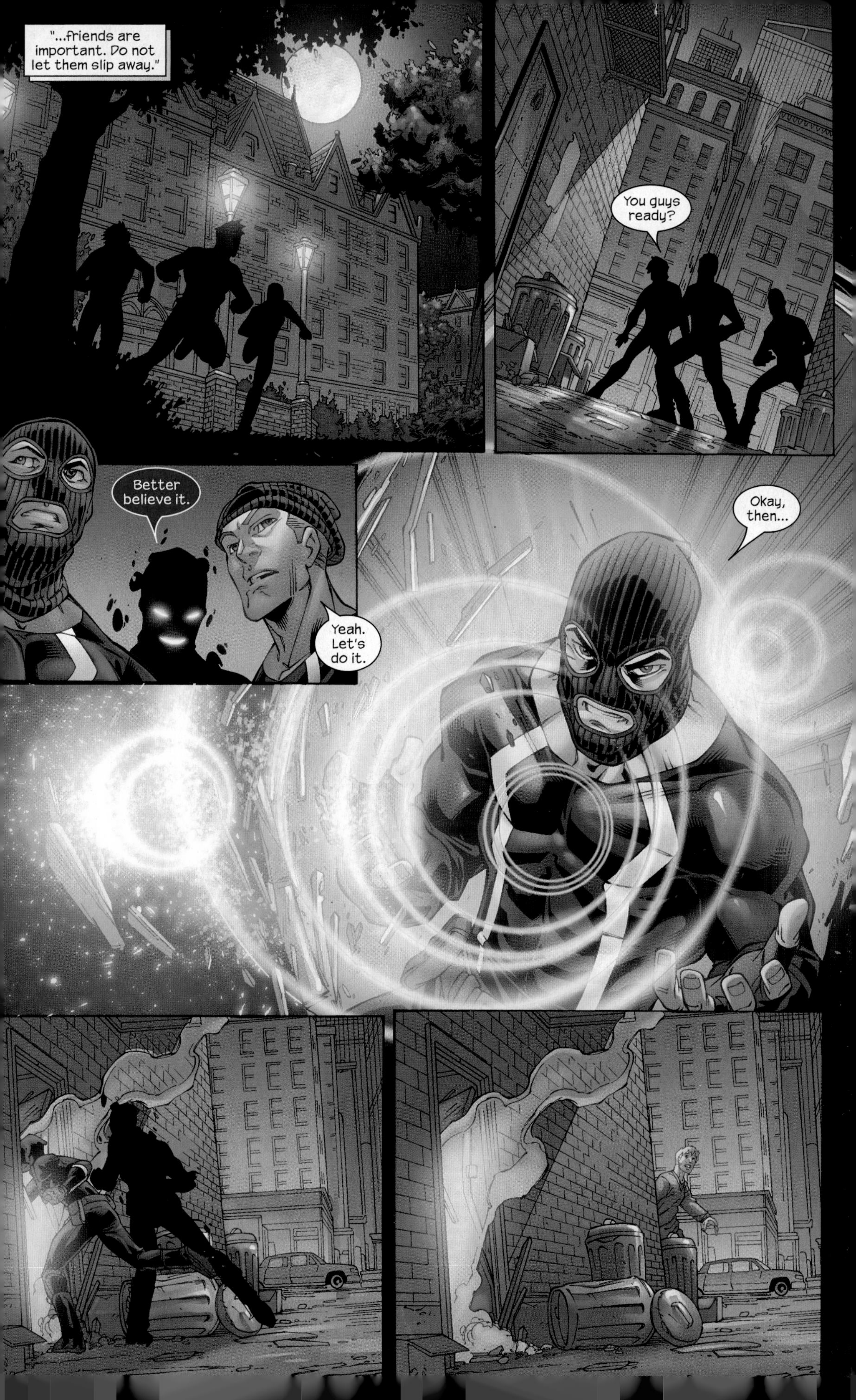
"...friends are important. Do not let them slip away."
You guys ready?
Better believe it.
Yeah. Let's do it.
Okay, then...

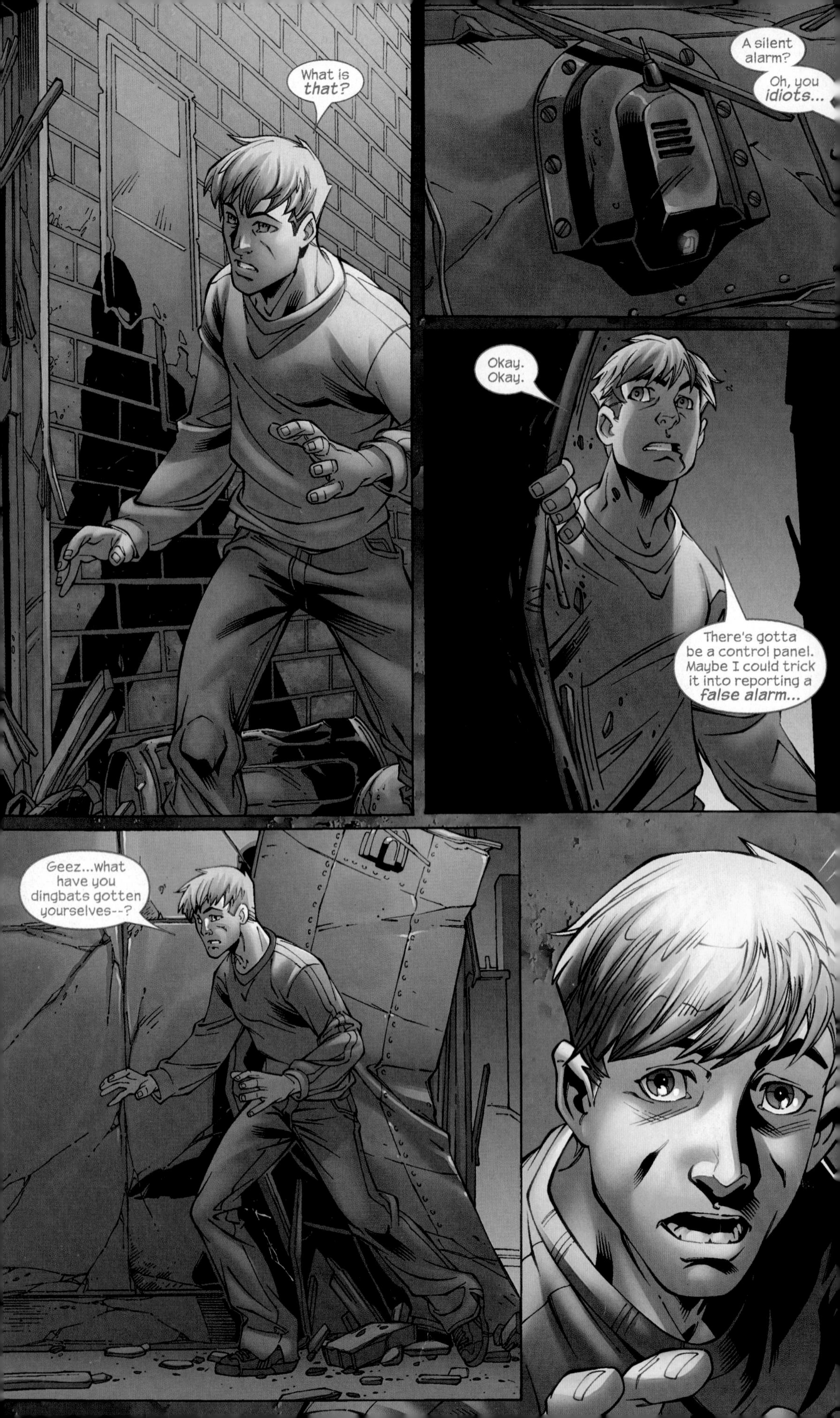
What is *that?*
A silent alarm?
Oh, you *idiots...*
Okay. Okay.
There's gotta be a control panel. Maybe I could trick it into reporting a *false alarm...*
Geez...what have you dingbats gotten yourselves--?

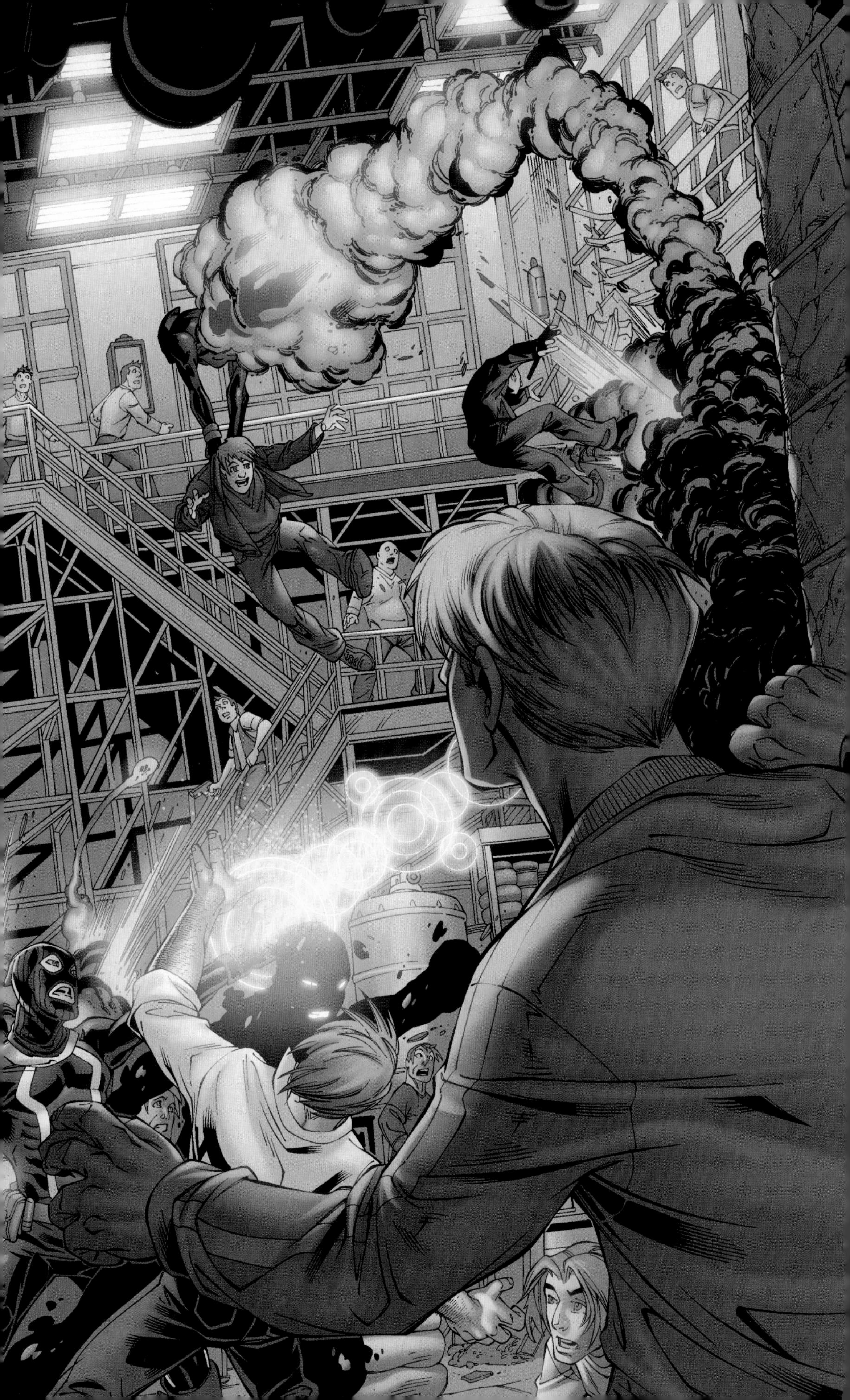

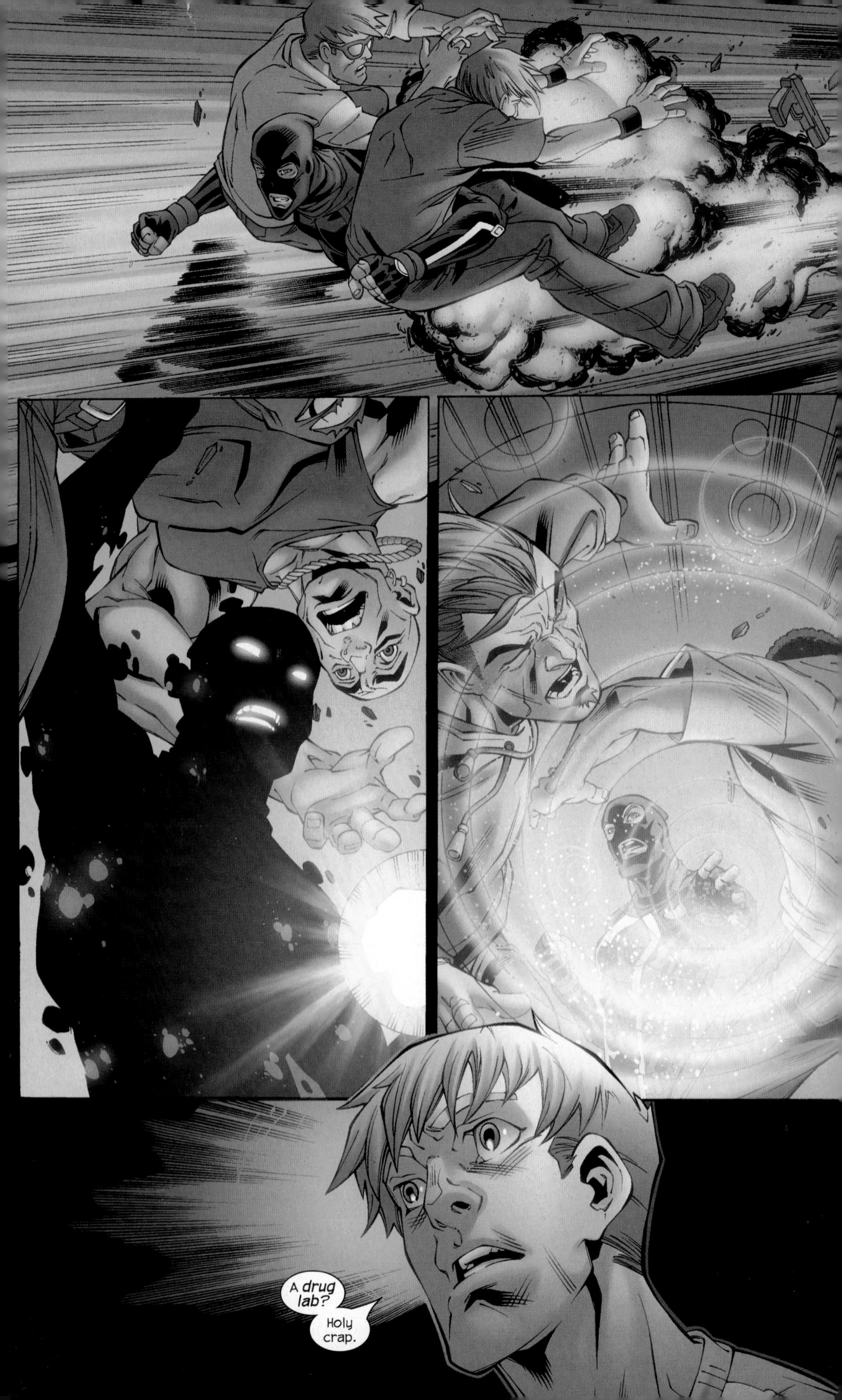
A drug lab?
Holy crap.

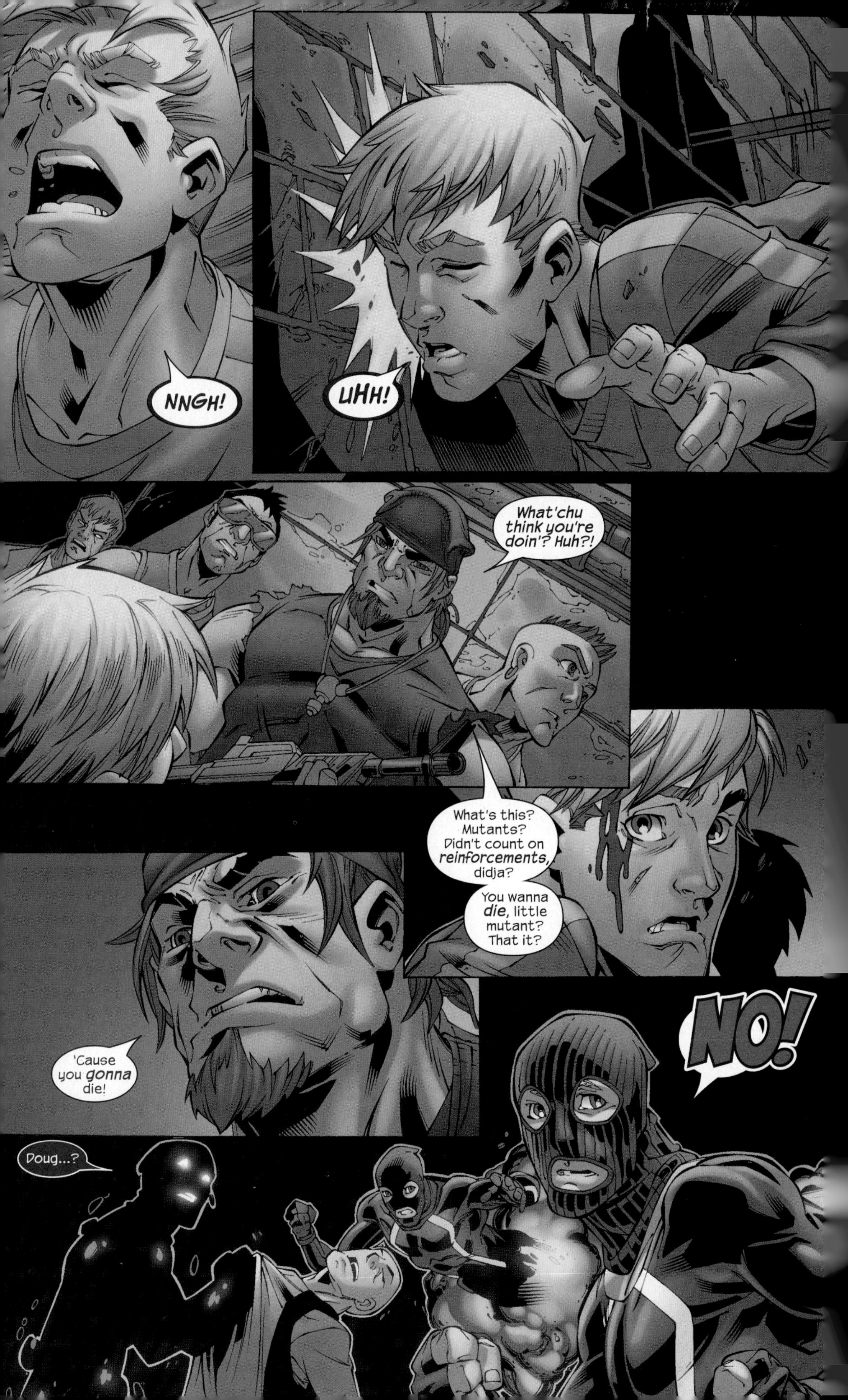
NNGH!
UHH!
What'chu think you're doin'? Huh?!
What's this? Mutants? Didn't count on reinforcements, didja?
You wanna die, little mutant? That it?
'Cause you gonna die!
NO!
Doug...?

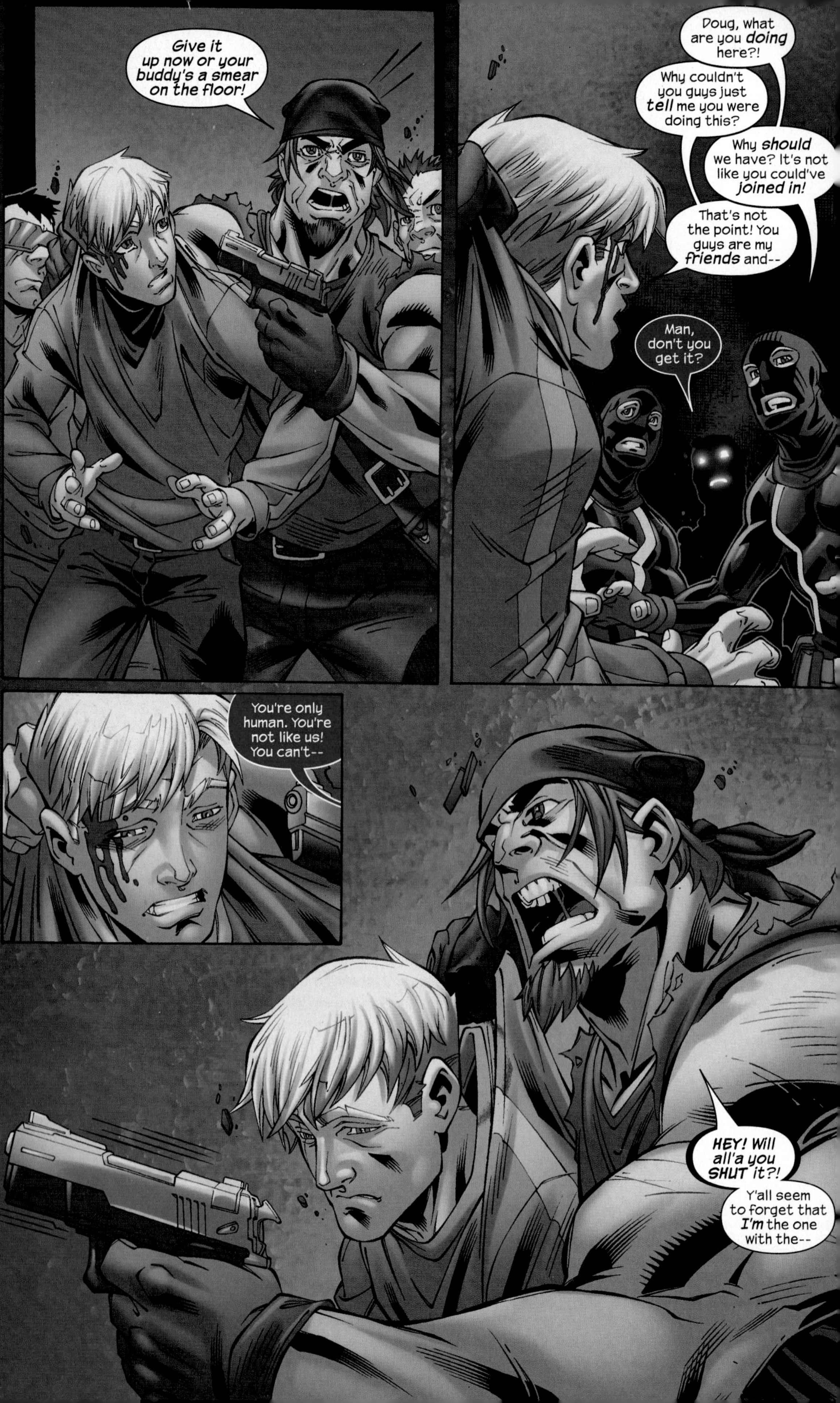
Give it up now or your buddy's a smear on the floor!
Doug, what are you doing here?!
Why couldn't you guys just tell me you were doing this?
Why should we have? It's not like you could've joined in!
That's not the point! You guys are my friends and--
Man, don't you get it?
You're only human. You're not like us! You can't--
HEY! Will all'a you SHUT it?!
Y'all seem to forget that I'm the one with the--

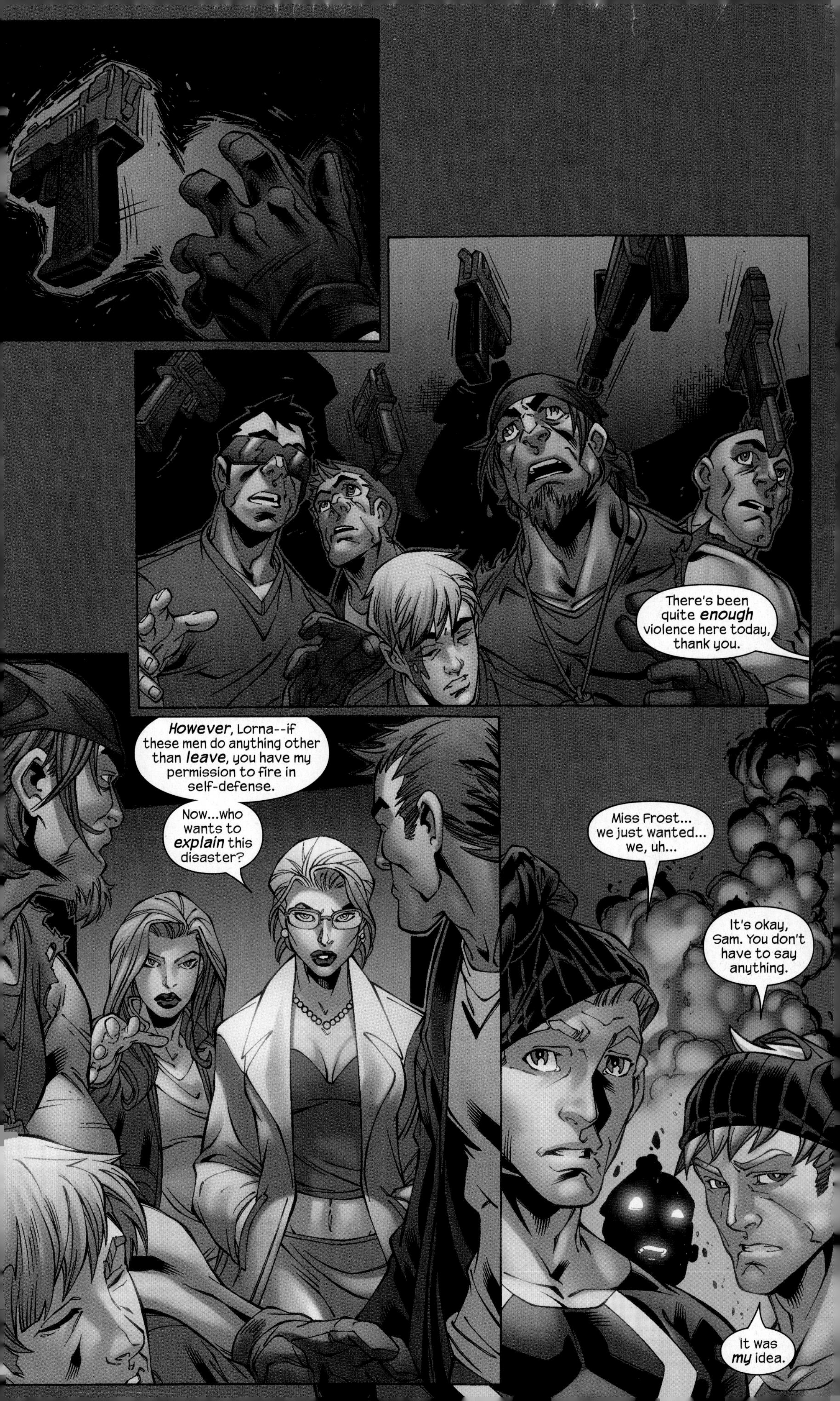
There's been quite enough violence here today, thank you.
However, Lorna--if these men do anything other than leave, you have my permission to fire in self-defense.
Now...who wants to explain this disaster?
Miss Frost... we just wanted... we, uh...
It's okay, Sam. You don't have to say anything.
It was my idea.

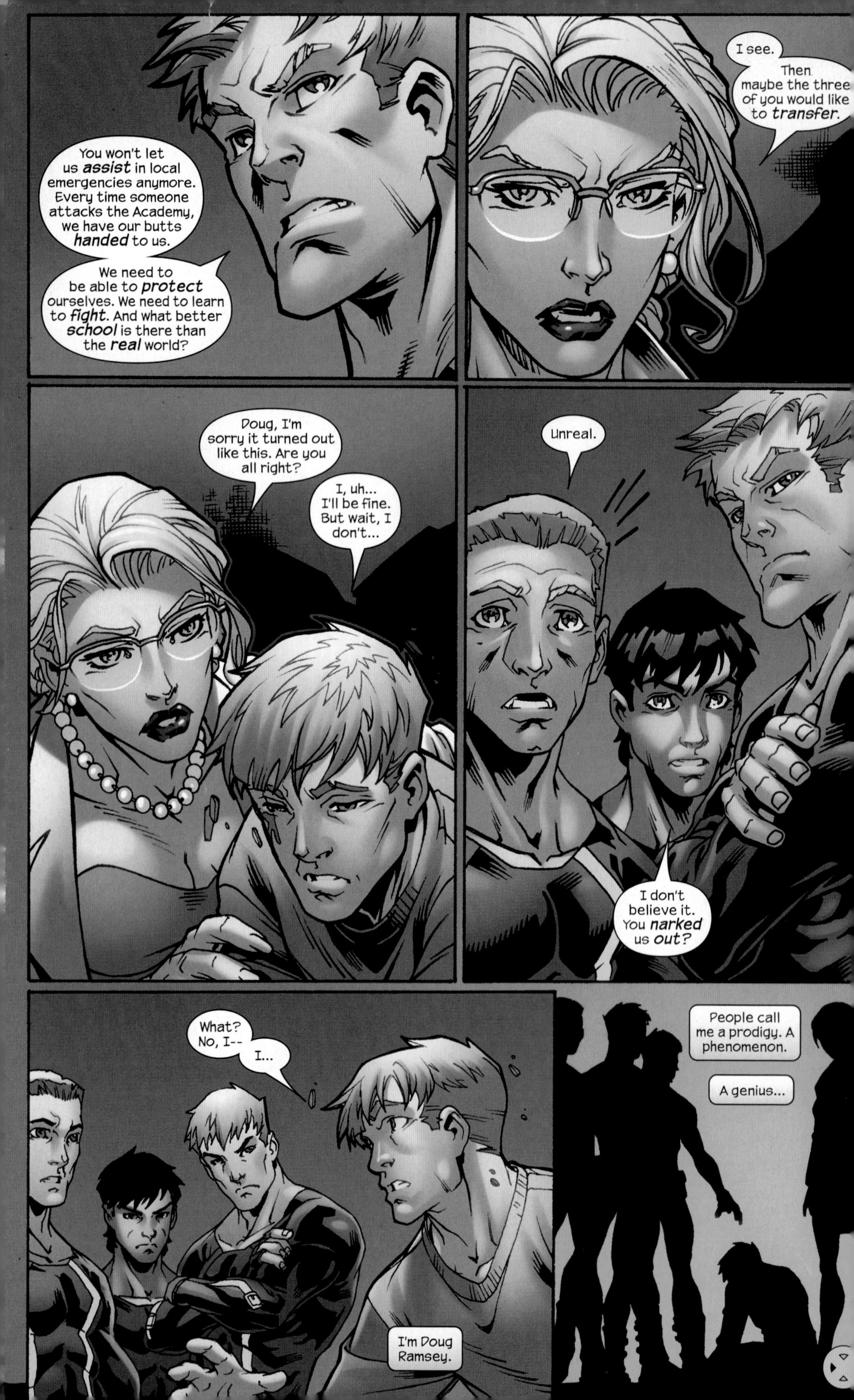
You won't let us assist in local emergencies anymore. Every time someone attacks the Academy, we have our butts handed to us.
We need to be able to protect ourselves. We need to learn to fight. And what better school is there than the real world?
I see.
Then maybe the three of you would like to transfer.
Doug, I'm sorry it turned out like this. Are you all right?
I, uh... I'll be fine. But wait, I don't...
Unreal.
I don't believe it. You narked us out?
What? No, I--
I...
I'm Doug Ramsey.
People call me a prodigy. A phenomenon.
A genius...

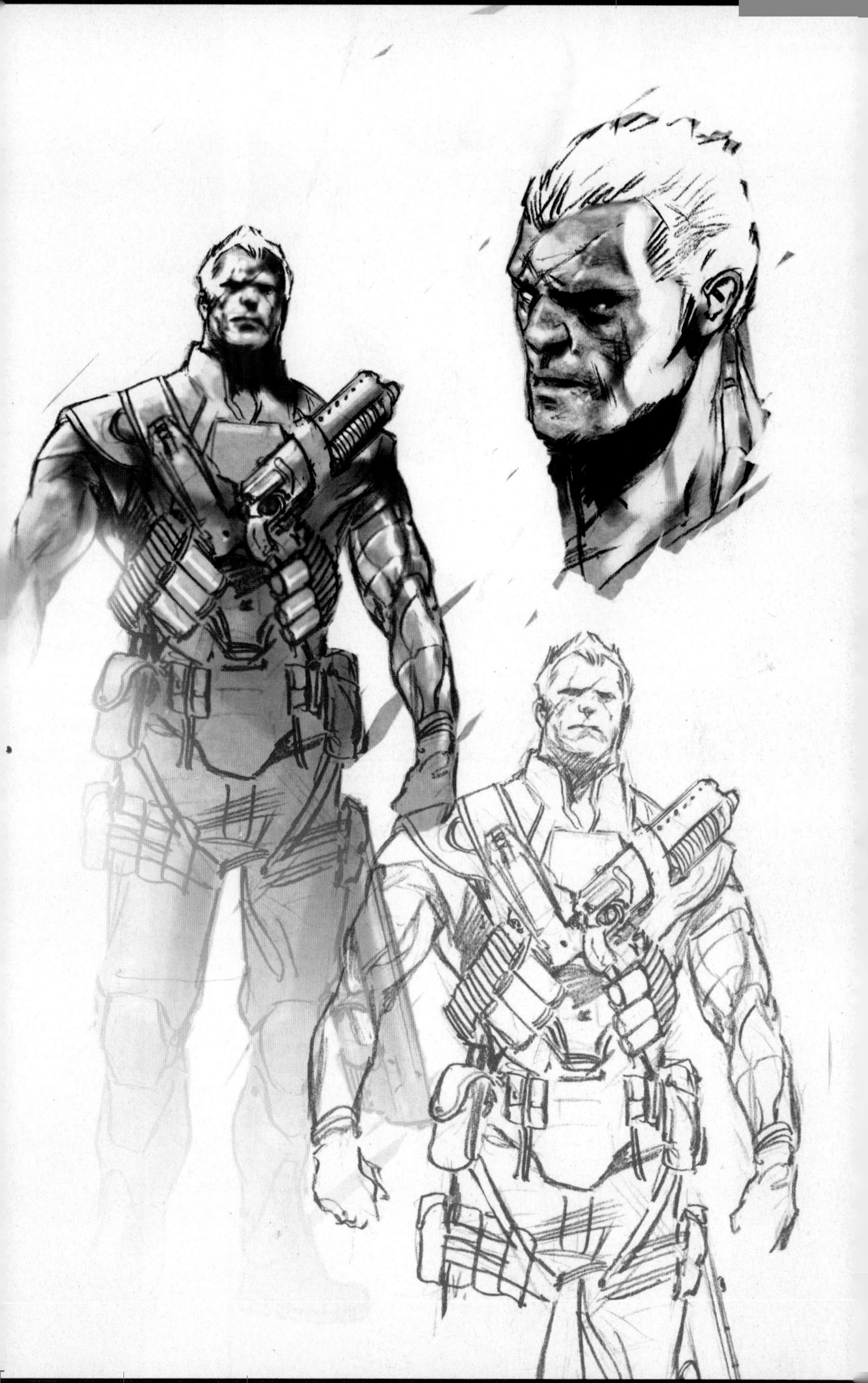

Yanick Paquette

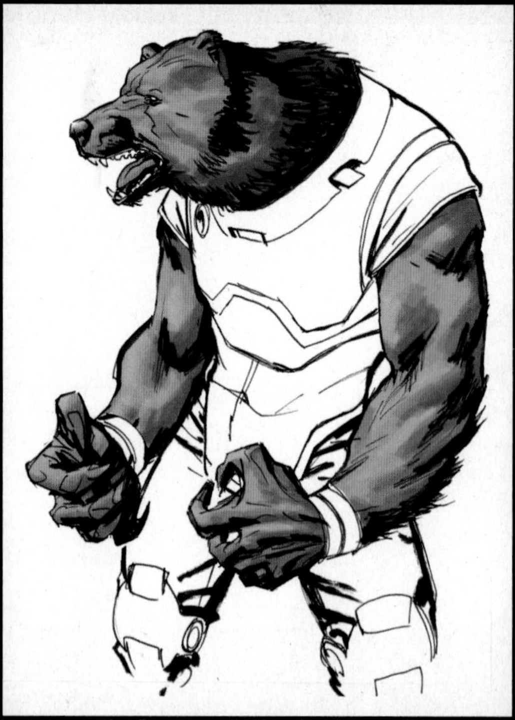

Yanick created this to show Ben (who wa
issue #78) where Wolverine would be injur
welcome Ben to the world of fatherhood,
why Ben didn't draw #77.

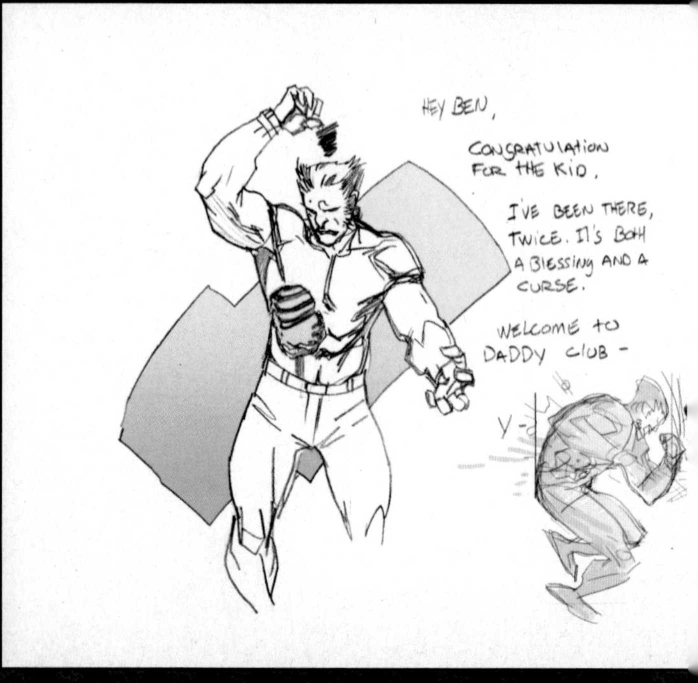
HEY BEN,
CONGRATULATION FOR THE KID.
I'VE BEEN THERE, TWICE. IT'S BOTH A BLESSING AND A CURSE.
WELCOME TO DADDY CLUB -

Issue #76 Cover Process by Ben Oliver

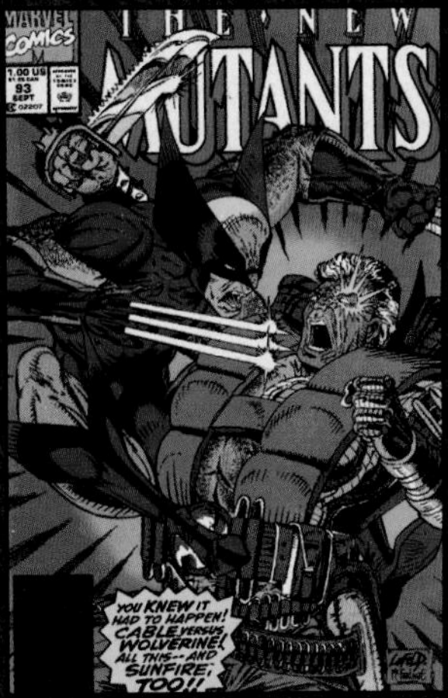
MARVEL COMICS
THE NEW MUTANTS
1.00 US
93
SEPT
YOU KNEW IT HAD TO HAPPEN! CABLE VERSUS WOLVERINE! ALL THIS-- AND SUNFIRE, TOO!!

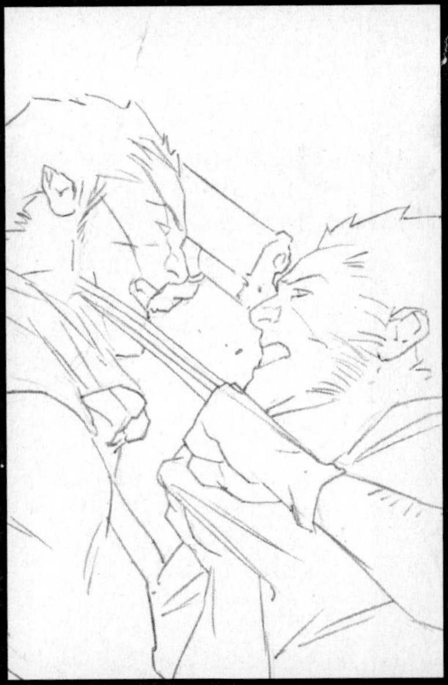

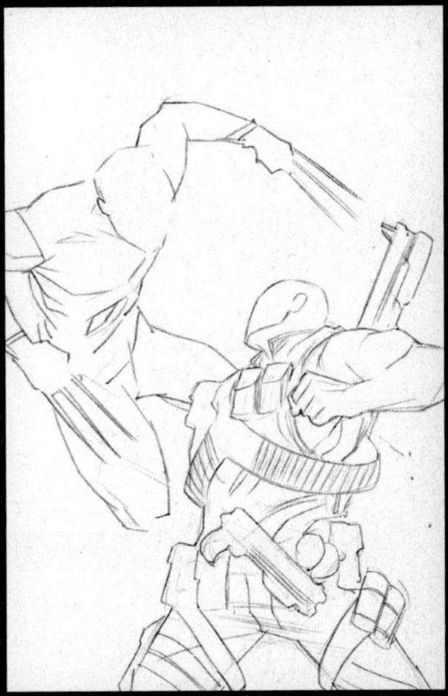

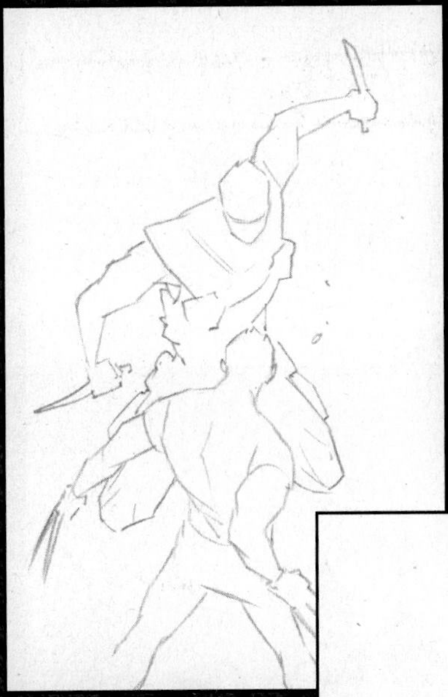

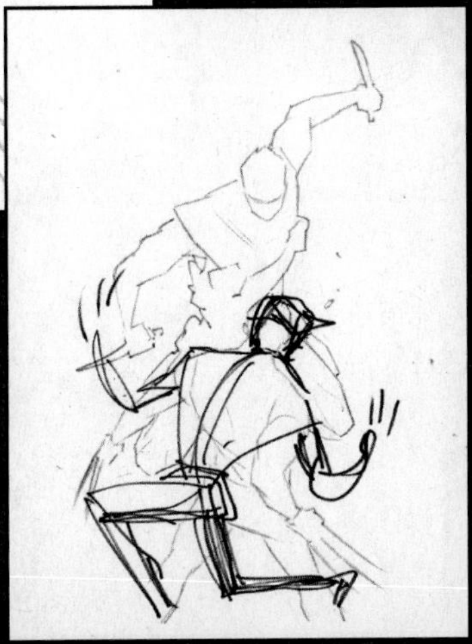

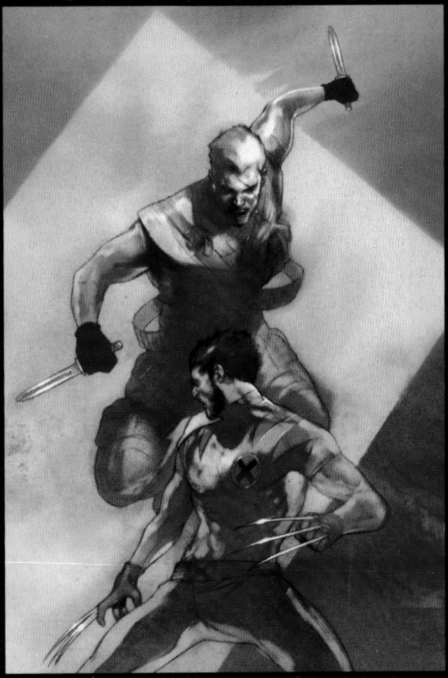

Issue #78 Cover Process
by Ben Oliver

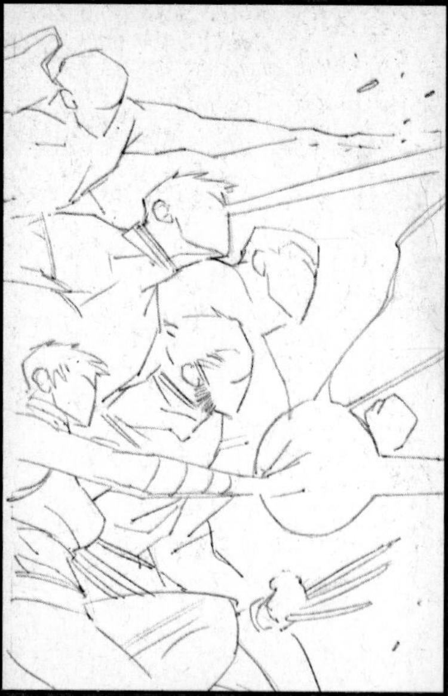

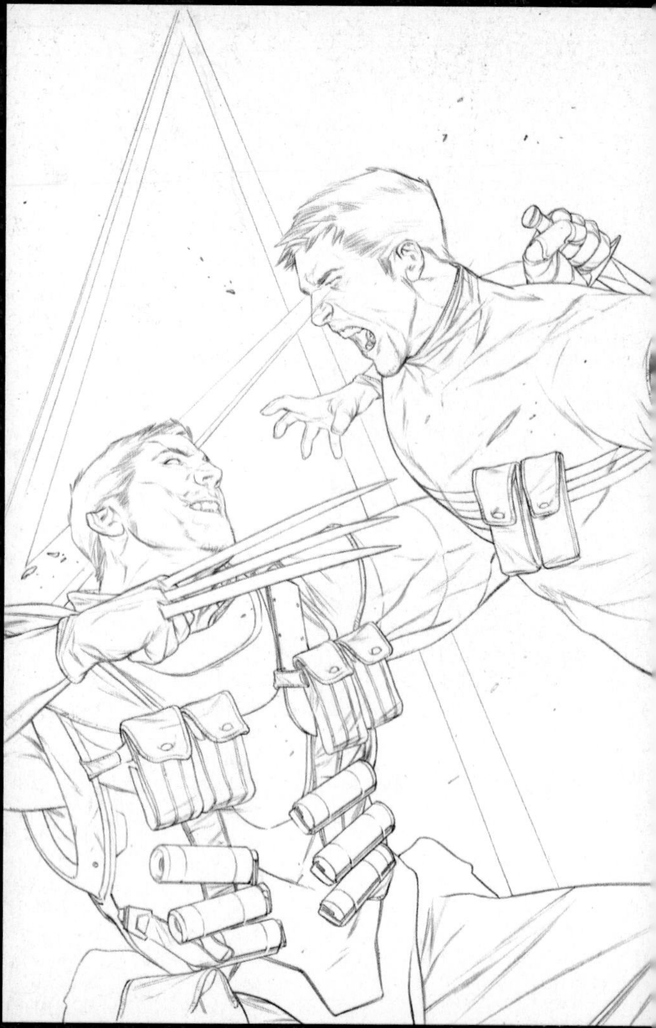

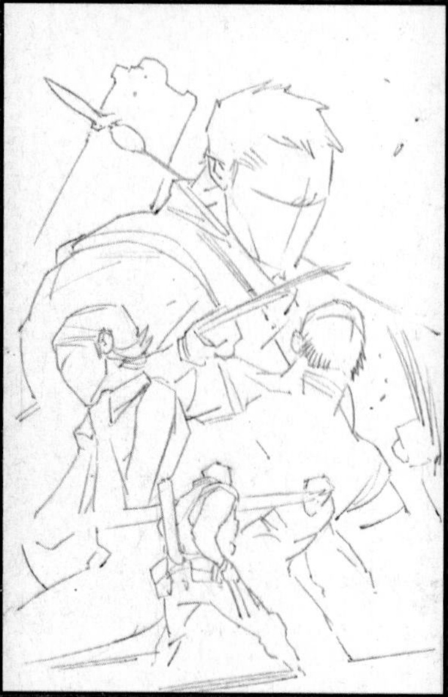

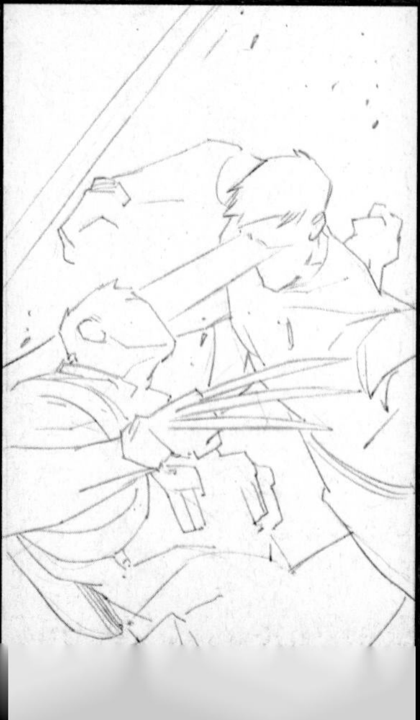

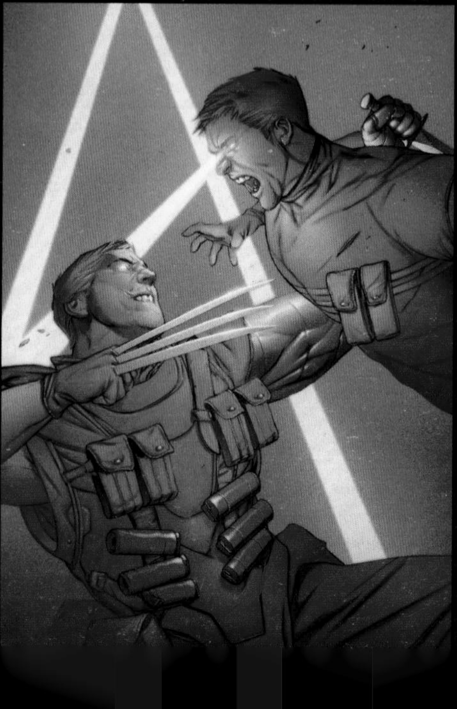